Photo essay
by Monica Larner

1 Matera, Basilicata

20 Central square, Sperlonga

18 Portovenere, Liguria
19 Piazza di Spagna, Rome

Kate Carlisle

Working and Living
ITALY

CADOGANguides

Contents

Author's acknowledgements

To all the many who have given help and advice. Monica, Cathy, Greg, Prudence, Alina, Paul and Stefano, who has given me an insight to his country that would have been impossible without him. And of course, my family. Thanks to all.

About the author

Texan native **Kate Carlisle** has been in and out of Italy for twelve years, and based in Rome for eight of those. As a feature writer for various publications, such as *Italy Italy*, she has written on the country's claims to fame such as fashion events and gastronomic wizards. As a special correspondent for *Business Week* magazine, she was the recipient of the Sidney Hillman award for her investigative cover story on human trafficking and slave labour in Europe, and also nominated for the Livingston Award for the article 'From Bad to Worse in a Gypsy Ghetto'. She has contributed to several books, including the Time Out guide to *Tuscany and Florence* and the ultimate football guide to European matches, the *Fan's Guide to Europe*, as well as the *Expatriate's Guide to Hungary*, where she lived for five years.

Conceived and produced for Cadogan Guides by:

Navigator Guides Ltd
The Old Post Office, Swanton Novers,
Melton Constable, Norfolk NR24 2AJ
www.navigatorguides.com
info@navigatorguides.com

Cadogan Guides
Network House, 1 Ariel Way, London, W12 7SL
info@cadoganguides.co.uk
www.cadoganguides.com

The Globe Pequot Press
246 Goose Lane, PO Box 480, Guilford,
Connecticut 06437–0480

Copyright © Cadogan Guides 2004
"THE SUNDAY TIMES" is a registered trade mark of Times Newspapers Limited

Cover design by Sarah Rianhard-Gardner
Cover and photo essay photographs © Monica
    Larner and © Corbis Stock
Photo essay design: Smith, Cowan and Wilkinson
Maps © Cadogan Guides,
    drawn by Map Creation Ltd
Editor: Susannah Wight
Series Editor: Linda McQueen
Proofreading: Carla Masson
Indexing: Isobel McLean

Printed in Italy by Legoprint
A catalogue record for this book is available
    from the British Library
ISBN 1-86011-130-0

Introduction

There's a world of difference between holidaying in a country and moving there. Yet often the itch to up-sticks and head to a faraway land is born from an idyllic holiday or pleasant brush with a destination. Italy is indeed a culprit in the field of charming its visitors, and more than one traveller has decided to make Italy their home after just a brief sojourn. That Italian magic can be unstoppable when it strikes.

Once you are packed up and there, some of your favourite daydreams may well bloom into reality, while other unexpected differences might throw the new-found bliss off-tilt. Stereotypes abound, but don't always help you navigate troubled waters or resolve sticky situations. Without some road signs, it can be hard to find the way.

This book is meant to provide those road signs to indicate the way, without weighing in with too many opinions. Alas, it is impossible to remove all hint of personal authorial preferences or inclinations. But this companion guide has a mission – to offer information to help iron out the rough spots and to provide a better understanding of the world the reader is about to dive, or has already plunged, into.

Chapter 01 is there to get you started with climate and geography descriptions, a historical overview and a look at the Italian language and the many dialects and accents throughout the country. After that, Chapter 02 breaks down each region to help you better understand their unique qualities and decide once and for all where you want to live. Chapter 03 launches into the make-up of the country today – political parties, religion, women's role, what you will be seeing and reading, economics and internal issues, and the real stuff of life: culture, art, eating and drinking. The following chapter runs through the first steps of getting to Italy, and addresses some initial questions regarding working and living there.

While underlining problem areas and potential frustrations, this book also explains how to navigate the roadblocks as expediently as possible. That is where Chapters 05 and 06 step in. Chapter 07 winds up with nitty-gritty issues about Italy's labour market, work etiquette, with ideas and information about what is needed to make a living in Italy.

Spectacularly beautiful, stuck in its ways almost to a flaw and burdened with more stereotypes than probably any of its other European counterparts. Italy can drive you crazy with passion and frustration. As with your own home country, there will be moments of joy and those of maddening misadventure. If Italy becomes your permanent home, this book will no doubt become flagged, then updated with your own observations and notes. As Leonardo da Vinci said, '*La sapienza e figliola della sperienza*' or 'Knowledge is the child of experience', and yours will certainly be as unique as this author's. But, for the common threads that run through the fabric of life in Italy, count on finding answers and insights throughout these pages.

Getting to Know Italy

01

Getting to know Italy means being brave enough to explore a mishmash of regional and provincial realities, and realizing that there is no single, homogenous Italy. Postcard Mediterranean panoramas with white-sand beaches and sun-baked deserts are as easy to stumble upon as pristine mountain passes more likely to bring to mind Heidi than Gina Lollobrigida. Numerous microclimates, air currents, visiting breezes and altitudes have moulded a country for all seasons. Both cold-weather-lovers and solar-powered individuals are in luck nearly all year long. The dizzying height of the Alps provides a guaranteed cool retreat in the summer, and the proximity of Italy's southernmost island, Pantelleria, to Africa keeps the country warm.

Although it was only unified politically – by Garibaldi – in 1861, Italy has existed for centuries, serving not only as the homeland to ancient cultures, but historically as the crossroads between Greece, the Balkans, Middle East and Europe. With strong local identities and dialects galore, sometimes understanding one another isn't merely a question of attitude. Keep the idea of dark and sultry Sophia Loren types in mind, but add freckled redheads and blue-eyed blondes. The variety within the Italian population reflects the country's mixed history, as does the fact that, when local dialects are spoken, Italians often (sometimes intentionally) don't understand each other.

There is a saying that Garibaldi didn't unite the peninsula and its islands, but divided Africa. Spoken by Italy's separatists, known as the Lega Nord (Northern League), the comment has a biting undertone of discrimination. But considering the vast differences from one region to the next, it helps explain the various dichotomies of the country. Garibaldi himself noted after his victory, 'We have made Italy, now we must make Italians.' Not to worry. Italy has been made, as have Italians; even if they are Napoletani, Romani, Milanesi or Veneti – whichever they are first, they are always Italians in the end. After all, it not only depends on how it's sliced, but on how it's eaten.

Climate and Geography

Want to have breakfast gazing at the sunrise over the Adriatic Sea? Then dinner as *il sole* sinks into the Tyrrhenian waves? Not only is it possible in Italy, it is relatively easy, as the land mass at its narrowest is only 150km (90 miles) across from sea to sea. Hop in the car and drive across the peninsula, and you can see it all.

Italy seen as a serpent's tongue forks in two directions – towards the Balkans on the Puglia side and towards Africa and the Middle East on the Calabrian side, finishing in the throat that is Europe's doorstep at the northern border. It is a country that runs the geographical gamut of extremes – the cool and dizzying heights of the Italian Alps; a knotty spinal cord known as the Apennines; 4,100 miles of coastline; expanses of rice-producing plains; Tuscany's rolling, vine-covered hills; near-desert stretches; and island paradises.

Sliced into three geographical divisions and 20 administrative regions, the peninsula is the epitome of variation, both climatically and geographically. Sun-drenched countryside and picturebook coastal scenes are all within a maximum of several hours' drive, no matter where one is living. For beach-lovers, one of the longest drives for a dip in the sea is the 150km (90-mile) dash from Milan to Genoa, and anyone living near the seaside can be slaloming down an acceptable ski slope in just a few hours by car or air. Measuring time by distance, that is. Horrific weekend traffic snarls along Italy's main routes can alter those times by hours (see **Living in Italy**, 'Transport', p.197). And as Italians are big fans of getting away for the weekend, or day outings on Saturday and Sunday, it is guaranteed that travelling on those days from any major city to destination can be a hair-raising experience.

A good deal of Italian metaphors and imagery harken from the deep south. Arid and dotted with prickly-pear cactus, whose fruit is greedily consumed by locals, its rocky white coast juts into the Ionian sea. Desert-like conditions, in part the result of agricultural mismanagement, and stone-cracking heat, are daily bread and water. Puglia, Calabria and Basilicata are the three regions that dominate the tip of the peninsula, and across a strait of 3km (1.8 miles) radiates Sicily, an autonomous region and island. Smaller isles south and northwest of Sicily, such as Lipari, Stromboli and Salina, make up the Aeolian Islands and south of Sicily are northern Africa's sisters, Pantelleria and Lampedusa. Brindisi, one of Italy's handful of natural harbours, sits on the east coast under Bari. Nuzzled up to the deep south conglomeration is the region of Campania, Naples being its capital. All of Italy's, indeed Europe's, volcanoes are located in the south and they still blow off steam, sometimes exploding, in Sicily, Etna and Stromboli and outside Naples at Vesuvius, which last went up during the Second World War.

At the other end, the northern border of Italy is girdled by Europe's largest mountain system, the Alps, called the Dolomites as they flow towards the east, dividing the country from continental Europe. One of the most famous first crossings of the Alps was by the African general Hannibal in the 2nd century BC, carried out with elephant-mounted troops – no small feat in his day and age. Today, despite their daunting and majestic appearance, the 1,200km (720-mile) range, with or without pachyderms, can be crossed without difficulty using the well-developed state highways and tunnels. Monte Bianco or Mont Blanc (4,810m/15,780ft) – the highest point in Italy and the Italian Alps – and the Cervinia or Matterhorn (4,478m/15,690ft) are two of the continent's most spectacular mountains.

Directly south of the Alps is the Po river valley and the Pianura Padana, spanning three regions – Lombardy, Veneto and Emilia-Romagna. Its colder winters and four well-defined seasons give it more in common with the central

European land mass than the Italian peninsula proper: its climate is closer to the rest of Europe than to the Mediterranean. In fact, snow falls regularly during the winter in the Po Valley, and at the river's mouth great swampy marshes – historically a breeding ground for malaria mosquitoes – are often shrouded in thick fog that has been damned for numerous fatal road accidents.

The rugged Alps soften into the 1,050km (650-mile) Apennine mountain spine that runs down the length of the peninsula, slicing the other two major geographical regions in half. On the eastern, Adriatic side, a narrow strip where the mountains descend to meet the sea widens into a stretch of white sand beaches known as the Adriatic Riviera. On the west side of the Apennines are wide expanses with valleys and plains that stretch towards the Tyrrhenian sea where Italy's second largest island, Sardinia, lies just south of the island of Corsica in the blue Tyrrhenian Sea. Approximately 260km (160 miles) long, 110km (68 miles) wide and 185km (115 miles) west of the Italian mainland, what was an all-night or all-day journey up until the early 1990s now takes less than four hours by ferry. Smaller jewels, like Napoleon's exile island of Elba and the tiny isle of Giglio between Rome and Florence, or Ponza just south of Rome, are even closer to reach with frequent ferries. The Apennines themselves cut through the regions of Emilia, Toscana (Tuscany), Umbria, Lazio, Marche, Molise, Abruzzo and Campania, and are home to ski resorts, mountain hamlet towns and numerous nature reserves.

Three major rivers flow through the country, the longest and largest being the Po, which runs west to east across the Lombardy plains and flows out into the Adriatic. Its numerous tributaries (the Adige, Piave, Reno and Tagliamento rivers) help create the marshy areas throughout the Po Valley. Meandering southwest across Emilia-Romagna, Umbria, into Lazio and finishing off its cross-country trip 24km (15 miles) west of Rome after cutting through the capital is the Tiber river. And Tuscany has the Arno river all to itself as it graces Florence and Pisa after running for many miles through the region. Other major bodies of water are Lake Garda straddling Veneto and Lombardy, Lake Como and Maggiore in Lombardy, Lake Trasimeno in Umbria with its two islands Isola Maggiore and Polvese, and the smaller but equally refreshing lakes scattered throughout the country.

There are numerous microclimates – on the Ligurian coast around Genoa, on the Amalfi coast near Naples, and on the islands scattered throughout the Tyrrhenian and Adriatic waters – and these areas almost never feel the chilled-to-the-bone cold that mountainous regions do, and are often winter retreats for cold-weather sufferers. Though the capital Rome is stroked by the cool *ponentino* breeze in the summer, its humid heat can be devastating, as xan that of land-locked Milan and Florence.

Apart from the occasional summer heatwave or killer winter storm, Italy's weather is where Europe finds its balance. Hotspots such as Rimini and Riccione have long been travel destinations for Europeans and Italians alike. Even in the heart of winter, parts of Italy all the way up to Turin can be ravaged by the African wind known as the *scirocco*, which brings with it hot air, red sand and a series of health problems such as headaches and 'temporary madness'. Trieste is whipped by the *bora*, winds that reach up to 150km per hour (93mph), and droughts strike throughout the country every year.

Adding to the discomfort of temperature highs and lows is the fact that air-conditioning, despite being on the increase, is still a rarity. Cold-weather sufferers should be aware that southern cities like Rome often have buildings that have been constructed to stay cool during the long hot spells in the summer, rather than warm through the brief winter cold. Marble floors and thick stone walls are a refreshing relief when it is 40 degrees outside. But in the winter you will often find chilly pubs and restaurants where clients never take off their coats and shiver from one serving to the next. The buildings in northern towns like Turin and Milan have been constructed more solidly because of their longer and harder winters, and generally have toasty-warm public buildings.

For average temperatures, barring meteorological anomalies, *see* **Reference**, 'Regional Climate Charts', p.282. A sunny November day in Lampedusa is just as predictable as fresh snow in the Alps in December. There are usually seasonal forest fires during the dry summers in Sardinia but autumn rains begin at the end of August throughout the country. Whatever climatic preferences you may have, a short plane-ride or drive to another part of Italy will bring a refreshing change of temperature.

Historical Overview

Wherever you start to dig into Italian history, a piece of it will say something to you. Though it is strange to think of Italy as a relatively new country, it is younger than most European, many Asian and even some African republics. But its richly organized Roman history spans back to 21 April 753 BC, which, according to empirical annals, is when Rome was officially founded. Before that, the land mass that is now known as Italia was home to Etruscans, Greeks, Latins and local tribes. Yet even before that it was chock-full of prehistoric inhabitants, one in particular of whom rose through the glacial ranks to become the world's most famous mummy when discovered in the Italian Alps in 1991. More than 7,000 Nuraghe, or large truncated conical towers of boulders and hewn rocks, from 1800 BC pepper the island of Sardinia.

From Romans to Renaissance, there are fragments of Italian history in almost every corner of the earth. The emperor Hadrian left a wall in northern England, which marked the end of his empire; other emperors left thermal spas in Bath; and even the name of the United Kingdom's capital, London (Londinium), is a hangover from the Roman expansion. St Francis of Assisi made it as far as

California, at least in name, when Spanish missionaries founded San Francisco. Los Angeles was named after Santa Maria degli Angeli (Our Lady of the Angels) where San Francesco rebuilt his first church. Marco Polo certainly got around, and one of Italy's most famous paintings, *La Gioconda* (*Mona Lisa*), still graces the halls of the Louvre in Paris, despite a national desire to bring her home, and one failed robbery attempt in 1911 to do just that. To list all the Italian finger-prints left around the world would take volumes and years.

All the more so, then, in Italy itself, where it is impossible to take a step without tripping over history's reminders. More than 70 per cent of Europe's artistic heritage is in Italy, and the country is packed with 3,554 museums, compared with 1,400 in France and 2,500 in the UK. So accustomed are Italians to living next to thousand-year-old remains of the past that they often treat them with a flippant disrespect. In 1997 two 'boys' (*ragazzi*), as they were called by the papers (they were both in their early 40s), were arrested for diving from the tail of Bernini's famous fountain of the four rivers and breaking it off. Baffled by their arrest, one of them objected, 'I just did a little dive...light as a feather.' Often that familiarity with national treasures is played out in vandalism and defacing; you will see an infinite amount of graffiti plaguing major cities. But the heat is on in many regions to put an end to vandalism, and Italians are not only proud of but generally knowledgeable about their history and will expound for hours when asked.

Etruscans, Greeks and Romans

Mysterious, subversive and oh, so misunderstood by the Greeks and Romans, the Etruscans often begin Italian accounts of recorded history. Major cities like Bologna were Etruscan and, according to one anthropologist, the Etruscan 'stamp' can still be seen in the dark, almond eyes, black straight hair and pronounced cheekbones of inhabitants in towns like Viterbo. They called them-selves Rasenna, but the Greeks and Romans transformed their name into Etrusci, Tusci and several other variations. Three thousand years later, the name of the sea that they sailed, the Tyrrhenian, comes from one of the Roman varia-tions of their one of their names, Tyrrheni.

Most of what is known about the 'long-nosed, sensitive-footed, subtly smiling Etruscans', as D.H. Lawrence called them, comes from second-hand sources, and their history is often plagued with bias or misinterpretation. The Greeks couldn't grasp their values and the Romans simply wanted to conquer them for patriotic reasons. To be noted is the Greeks' unabashed disgust for the equal status in society shared by Etruscan men and women. Indeed, one of the world's best-preserved ancient artefacts found in the town of Cerveteri near Rome is the Sarcophagus of the Married Couple from the 6th century BC, showing a husband and wife reclining side by side, united and equal in death as in life.

At their height, the Etruscans controlled most of the Mediterreanean, both commercially and militarily. They were metalworkers and skilled potters. Tuscany, named after the indigenous inhabitants, was their 'homeland' and somewhere between the 10th and 8th centuries BC they began establishing close-knit communities instead of scattered habitations, draining marshes, cultivating and burying their dead – the last fact leaving excellent necropolises that have given scholars a great insight into their life and society. Then they cleared the shepherd ghettos around the Tiber and on the Palatine hill, and laid the basis for what is Rome today.

While snazzying up its bulk export of metals from the Tyrrhenian coast and continuing to develop rituals and systems that were copied by the Romans, such as the military grid pattern, Etruria continued to expand. By the 7th century BC parts of northern Italy, the Po Valley, Lazio and Campania were either under the political sway of the Etruscans or inhabited by them. But it was then that the Roman legions began their onslaught, conquering region after region, absorbing or eliminating as they went. Note, however, that three of the seven Roman kings were Etruscan, and Etruscan soothsayers showed up in Roman writings reading the intestines of slaughtered small animals way into the 5th century AD.

Romans – Monarchy, Republic and Empire

Don't think that Roman history isn't alive and well. Every year on 15 March – the Ides of March – many inhabitants of Italy's capital city flock to the statue of Julius Caesar to lay flowers at the feet of the statue erected in his honour. The day Rome was founded in 753, 21 April, is a local holiday when employees have a paid day off. In the 1970s, the fad of tattooing SPQR as a proud proclamation became nearly as popular as tattooing girlfriends' names, 'mom' and thorn-choked hearts. Even the desire not to let the memory of Roman soldiers die has become a touristy mainstay around the Colosseum and other monuments as modern gladiators wave swords and blow kisses at giggling foreign visitors.

What makes the Roman Empire's rise and fall so evergreen in our imagination? The intrigue, for sure. Those who ruled Rome and its colonies were some of the most ruthless (viz Caligula slicing open his pregnant sister), and some of the most tender (Mark Antony killed himself out of lost pride, but his love for Cleopatra did play a part in the suicide). They also built an empire that dazzles to this day, and is constantly being scrutinized by historians and politicians for its success and failure, not to mention its inextricable religious links with Christian and Jewish history for the millions of pilgrims who visit yearly.

The Romans' successes were legion. Kings and emperors, one after another, ruled numerous populations and cultures. Some like to say that Roman rule was superior to 'modern' colonialism since the conquered were allowed partial or complete Roman citizenship, which meant they had rights; they also paid penalties such as taxes. The saying that all roads led to Rome was true. Between 334 and 170 BC six major roads that still serve as the ingoing and outgoing veins to the capital were established. Those roads are still around as the Appian Way, Salaria, Aurelia, Cassia, Flaminia and Latina.

Among the most well-known Roman rulers, Julius Caesar reached such dizzying heights of power that he was almost made king – until friends, Romans and countrymen were asked to lend their ears to Marcus Junius Brutus, who explained why he had him stabbed to death in the Senate on 15 March 44 BC. Beware the Ides of March. But with his death, the Republic continued its transition into an empire.

The immediate successor of Julius Caesar was Marc Antony, a Roman general who assumed control by seizing Caesar's papers and wealth. Intent on expanding the Republic, Antony met Cleopatra at Tarsus in 41 BC. It is said that she seduced him and kept him hanging around Egypt for a year. When Antony eventually returned to Rome, still smitten with Cleopatra, he made peace with Caesar's willed successor, Octavius. That peace, however, came with a package. Soon Antony found himself married to Octavius's sister, Octavia. That didn't stop him from openly marrying Cleopatra in 36 BC, an event that infuriated Octavius, who immediately gathered western legions and defeated Marc Antony at the Battle of Actium in September 31 BC. Cleopatra fled to Egypt with Antony trailing closely behind. A year later, he committed suicide in disgrace and Cleopatra, unable to retain her rule of Egypt, followed suit with the help of an asp.

Octavius, awarded the name of Augustus, stepped in and lived up to Caesar's legacy. He was, after all, Caesar's great-nephew. His ruling style created the cult of the individual, gave little support to the applied arts and showed favouritism towards anyone who helped increase his empire. In fact, tax breaks and subsidies were given to families with numerous children, and the birth rate shot up to an all-time high.

Many historians and scholars have written about the Roman Empire in far more detail than can be covered here. To simplify, during the period that arguably laid the foundations for Italy as it is today, it can be said that public order was restored by the Caesars (planned by Julius but brought to fruition under Augustus). Either directly or indirectly, by 49 BC Rome ruled the entire Mediterranean world, because all political, commercial and cultural pathways led straight to the capital (*caput mundi*). And, much like today, the urban lure of the potential for wealth and glory to be found in the capital drained other Italian communities of human resources. Foreign imports, especially agricultural ones, hurt local farmers and landowners. Municipal governments faltered, and civil wars ensued. On the eve of the birth of Christ, Rome was a mighty empire. But the cloth was beginning to wear thin.

Christian Rome

The decline and fall of the Roman Empire wasn't immediate. But the last two hundred years of the Roman Empire were just years of stress, stress and more stress, with the 'Christian problem' plaguing emperors since Jesus' birth and crucifixion, and barbarians pushing their way in from the northeast.

Constantine, the emperor who converted to Christianity and legalized the practice of the religion, became emperor in AD 306. In 330 he made Constantinople (previously Byzantium) the new capital of the Empire, moving the administrative functions away from Rome altogether. The barbarians had been invading and rampaging, and the menace of an attack on Rome increased greatly. With the move of the capital to present-day Turkey, the best Roman artisans, politicians and public figures left Rome: Constantinople became a city renowned for its splendour, intrigue, jealousies and passion, while Rome languished in neglect. When the empire split in two, the western capital was moved to Milan, then Ravenna. Rome was sacked by Alaric the Visigoth in 410, which was the beginning of numerous assaults to come. No author describes this better than Edward Gibbon, in the historically intimidating book *Decline and Fall of the Roman Empire*.

The Middle Ages

After the fall of the Roman Empire, citizens who once had a political structure guiding their existence found themselves in the hands of powerful families and individuals who formed kingdoms and city-states. Political organization started to take shape as city-states (*comuni*), and republics. The Lombards, a warring tribe from Pannonia (present-day Hungary) ruled the north from 568 until the 700s, at which point they began to become Italian, adopting the language and dress. The Byzantine monarchy in exile regularly clashed with the Lombards, while the common citizen lived in abject poverty and was indifferent about who won the clashes, since it had little impact on daily life.

With no overseeing government defining laws and regulations, any sense of order and structure that existed was driven by monasteries and friars. The Church, through its keepers, began its transformation into a state. Friars and monks tended to everything from agriculture to medicine, transcribing and writing, praying and sustaining. They were the caretakers of learning and preservation ... and sometimes the destroyers. The popes of yore were hardly virtuous representatives of God. More than anything, they weakly administered Byzantine law in Italy to avoid the Lombards running amok and taking over the entire peninsula. It was during this time that many of Italy's festivals and ceremonies that are still celebrated today were born, mostly springing from conflicts between cities with opposing rulers. Arezzo and Siena are bitter rivals even today, after a clash between the Lombards and the pope in the late 600s.

When the Lombards got to be too much, the Franks descended into Italy to support the pope. Pepin III was happy to swoop down, defeat King Aistulf in 755 and abscond with some booty back to Francia. When the going got tough again in 772 at the hands of the more ambitious Lombard king Desiderius, Charlemagne answered the call, and stayed. For over two centuries Italy was to remain in the orbit of the Carolingian dynasty, which ended up substituting the Lombards in the Kingdom of Italy. In justification for the extended visit, the document *Donatio Constantini* (Constantine's Donation) was miraculously 'discovered', allegedly giving the papacy the right to rule the entire western half of the Roman Empire.

Pope Gregory I, known as Gregory the Great, started work in the 6th century to increase the power of the papacy, making it a major landowner in Italy. The popes of the 7th and 8th centuries built on Gregory's legacy. They created and ruled a Papal State in central Italy and declared independence from the Byzantine Empire. The state was, however, a vassal of the Holy Roman Empire. The Lombards hung on until the beginning of the 11th century, keeping the Duchy of Benevento, which was later transformed into a principality. The southern towns of Salerno and Capua originated from that duchy after developing into principalities in their own right.

During the 9th century Arab expansion became another concern. Over the years 827–902 Sicily fell entirely into Saracen hands and became the starting point for coastal and interior raids of the Italian peninsula. City names today, such as Caltanissetta (Calat-en-Nissah) and Marsala (Mersah-el-Allah), food like local *cuscus*, and Moorish architecture are direct hangovers from Arab Sicily (*see* **Profiles of the Regions**, 'Sicily'). At the same time, in the south of Italy, the first independent city-states began to develop, with the formation of *signorie* at Naples, Amalfi and Gaeta. With the sea at their doorstep they were able to develop a mercantile economy that could avoid the northern barbarians while at the same time defining an economic niche. These are the first examples of the free *comuni* that were to flourish slightly later in central and northern Italy, such as Pisa, Genoa and Venice.

With the disorganization of the Holy Roman Empire and fluctuating foreign overlords, rural Italians were left to self-govern within their *comuni*. Italy had become a patchwork of independent towns and small principalities whose borders were drawn and redrawn by battles, diplomatic negotiations and marriage alliances. During the 14th and 15th centuries petty principalities consolidated into six major political units – the kingdoms of Naples and Sicily, the Papal States and the three major city-states of Florence, Venice and Milan. Other minor city-states co-existing alongside these larger powers made political stability in Italy more tenuous as their loyalties swung from one main force to another.

For the first time, starting around the 11th century, a new class appeared. During these late Middle Ages, modern Italy started to take shape. Wealth created in the *comuni* and republics began feeding the upcoming bourgeoisie, and the merchant class and traders began to inject the economy with money from their endeavours. Art flourished. With the strengthening of Italian *signorie*, the vying for notoriety often brought increased investment in architecture and art as a way to appease the Church and impress the masses. Powerful mogul families such as the Medici, sought to enhance their standing by financing architectural projects, paintings and sculpture. Italy's literary language, the Tuscan dialect, was being used by poets and writers such as Dante, Petrarch and Boccaccio, and was soon to become the nation's official spoken language (*see* 'The Italian Language', p.20). By 1300, a broad belt of some three hundred virtually independent city-states stretched from central Italy to the northernmost edge of the peninsula as the Renaissance was dawning.

Then the plague struck, halting city works and decimating populations. Florence was particularly hard hit, losing as many as 65,000 inhabitants. Petrarch lost his beloved Laura to the disease in Avignon, France. Boccaccio framed his most famous work, the *Decameron*, around a group of people fleeing Florence to the Tuscan countryside in refuge from the plague. In Siena, half of the population succumbed and coffers for church-building were drained to deal with the health crisis. By the end, Europe's population was nearly half what it had been. But the Renaissance had not been killed off.

The Renaissance

Whether it was the rise in powerful banking societies, economic success and excess or sheer post-plague enthusiasm that kicked off the Renaissance is debate material for the historians. But one thing that most do agree on is that *il Rinascimento* started in Florence. 15th-century Firenze was a self-governed, independent city-state. Twelve guilds regulated the trades, and wealthy guild members held influential positions in government and society.

Roman and Greek literature were exhumed and brought to life as valuable cultural assets. With the Byzantine Empire doomed and the advance of the Ottoman Turks on Constantinople, many Byzantines looked towards the Christian West as an escape route. Italy was not only the closest safe destination, but in the 1400s it also offered a dynamic atmosphere refreshing to many Byzantine intellectuals. Though the Greek émigrés who reached Italy during the 15th century were not all scholars, they played an important part in spreading the knowledge of the classical Greek language and ancient Greek literature in Italy.

Despite the intellectual and artistic advances that were made during the Renaissance, despotism in the cities was common. Totalitarianism driven by hereditary dictatorships and ruling élites replaced city governments. The city dictators seized power in numerous cities, installing dynastic rule for their families. Those cities that resisted the *signori* grasp – Venice, Florence, Siena and

Lucca – vacillated between republic-style governments and oligarchies. Almost every major Italian city today is graced by the remnants of the booming economies and expansion during the Renaissance. Florence had the Medici family that ruled the city *de facto*, emptied the communal coffers but patronized the arts generously. Venice's distinct oriental feel comes from centuries of trade and exploration. Marco Polo, the emblematic Venetian, embodied the daredevil pursuit of wealth and interests, and showered the city with legends, as well as jewels.

During the Renaissance, improvements in navigation and map-making made it possible to travel farther than before, and there was a lively trade in exotic spices, gems, fabrics and precious metals, especially when the Americas started to be exploited for their wealth. One of the Vatican cathedrals in Rome, Santa Maria Maggiore, has spectacular mosaics laid with gold brought directly from the new world. By the time the Renaissance puttered out around the end of the 15th century, the Middle Ages had been pushed far into the pages of history – or had they?

Symbolically, the Renaissance was crushed along with Rome, during the sack of 1527. For some this was a divine sign that Italians had taken a wrong turn down the religious road. Divine or not, it kicked off a century and a half of Spanish domination and pushed Italy on to the sidelines of European affairs. The Inquisition began burning and banning, planting fear left and right. Intellectuals like Galileo Galilei were questioned and imprisoned. Others, like Tommaso Campanella and Giordano Bruno (whose statue shadows Campo de Fiori in Rome), were burnt.

Economic decline led to general unrest and increased criminality in the way of bandits and roaming gangs. Spanish domination continued with the support of the Italian nobility, but was poorly carried out and at times brutal. Rome, under papal dominion, spent years stripping valuable materials off monuments like the Colosseum to build a more cosmopolitan city. Yet Rome suffered the trappings of a parasitical existence with no real means of generating income except by taxation.

The defeat of the Spanish in the War of Succession and the subsequent Peace of Utrecht treaty in 1713 did not bring significant changes. In the 18th century Italian aristocratic families owned almost everything there was to own, lived in opulence, and left the poor to grovel. Crime had supposedly spun so far out of control that in Venice a bizarre justice system was invented in which the judge, lawyer, priest and hangman would cruise the city together and wield sentences for misdeeds on the spot.

The enlightenment was on its way into Italy from France. When the French Revolution broke out and Corsican Napoleon Bonaparte began his military campaign, the enlightenment was interrupted. But in all of his comings and goings, Napoleon planted one decisive seed that would take root in the following years – the idea of a united Italy.

Risorgimento and Unification

Italy's desolate pre- and post-Napoleanic state had as much to do with geographical features as with the mismanagement by domineering rulers. While the northern farmers on the Pianura Padana had turned their marshes into productive rice paddies, central Italy suffered from malaria originating from unclaimed marshland. Deforestation in burnt, southern Italy made productive agriculture almost impossible in bulk. Trees were felled along the coastline for shipbuilding over the centuries. The alternative animal herds that made the cheese that is relished in the south even today, brought more environmental woes as the goats' hooves broke up the topsoil, leaving the land ready to flood at the first rain. A deficit in raw materials held the country back from taking part in the industrial revolution, and relegated the country to a lower place on the economic totem.

Within the confines of the peninsula, cultures, customs and languages couldn't have been different. In 1860 Metternich reproachfully said of Italy that it was merely a 'geographical expression', not a nation. But three characters whose names grace streets and squares all around Italy set their sights on a united Italy – Vittorio Emanuele II, Camillo de Cavour and Giuseppe Garibaldi. The unification (*risorgimento*) of Italy began in 1861 and by 1870 the nation was born. But 134 years after the *risorgimento*, Italy is still short on patriotic fervour. A recent survey showed that 65 per cent of Italians cannot sing the national anthem and 40 per cent confuse the Italian tricolour flag with Mexico's (which one has the eagle?). But the *risorgimento* made Italia and the Italiani the jigsaw they are today.

There is a saying that Italians only unite for wars and soccer matches. Post-unification brought the individual kingdoms into one, the Kingdom of Italy. But it wasn't until the First World War that nationalism reared its head – in the ugliest way, when, feeling jilted by post-war agreements, the country took a step away from the liberal state closer towards fascism. The demagogic poet Gabriele D'Annunzio began stirring the crowds into an incensed frenzy, and charismatic Benito Mussolini stepped in to give the movement a name. Remnants of fascist architecture and development stand side by side with ancient monuments. Entire towns, like the seaside resort of Saubaudia south of Rome, and neighbourhoods, like EUR in Rome, built with severe, white marble, are reminders of a not too distant and enduringly controversial past.

After the Second World War the first Italian republic was formed. After years of revolving door governments, and a number of corruption scandals, a second republic was born, supposedly purged of rotten elements through the trials called *Mani Pulite*, or Clean Hands. *See* **Italy Today**, 'Major Political Parties, Alliances and Elections', pp.60–64, which covers the last forty years of Italian politics.

The Italian Language

It wasn't until the advent of television that Italians began to understand and speak Italian. At least that is what has been said. Even today, a recent study reported that nearly half the population do not use standard Italian as their mother tongue. Just think that in 1861, when Italy became a unified nation, only 2.5 per cent of the new Italian citizens could speak what was considered standard Italian by the Piedmont administrators.

Not only are colloquial accents and Italian-related dialects widely used, but more than 11 distinct languages are spoken by ethnic minorities, some of which date back as far as the 10th century. Albanian, Croatian, Catalan, Occitan and Greek are five of the languages that have been spoken continuously for centuries in Italy. The Judeo–Italian dialect, Italkian, is spoken mainly in Rome, central and northern Italy (especially in Livorno). Originating in the 10th century, this fading dialect is a mix between Italian and Hebrew (as Yiddish is a mix between German and Hebrew). Only a tiny number of people speak Italkian fluently today and fewer than 4,000 people still use it in their everyday speech.

Each regional dialect is something like an insider's joke that coexists with the standard language, and one local tongue is generally unintelligible to speakers of other dialects. Piemontese and Sicilian are distinct enough to be classified as separate languages by the Italian Ministry of Culture. Venetian and Lombard are also very different and Neapolitan is unintelligible to speakers of standard Italian. For the linguistically curious, local dialects will never cease to amaze. Accents creamy enough to be cut with a butter knife, like Neapolitan, the rifle-precise staccato of Milanese and the countryside languor in the south all reveal the underlying fact that Italy was politically united, but did not have a homogenous development linguistically. This is not just a problem for newcomers to the Italian language. Italians themselves stumble over dialects. A Roman at a local fruit market in Naples hears what he or she calls *pomidori* referred to as *pummarole* in Naples. Many Roman words come directly from the heritage of the empire. *Fora*, or 'outside', in Roman slang, comes straight from the Latin *foro* – hence the Roman forum, *Foro Romano*, ruins that in ancient times were part of the outdoors Roman downtown.

Unlike other colonial countries such as France and Spain there is no country besides Italy (and the tiny San Marino within the borders of Italy) where Italian is the official language. According to a recent study, 55 million Italian-speakers – some of whom are native bilinguals of Italian and regional varieties, and some of whom may use Italian as second language – live in Italy. And some 62 million people throughout the world – in countries where Italians emigrated – speak Italian as their mother tongue. Countries where short-lived fascist colonialism developed, like Somalia, Ethiopia, Eritrea and Libya, still have many Italianisms, and several of the war generation still speak some Italian, but Italian is not the

What's in a Name?

'Romeo, oh Romeo,' sighed the young girl, in the back seat of her 1999 Fiat Uno, 'time to go home before my father shoots you.' Those names that seem like literary hangovers are alive and passing down from generation to generation. Here is some classic nomenclature that keeps coming back for encores on birth certificates around Italy, names so specific to Italy that you'll be happy you heard them here first.

Calogero – after Calogerus, a 5th-century Greek hermit saint who settled in Italy; Calogero is a melding of the two Greek words *kalos*, or beautiful and *geraios*, old age.

Cesare – Caesar, as in Julius (Giulio, another common name).

Cosimo – the elder Medici who founded the 15th-century Tuscan empire, and a name that smacks of something stellar.

Dante – still a first name and especially loved by the Tuscans.

Remo – a name still heard in the alleys of Trastevere in the capital; Romolo was the doomed brother of the mythical duo Romolo and Remo (Romulus and Remus) who founded Rome; Romolo was obviously the winner.

Ercole – Hercules never goes out of style.

Italo – legendary father of Romulus and Remus ... but wait, weren't they orphans?

Ottavio and Ottavia – in Roman times it meant eight.

Tiziano and Tiziana – Titianus, or Titus, was and still is a Roman name; there is a high percentage of Tizianos and Tizianas born in the 1960s – it's a popular name among mothers of the era.

Italian jokes often revolve around amusing situations that crop up as a result of regional differences. Stereotypical names that are inextricably linked to some of Italy's major towns and cities are:

Rosalia – a Sicilian name, especially in Palermo where the patron saint is Santa Rosalia.

Ambrogio – Milan's patron saint.

Nicola – good old St Nicholas, whose remains are in Bari.

Gennaro – the patron saint of Naples; two other names, Ciro and Salvatore, run a close second and third for stereotypical names.

first language in these countries as Spanish is in central and South America, or French in Francophone Africa.

However, today's official language in Italy is Italian, and Latin is its origin. Ancient Romans spoke and spread Latin throughout the continent, making it the *lingua franca* for commerce and business throughout the empire. Local dialects (*vulgare*) spun off Latin and were spoken by the populace. And the Latin that was dispersed with Roman expansion developed into Italian in Italy, Spanish in Spain, French in France, and so on.

The earliest Italian documents are written in vernacular. and over centuries Italian writers continued to use their native dialects, making way for a number of competing regional schools of literature to spring up. But during the 14th century the Tuscan dialect began to predominate. Dante, considered the father of Italian literature, wrote in the Florentine vernacular of the time. Tuscan, it was maintained, departed least in morphology and phonology from classical Latin. Towards the end of the 15th century Aldo Manuzio began commercial printing in Venice, reproducing the classics such as Homer and Virgil in Latin, but also Dante in *vulgare*, indicating to all of Europe that the shift from Latin to Italian had been accepted. When Alessandro Manzoni wrote *I Promessi Sposi* in 1827, the final cut was made from Dante's Italian to the form that is spoken today. And of course, television has added the final touches.

Profiles of the Regions

02

Non è questo 'l terren, ch' i' toccai pria?
Non è questo il mio nido,
Ove nudrito fui sí dolcemente?
Non è questa la patria in ch' io mi fido,
Madre benigna e pia,
Che copre l'un e l'altro mio parente?
Per Dio, questo la mente
Talor vi mova; e con pietà guardate
Le lagrime del popol doloroso,
Che sol da voi riposo,
Dopo Dio, spera: e, pur che voi mostriate
Segno, alcun di pietate,
Vertú contra furore
Prenderà l'arme; e fia 'l combatter corto;
Ché l'antiquo valore
Ne l' italici cor non è ancor morto.

                    Petrarch (1304–74)

Is not this precious earth my native land?
And is not this the nest
From which my tender wings were taught to fly?
And is not this soil upon whose breast,
Loving and soft, faithful and true and fond,
My father and my gentle mother lie?
'For love of God,' I cry,
Some time take thought of your humanity
And spare your people all their tears and grief!
From you they seek relief
Next after God. If in your eyes they see
Some marks of sympathy,
Against this mad disgrace
They will arise, the combat will be short
For the stern valour of our ancient race
Is not yet dead in the Italian heart.

                    trans. William Dudley Foulke LL D (1915)

There's no doubt about it, Italy has a little of something for everyone. Have you dreamt of a sunny seaside retreat, an expanse of snow-capped mountains outside the living room window, or an arid desert landscape dotted with prickly pears in bloom? Do you prefer an ancient city centre where time refuses to loosen its grip on tradition, or a modern metropolitan hub where fashion and design reign relentlessly? Well, thank goodness you're moving to Italy. The choices abound.

Italy is an old land, but a very young nation, and far from a homogenous entity. Every region has its own particular character – often more than one – that comes from centuries of independent city-states scattered throughout the peninsula. Everybody rings their own region's bell in a very Italian attitude known as *campanilismo* – having an overwhelmingly strong sense of identity and devotion to citizens' native region or town. When abroad and asked where they are from, Italians will inevitably respond with the name of their home town first, and perhaps follow this up with the country.

But this isn't usually necessary when the town in question is Naples, Venice, Rome or Florence. These cities, with their vibrant and intriguing pasts, have made a name for themselves in the annals of history and in the collective imagination of the world. And that is exactly what *campanilismo* leads us towards. Italy, like a fine da Vinci painting, would lose its meaning if any one region were removed. It is as part of the whole that each individual area shines the brightest. To find out about the regional food and wine specialities of Italy *see* **Italy Today**, 'Regional Cuisines and Specialties', pp.89–94.

Central Italy

Sometimes called the beating heart of the land, at other times accused of being the breeding pot of corrupt government officials, central Italy has some of Italy's most celebrated towns, cities and historical backdrops. It is an area where the Vatican state wielded its power for centuries, shaping the psyche of politics and people. Lazio, the area around Rome, holds historical riches and is largely neglected as the masses gravitate to the capital city itself. Tuscany and Umbria have ever-popular tourist hotspots, and many expats who move to 'idyllic' Italy. Marche and Abruzzo, Central Italy's two forgotten territories, are climbing up the charts of popularity as a result of their rugged beauty and comparatively modest prices.

Abruzzo

Roughly the shape of a semicircle, with a diameter of about 150km (90 miles), Abruzzo is right in the middle of the peninsula. Abruzzo's handicap is also its blessing. Craggy, remote mountains make parts of the region difficult to access, especially during the winter months of snow. Monks, hermits and saints have gravitated to Abruzzo's remote and mountainous terrain seeking peace and isolation. Sanctuaries grace some of the most spectacular and hard-to-reach spots throughout the region; many are still beautifully preserved and open to travellers looking for a quiet alternative. Yet those same mountain passes that protected loners from unwanted visitors have been penetrated by modern highways, and now the region boasts modest yet well-frequented ski resorts, which attract central and southern winter sports fans. On a clear day, skiers and snowboarders get a great view of the sea in the distance.

The region's inhabitants have traditionally lived unassumingly on the land or else moved elsewhere – Dean Martin and Sylvester Stallone are two of the region's exports. Conveniently, the region's four provinces are geographically varied. The province of L'Aquila is characterized by mountains, whereas in the **Chieti** area hills prevail, and the provinces of **Pescara** and **Teramo** have an equal sprinkling of both. There are no plains to speak of except for the Piana del Fucino, created last century by drying up Lake Fucino.

The relatively short coastline of 129km (80 miles) stretches from the river Tronto to the Trigno and constitutes the eastern boundary of the region, while the north borders with Marche, the south with Molise and the west with Lazio. The land boundaries of the region are 467km (290 miles) long.

Beautiful urban developments like **L'Aquila**, the regional capital, with a view of the ominous Gran Sasso mountain, have noble backgrounds and were built when the region was at its most desolate. L'Aquila was founded by Frederick II in 1254 and nestles near the Parco Nazionale dell'Abruzzo, an enormous, 518 sq km (200 sq mile) natural reserve where the king used to do his hunting. Teramo is a 1st-century AD Roman town, like Chieti, with a theatre still used for shows and performances.

Mysticism and superstition run deep for the inhabitants of this remote and rugged terrain and, as in most of the rest of Italy, are exorcised through annual festivals and rituals. La Panarda, one of Abruzzo's most fanatically celebrated festivals, is an all-night feast with 30 to 50 servings of gargantuan proportions, held to celebrate the legendary divine intervention of St Anthony Abate when a mother returned home to find her newborn in the jaws of a wolf.

Lazio

Italy's capital city overshadows the region that encompasses it. What a pity. But it hasn't always been that way. Lazio – or Latium, meaning abundant territory – has nuggets of scenic getaways, seaside towns that Roman emperors flocked to, gardens, villas and mountain sanctuaries fit for the popes. But despite all that, for Lazio, having **Rome** as a capital city is like having Naomi Campbell as a big sister.

When Rome acquired the title *caput mundi*, or capital of the world, not many raised their voice in protest. And the eternal city holds her grip today. Impossibly chaotic, lagging light years behind other European capitals in development and modernization, loud, polluted and suffocating, Rome is a city that makes no pretences. Romans don't care if you love their city, or if you criticize its inefficiency. If it hasn't changed in all these years, your bit of nagging isn't going to count any more than the coin you throw in the Trevi fountain. That insistence on

Spaghetti Western

In the deep south of Tuscany and northern zone of Lazio, known as the Maremma, some locals meander in boots with spurs and are just as expert at roping cattle as any Texan on the range. A Tuscan cowboy (*buttero*) is no less a rider, breaker, lasso-thower and whisky-drinker than John Wayne in his best western. In fact, the *butteri* gave Buffalo Bill a lesson when he brought his superlative riders from America and challenged them in Rome. Bill went back defeated. The *butteri* went back to their longhorns in the dusty-pale countryside, richer and victorious.

coping with change slowly is what has preserved the city's character and kept her so well known, and often shunned by neighbouring regions.

Beyond the city limits, the pull of the Eternal City becomes background noise, getting quieter with every mile's distance from the roar. Stretches of wide beaches, great pinewoods, mountains, gentle hills and expansive plains make sure of that. Especially stunning necropolises and museums with Etruscan relics dating as far back as the 8th century BC at Tarquinia, Cerveteri and Tuscania have attracted the likes of D.H. Lawrence and Gustav VI, king of Sweden. Towns such as Rieti, Viterbo, Latina and Frosinone have Roman ruins as ancient as those found in the capital city itself. Villa Adriana in Tivoli and the Renaissance Villa d'Este, with its spectacular fountains, are less than a 40-minute drive from the heart of Rome. The Vatican's same grandiose style is projected and duplicated outside Rome with the abbeys of Montecassino, Casamari and Fossanova, and the monasteries of Subiaco.

Hunkered in the territory between Tuscany, Umbria and Campania, identities bleed over the borders. In the **Maremma Laziale**, the northern part of the region, the letter 'c' turns into an 'h', in the distinct Tuscan accent. Due south, the coastal towns of **Sperlonga** and **Gaeta** with their Neapolitan flair and tubs of white *mozzarella di bufala* are closer to Naples in atmosphere, despite being only an hour's drive from Rome. It just goes to show that Lazio is not just Rome, as Rome will never be all surrounded by Lazio.

The Marches

Hailed today as the untouched Tuscany, Le Marche is a region that is only starting to gain notoriety outside Italy. No surprise. Unspoilt and modest, it is refreshingly free of pretentious developments, cheesy tourist traps and heavy industry. But being untouched does not leave the Marches without a history. The Etruscans established settlements near the coast and numerous archaeological centres have been exposed by the region's excavation efforts. Massive monasteries deeply affected the social structure of the region by introducing agricultural reforms that gave peasants sharecropping rights, known as the *contratto di mezzadria*, which meant the end of starvation for poor farmers.

The region shares the border and part of the Apennine mountains with Emilia-Romagna and has Umbria to the southwest and Abruzzo to the southeast. Though Ancona is the capital of the region, Le Marche is really a patchwork of self-sufficient communities of farmers and artisans. Hundreds of towns of nearly equal measure and importance today carry on a castle and villa economy stemming directly from the Middle Ages.

Coastal capital city **Ancona** is the junction for the region. Greek refugees from Siracusa gave the city its name, which means elbow in Greek, because of the way it juts into the Adriatic. The Romans came and went, as did the Barbarians, all leaving their mark. Ancona was bombed in the Second World War and has been shaken by earthquakes, but is still graced with splendid architecture. Ascoli Piceno, Macerata and Pesaro-Urbino are other major towns.

Le Marche has its share of legends. In the heart of the Sibillini mountain range that runs through a national park by the same name lies the cavern entrance to the land of endless delights, the queendom of none other than Sibilla. Near the tiny town of Montecasiano, **Lake Pilato** is where the Roman governor Pontius Pilate's body is said to have been brought and dumped. The town of **Loreto** has something no other town in the world can boast of – the Virgin Mary's house, which arrived on 10 December 1294, some say delivered by angels, the only known form of air transport at the time. Not to be forgotten, one of Italy's most famous artists, Raphael, is from the town of Urbino, though he painted angels instead of cavorting with them.

Traditionally known as the region of tax collectors for the Papal States, Marchigiani gained a reputation for being thick-skinned and pragmatic. If there is a job to do, they get it done, but at their own pace. Today, most of Italy's fine shoes are cobbled in Le Marche, known as the shoe capital of the country.

Tuscany

Poor, over-clichéd Tuscany suffers the same brutal stereotyping as all of Italy. Florence, sometimes called a Renaissance Disneyland, gets massive waves of brush-over tourism, and a handful of the selective kind. Notorious **Chianti** has

Mary's Girdle

Not wanting to leave her followers without a momento, Mary left her girdle (*cintola*) to Thomas the Apostle in a brash, last-minute performance. Think of Mary's moment of assumption as something of a rock concert finale. While rising above the crowds, she tossed a piece of attire to the first person who could catch it. Legend goes that Thomas faithfully kept and protected the item of clothing and it was passed down to a priest and his descendants. It arrived in Prato after one of the crusades as part of a young bride's dowry in the Middle Ages, and is taken out several times a year and displayed for all to see.

Tuscan Writeaway

Not only do authors write about Tuscany, they go there to write. A 15th-century medieval farmhouse, not far down the road from Sting and no more than a 20-minute train ride from Florence, Santa Maddalena has hosted many authors in need of sanctuary and inspiration. Run by Beatrice Monti della Corte, the house was turned into a retreat after her husband, novelist Gregor von Rezzori, passed away. Zadie Smith is among the famous pen-wielders who have sought and received the ancient stone house's blessings, along with Irish writer Colm Tóibín, Michael Ondaatje, author of *Anil's Ghost*, and film director Bernardo Bertolucci, to name a few.

been dubbed Chiantishire for its overgrown expat community that jacked up property prices for good. Beyond the clichés, Tuscany is more than any other region a direct descendent of the city-state structure. There are uncountable old bones to pick. Florentines still moan about the Sienese, who defeated them in the battle of Montaperti in 1260. The saying *'meglio un morto a casa che un Pisano all'uscio'* or 'better to have a dead person in the house than a Pisan at the entrance' shows just how much everyone loves Pisans. Not only does history run deep, the waters are full of flotsam that keeps rolling to the shore. In other words, history is still alive for most Tuscans, and one reason is as good as another for having a heated discussion, if not an out-and-out fight. Friendships and alliances go back, too – the Puccis' ancestors rubbed elbows with the all-mighty Medici in the days when true friendship could help keep your head on your shoulders, and not rolling on the ground.

Dante, a Florentine himself, said that his compatriots were an envious and proud lot, and Machiavelli laid out the rules for just how much citizens needed to be punished and kept in line. Florentines like to say that they invented the Renaissance – something like creating the modern world. From the Middle Ages to the Renaissance there was no other city that could match the city's power and wealth. No matter how much they wish they could, no Italian can deny the vast culture that Florence and Tuscany generated. From Boccaccio to Botticelli, Michelangelo, da Vinci and Galileo, the stream of art and literature goes on and on.

Florence is a chic city. Gucci and Pucci are fashion icons cut from Tuscan cloth, and the abundance of leather and gold drip from the city's many so-called outlets. The real bargain basements, however, are near another Tuscan town, Prato, where the girdle of the Virgin Mary is displayed in the main cathedral and flocks of shopping tourists take numbers and queue outside warehouses for hours to pick through designer labels at a fraction of shop prices.

Tuscany is not monopolized by Florence, by any means. Russell Crowe, Sting and the likes, all of whom purchased homes in the countryside, will attest to that. But nor is it the abundantly filmed, over-depicted and foreigner-filled

Chianti. To the northwest loom the massive **Alpi Apuane**, with snow- and marble-covered peaks, ski resorts and nature trails. The remote stretch of valleys between the Alps and Apennines known as the **Garfagnana** is a far cry from the rolling hills of Chianti. The same goes for the plains to the south, the **Maremma**, a territory that has its other half in the northern part of Lazio.

Umbria

Maybe it was the peaceful St Francis who left his mark on Umbria. Timeless and mystical, the green heart of Italy appeals to the pensive soul of nature-lovers and those who revel in the quiet of the countryside. Sparkling hilltop towns are bastions of art and architecture dropped in the midst of a verdant expanse. With its few – but mightily precious – tourist attractions, Umbria has sidestepped the push and shove of its closest neighbour Tuscany. It is only recently that foreigners have started to buy up properties that, compared with the expat-saturated Chiantishire, are still relatively inexpensive.

Second only to the Vatican as a spiritual magnet, fans of St Francis and St Clare come by the busload to walk up the steep and winding road leading to the basilicas of **Assisi**. Perhaps no single figure sent waves through the church as St Francis did, with his unabashed criticism of opulent church spending and love of nature. It was his inspiration that encouraged Giotto, who set paintings and frescoes in recognizable scenes, turning what had once been sterile and faraway icons into images familiar to all. He stripped naked in front of the town's bishop, refused his earthly parents and claimed he had only one heavenly father. So great was his impact on the Church that if his had not been incorporated as an order, Martin Luther might not have been the first Protestant.

Perugia, Assisi's sworn enemy for centuries, holds less spiritual appeal but plenty of interest artistically. Crowning a tall plateau, the ruins from its Etruscan and Roman origins still surround the city's base. An elegant, modern town now, it hosts one of the country's best-known language schools and a yearly chocolate festival that brings in sweet revenues, as well as tons of luscious stuff in every shape and form imaginable. Several valleys away, **Spoleto** becomes one of Europe's hottest music venues each summer with its annual music festival.

Though landlocked, Umbria has an abundant amount of water. **Lake Trasimeno**, where the African general Hannibal ambushed and defeated Roman troops before moving south, has two small islands and miles of banks where one can perch before diving into the refreshing waters. The Tiber dissects the region, providing the needed vapour to create that city-in-the-mist look that increases the charm of many hilltop towns, **Todi** especially.

The South

No single region of Italy evokes the archetypal image of the country as the southern ones do. Hot in temperature and spicy in flavour, the combined regions of Calabria, Puglia, Campania and less well-known Molise and Basilicata suffer the burden of being labelled 'underdeveloped'. They all have their share of infrastructure difficulties, corruption and unemployment.

Calabria

When Italy was unified in 1861, underdeveloped Calabria had one road running from the southern town of Reggio to the north. No railroad connected the isolated hillside enclaves or coastal settlements. Years of tick-like rulers had sucked the populace dry through over-taxation and stripped the land of much of its valuable timber, the very origin of its present-day name, which originates from the Hebrew *kaleb*, or land of woods. Over the last century, especially, Calabria has seen a constant trickle, if not flood, of fleeing natives in search of opportunity – a problem endemic in the south, and even more so in Calabria.

When the Greeks arrived they landed in a territory called Brutium after a tough Italic tribe that had occupied the land. Previously, it was known as Enotria after another tribe. Towns like the southernmost **Reggio di Calabria**, **Crotone** and **Cantanzaro** all have their roots in the Greek colonies of Magna Grecia. Romans referred to the region as 'Italia' probably after Italic tribes who inhabited the region, and were nicer than the occupants that caused its name to be demoted to Brutium – not a pretty name. Romans came and went, wielding their brand of development and founding the town of **Cosenza**.

What Calabria has always had in abundance, apart from misery, is sun. Hundreds of miles of coastline and crystalline waters have been a boost in developing tourism over the last decades. Yet the inhabitants have been called daunting and dry; certainly old-fashioned etiquette and an over-exaggerated use of titles hang on stubbornly. There are pockets of self-contained communities, such as the Grecanici who live along the slopes of the dried-out Aspromonte rivers, protecting their traditions and secrets and tracing their roots back to the survivors of the Trojan war. Enclaves of Albanian descendants, refugees from the 15th-century Ottoman invasion of Albania, where a modern version of ancient Arbëresh is still the norm, are scattered throughout the highlands of the Sila, Calabria's magestic mountain range.

Despite having a blighted reputation for kidnappings and an overwhelming presence of local mafia, 'Ndrangheta, the region has a time-frozen beauty that tourists are beginning to recognize. Food and wine tend to be spicy, redolent of a strong Greek influence.

Puglia

When in Puglia, the rolling hills of Tuscany and glimmering canals of Venice could not seem further away. Luminous and sun-drenched, the arid landscape that spans Italy's heel is lapped by the Ionian and Adriatic seas and saturated with a magical history.

Landing ground to many throughout the centuries, the faces, accents and cuisine of the region sing of ancient Greece, Spain and the nearby Balkans. Whoever sighs that the accent is 'all Greek to me' is closer to the truth than they think. Many words in dialect, and names, are remnants from the old Greek colonies. The tarantella, a wildly rhythmic jingling dance to music performed by shaman-like musicians, once used to cure spider bites, is still stomped and spun out, as it was in the beginning in honour of Dionysus (the patron god of wine) of ancient Greece.

Another distinctive element of Puglia is the conical-shaped *trullo* building, which shows up in endless rows throughout the region, but especially near the settlement known as **Alberobello**. Decorated with mysterious signs, and still inhabited today, the origins of the building are unknown. Where the plains flatten out near Ostuni, west of Bari, sprawling ranches known as *masserie* give the country a far west feel.

Once a den of danger and despair, until recently the historic centre of the capital city **Bari** was considered off-limits to the uninitiated. Nowadays the old quarter (*bari vecchia*) is openly flaunting its Byzantine and Romanesque architecture. Further south and down the coast are the towns of Salento, Lecce and Brindisi, where ferries depart for Greece and the Balkans. On the inside of the heel, the island of **Gallipoli**, connected by an isthmus, sighs with oriental memories of the Saracen rule. Sea-lovers swear that the water is at its bluest off the **Salentine peninsula** on the Gulf of Taranto, where Gallipoli floats near the coast. Along the strip of land sometimes called the spur of the heel, the **Gargano promontory** is known by locals for a series of mysterious and irresistible caverns cut by years of wear from wind and water. Each grotto has a name that gives away its story, like the smugglers' cave (*grotto dei contrabbandieri*) or the cave of the swallows (*grotto delle rondini*).

Campania

If you don't give your heart to **Naples**, she will take it from you. The capital city of the region of Campania has brought tears to the eyes of many, put joy in poets' hearts, nursed imaginations and been cursed by nations for centuries. Goethe was right, 'see Naples then die', because it is hard to top her.

Neapolis was the new city for the Greeks, who established an outpost on the bay in 750 BC. Most of the city's character comes from later rulers – the Spanish Aragonese and the French Bourbons under Charles – as do popular names like

Alfonso, words in Neapolitan dialect and a strong distaste for authority. Even San Gennaro, the city's patron saint, is something of a renegade, since the Church half-heartedly canonized him, realizing that if they didn't, Naples would turn its back on the Church in favour of Gennaro. And in the city where superstition reigns supreme, his name is evoked for everything from sick family members to playing the lottery.

Its long history as a regal capital and international metropolis (it was the third largest city in Europe in the 18th century) has also left a culinary legacy of complicated aristocratic *pièces-de-résistance*, such as the rice casserole *sartù* and a tradition of sweets installed by Swiss pastry-chefs, featuring the rum-soaked *babà* and the ricotta-filled *sfogliatelle*, which often accompany the world's best espresso.

Away from the city's pull, some of the best day trips from any Italian city leave from Naples. **Pompeii** and the lesser-known **Herculaneum** excavations are on the outskirts. A drive or walk up Vesuvius is all it takes for a dizzying view of the bay of Naples outstretched and sparkling. Cumae, a town in the middle of the gaseous Phlegrean Fields, is mentioned in the oracles related to the cult of Apollo and probably also of Hera. The Greeks, by the way, believed the fumes came from the decaying bodies of giants buried there. And the citrus-lined splendour of the winding **Amalfi coast** has arguably one of the world's most scenic roads.

Naples is unrelentingly appealing. Recent restoration and improvement schemes have paid off and the city is starting to lose its reputation for being dangerous and crime-ridden, something that never kept visitors away anyhow. But the city's inhabitants will always have that glimmer of cleverness (*furbizia*) that they are known for. It is one of the city's most frustratingly endearing characteristics.

Molise

Previously coupled with Abruzzo in a block-unit region known as the Abruzzi, Molise was issued its birth certificate in 1963 through an Italian regional reform. That doesn't mean that it is a region short on history and monuments. Palaeolithic settlements from more than 900,000 years ago, along with Roman amphitheatres and medieval castles, have been protected and preserved, as have the inhabitants' artistic, culinary and linguistic heritage.

Sparsely inhabited expanses make up the mid-ground between Abruzzo's steep mountains and Puglia's sweeping plains. Ferdinando I hunted wild boar in the verdant, rolling hills that are today some of the most immaculately preserved nature reserves in the country. Shepherds walk down the paths that were cut by their ancestors thousands of years ago. Around Christmas-time, wandering musicians known as Zampognari head to Rome from the hillsides of

Molise in shepherd-inspired clothing to play their bagpipe-like instruments under windows for money. Their wailing tunes usher in the holiday season for most Romans. **Campobasso** and **Isernia** are the two principal towns of the region, while the costal town of **Termoli** is on the way to becoming a modestly trendy resort with its 35km (22-mile) stretch of white-sand beaches.

Directly across the Adriatic strait lies Croatia. Immigration from the 15th and 16th centuries by Albanians, Serbian and Croatians has influenced the local dialect and looks in many of the towns throughout the region.

Basilicata

Once shockingly impoverished, beautifully barren Basilicata is crawling out from the shadow of obscurity. But it will take some time. This region continues to be shackled by unemployment, an underdeveloped infrastructure and little outside investment, keeping it cut off from the rest of the country. Carlo Levi's *Christ Stopped at Eboli* underlines its isolation. To which some respond, 'good'. Incredible landscapes with moon-like qualities, sparkling bays with no belching smokestacks and Byzantine churches carved into hillsides have survived untouched and are there for the enjoyment of those willing to cross the abandoned countryside to reach them. Isolation, it is said, has its advantages.

Despite having both the Tyrrhenian and Ionian seas lapping at its shores, the region hosts no major harbours. **Maratea** is the coast's most gracious town; it peers down from its rocky cliff where it is perched above a small harbour. Quiet and unassuming, the mostly undiscovered resort spot is not to be confused with **Matera**, a town completely cut off from the rest of the region, lacking any rail connections. Many of its inhabitants lived in abject misery in squalid, damp caves carved in the tufo rock that the town is built on until the government relocated some hundreds of sick and lice-infected children and adults into public housing.

The North

Cerebral and glamorous, northern Italy pulses glitz and shine, as it does agriculture and rural living. Proud of their industrial essence, Northern Italians are characterized as hard-working and organized, if also a bit dry. This upper third of the country is formed by the regions Lombardy, the Veneto, Piemonte, Valle d'Aosta, Trentino-Alto Adige, Friuli-Venezia Giulia, Liguria and Emilia-Romagna.

The northeast, or tri-Veneto as it was once called – made up of Veneto, Trentino-Alto Adige and Friuli-Venezia Giulia – is where Italians fought most of the First World War. Valle d'Aosta and Piemonte had a centuries-long umbilical cord connecting them to France, which was weakened but not severed with the unification of Italy in 1861 and the Second World War. If rebel-rouser and separatist Umberto Bossi from the Lega Nord (Northern League) had his way, he would have the entire region of Lombardy chatting away in ancient Celtic dialects to emphasize the region's distance from the rest of the country.

Despite the overall stereotype of this being an industrial region, each separate area has characteristics that date back to the peninsula's city-state heritage.

Lombardy

Industrialized and organized, the northern region of Lombardia is as no-nonsense as its inhabitants, and known as the industrial backbone of the country. 'Chi ghe volta el cú a Milan, ghe volta el cú al pan,' say the Lombards in dialect, meaning 'Who turns their back (ass) on Milan turns their back on food.' It is said that even the region's trademark, heavy fog, is created by the thousands of spewing industrial smokestacks as much as from the wet plains around the Po river. Though it lacks the pomp and flair of the exuberant south, it makes up for it with measured tempers and refined mannerisms. The Milanese themselves say Milan is for work, Rome is for living.

Supporters of the separatist movement and political party Lega Nord would have the world believing that i Padani – the inhabitants of the area defined by its geographical distinction, the Pianura Padana, or Padana Plains – are direct descendants of the Celtic tribes that lived in the area, not Roman. But, despite their political mythology, the region has in fact been influenced by Spanish overlords, Austrian invaders, French and Venetians, all of whom have left a delicious mingling of cultures and styles that burst forth in architecture, food and dialect.

Lombardy was part of the Roman empire's Gallia Cisalpina. The German barbarians known as Longobards (long beards) enjoyed heckling and raiding ancient Rome from the land they dubbed as Mailand (land of May), because of its comparatively mild climate. Landlocked with the Alps to the north, most of the region is spread across the Po River basin. Mountains help block the frigid air currents of the two major lakes – Lago Maggiore and Lago di Garda – keeping the weather mild enough for palms and citrus trees to grow along the banks.

The region's capital city, **Milan**, is ruled by fashion and finance. The country's exchange, the Borsa, gives the city a New York hustle and bustle feel. The whirl of Fashion Week, when Europe's designers unveil their latest, and the Salone dei Mobile, interior design's comparable event, bring visitors by the masses.

The aperitivo culture thrives in Milan like in no other city. It may be that hard work leads to serious play; certainly rivers of scrumptious snacks and finger foods appear on bars around the city as in no other Italian town, as business men and women spill out of their offices for a Campari-soda or other lightly alcoholic beverage to help them unwind before dinner.

Veneto

With one of the world's most dazzling cities getting all the limelight, Veneto has a hard time reminding tourists to get out of Venice and see the rest of the region. The sparkling allure of the floating city has entranced the world, and especially couples in love who dream of floating down the city's canals in curvy-bowed gondolas, serenaded as they go. And if Venice doesn't inspire enough cooing and eyelash batting, Verona, the city where Romeo and Juliet sighed and died, and where millions of lovers flock yearly to swear eternal love, is just a couple of hours away.

Bedazzling **Venice** is located about 4km (2.5 miles) from the mainland of Italy and spread out on 118 islands in the Venetian lagoon. It is connected to the mainland by road and railroad directly to Mestre and Porto Marghera, but once in the city itself the streets are refreshingly free of wheeled traffic, bicycles excluded. More than 150 canals and 400 bridges crisscross the city and provide the network for water ferries (*vaporetti*), which serve the same purpose as roads would – getting people and goods around town. Outlying islands, such as Burano, famous for its lace, the glass-making centre of Murano, and the resort town Lido, are administered by the city of Venice.

In the 7th and 8th centuries the Republic of Venice began to develop into an important trading centre and Mediterranean power. Venetian merchants gave the city one of its most prized relics in 848 by stealing the bones of St Mark from Alexandria. It gradually acquired territory in Greece, Turkey and on the Italian mainland, and by the 15th century had reached the height of its power. It was by arranging the transport in the Crusades that the city accumulated much of its wealth, and in 1204 Venice went so far as to conquer Byzantium and raked in booty worth seven times the revenue of the kingdom of England at the time, and the famous four bronze horses that grace San Marco.

Much of the Veneto was embellished by the works of architect Andrea Palladio in the 16th century, and a number of his villas and other works are scattered throughout the region, especially in his home town of **Vicenza**. **Padua** has the remarkable early 14th century Scrovegni chapel with famous frescoes by Giotto and the 14th-century Basilica di Sant'Antonio, where the saint's tongue and vocal cords are on display. Verona, apart from embodying lovers' dreams, is an important site for Roman ruins.

Piemonte

Natives of Piemonte, the Piemontesi, are known for their sober and serious demeanour. There is a story that a Sicilian living in Piemonte finds it hard to make friends. To help him strike up conversation, he decides to buy a cute, special little puppy – one that can walk on water. Not one head turns as the lonely southerner tosses a stick over and over into the pond of Turin's main park and his dog dashes across the surface to fetch it. Finally, desperate to exchange contact and conversation, he looks over at the man fishing next to him and says, 'Hey! See what my dog can do?' To which the Piemonte native replies nonchalantly, 'You'll never teach that dog to swim.'

The capital of Italy from 1860 to 1865, **Turin** looks anything but stereotypically Italian. With its wide, tree-lined avenues and 16km (10 miles) of porticoes it is a graceful town with all of its grandeur on display.

Turin was made the principal town of Piedmont by Amadeus, first duke of Savoy in the 13th century, and when the dukes were elevated to kings became the royal capital. Italy's fever for unification infected the peninsula from Turin and in 1861 it briefly became the capital city. The first Italian Parliament met in Turin's most beautiful building – the Palazzo Carignano, built in the late seventeenth century.

Torinese are fine connoisseurs. Superb food shops with their wood-and-etched-glass façades displaying beautiful cheeses, pastas, *grissini* (breadsticks, a city speciality) and *gianduiotti* (little ingots of chocolate and hazelnuts) create a Parisian feel. Locals will spend hours discussing the finer qualities of the chocolatier who roasts his cocoa beans over olive wood when compared with a competitor who instead roasts the hazelnuts before grinding them into a paste for his delicate pastries.

It is also a town that likes to stroll. The *passeggiata* is practised by everyone and the long stretches of parks and green spaces make the city human. There is a mass exodus out of town at weekends as the locals go off in quest of good food and fresh air. The best of precious white truffles are found near the town of **Alba** to the south, where the yearly festival sets world prices for this underground mushroom, which costs more per ounce than gold. Barolo, Barbaresco and Nebbiolo are just three of the prize wines produced in the region and many vineyards open their fields for walks and tastings.

Valle d'Aosta

When much of Italy is at its worst – during the depths of winter or height of summer – the country's tiniest region is at its best. A more picturesque entrance into Italy for those journeying from France through the Mont Blanc tunnel could hardly be dreamt up. Seemingly a lost land, leaning more towards France than Italy, Aostani proudly speak patois and link their history's development to the royal Savoy family, but not especially to France.

Winter in Valle d'Aosta tops any fairytale setting. Its two major ski resorts, **Courmayeur** and **Breuil-Cervinia**, are near enough to Piemonte for skiers to drop in at weekends, and spectacular enough for vacationers to drop the bucks and come for an extended stay. Inviting villages crafted from grey rocks culled from the mountains, which rise on all sides, have welcoming taverns where hand-carved bowls with spouts brimming with the local winter drink, *grullo*, made from hot coffee, spices, sugar and grappa, is passed around to knock the chill out of the bones.

Despite being known primarily as the stomping ground of serious skiers and hikers, the region's cultural sites abound. Although generally off the beaten track, for millennia, it was a well-trodden crossroads, in fact one of the main access routes between northern and southern Europe. Invading African general Hannibal marched his elephants through the steep passages in the 3rd century BC, as did generations of Roman legions, who built roads and bridges that are still visible today. Undaunted pilgrims trekked through on their way to Rome. All of this was before two of the great engineering feats, the Mont Blanc Tunnel and the Great St Bernard Tunnel, were built.

Trentino-Alto Adige

Just one step from Austria, in Trentino-Alto Adige you feel as if you are already there. Essentially, half of the region is. Alto Adige, also known as **Süd Tirol**, and its inhabitants, the Tirolesi, are German-speakers who live a life that is culturally very different from people who live at the other end of the region in Trentino.

Both German and Italian are spoken throughout the region, though depending on where you are the German often wins out. Maps get crowded up with the many double-names such as Bressanone/Brixen, Bolzano/Bozen, Corno Nero/Schwarzhorn and of course Corno Bianco/Weisshorn.

All may seem calm and orderly in appearance, but this is a deeply divided region, which has long struggled to find a homogenous identity for itself. Napoleon conquered this area and immediately turned it over to the Austrian Habsburgs, who ruled it until it was returned to Italy at the end of the First World War. Mussolini laid down the law in 1939, giving inhabitants the chance to choose Italian citizenship and stick around or take their *knudel* and go north. The overwhelming majority chose the latter option, and the rural territory was left even more underpopulated than previously.

Those who did stick it out in Alto Adige hardly became mandolin-playing Marios. In 1948 the Italian legislature took the politically expedient route and made Trentino-Alto Adige an autonomous region, deepening the internal rift between the two provinces. **Trentino**, despite its geographical closeness to Alto Adige, is unmistakably Italian. But to make it more interesting, sprinkled throughout the mountain valleys of both areas are about 80,000 residents who, clinging to yet another ethnic tradition, speak an ancient language known as Ladin. This utterly incomprehensible language is a combination of Celtic dialects and Latin from the 1st century BC, a mingling of northern colonists and Roman legions.

What most visitors go to the Trentino-Alto Adige for is not the cultural break-down but the inconceivably stunning **Dolomite mountains** and all the fun that can be had from their peaks to their valleys. **Madonna di Campiglio** and **Cortina d'Ampezzo** are by far the best known, and Cortina, especially, turns into a winter resort straight out of *Who's Who*. Those driving in from Austria take the Brenner pass with its outstanding view of the rosy-peaked mountains.

This is probably one of the few areas in Italy that can manage to make a bad pizza and overcooked pasta. That's because, even more than the language, the food is decisively German, including rye breads, sauerkraut and schnitzel. More beer is consumed than in southern Italy, but a fine array of white wines, like Gewürztraminer and Riesling, abound.

Friuli-Venezia Giulia

The last wall dividing eastern and western Europe came down on 12 February 2004 in nowhere other than Italy. One of Europe's last symbols of Cold War-era division finally removed, more than a decade after the fall of the Berlin wall.

But the removal of the metal fence that had separated the Italian town of **Gorizia** from its Slovenian neighbour Nova Gorica since 1947 was primarily symbolic. Friuli-Venezia Giulia shares its borders with Slovenia and Austria, but has rarely been divided from the Saxon and Slavic threads that run through the region's cultural and culinary fabric, despite tensions and old grudges.

Its main town, **Trieste**, perches on top of the Carso Plateau, running along the Slovenian border, with a spectacular view from atop a rocky peak carved by the famous Bora wind. Longobards descended on Trieste and plundered it in AD 586, and the surrounding territory now known as Friuli remained culturally Roman while slowly drawing closer to the Longobard ways through influence and often force. Institutions founded by the Longobards survived in Friuli well into the 15th century. In the meantime the Byzantine influence took root and the Avars and Slavs found a foothold. By the 18th century Charles of Hapsburg established the 'free ports' of Trieste and Fiume, giving the Austrian empire access to the Mediterranean Sea. Austro-Hungarian architecture, with its Mitteleuropa hues, dominates the city so loved by Maria Theresa in the 18th century.

With its shifting borders and unclear ethnic blurs, the region suffered the brunt of numerous, painful battles in the First World War, particularly around the ports and in the Isonzo valley. Gorizia was razed to the ground. The heavy hand of the Austrian police and the defeat of Caporetto in 1917 kicked off the exodus of much of its population. After the war, violent political debate still continued in the region, and a large number of Slavs found their borders switched overnight. What wasn't resolved was reborn with the Second World War, when an active Slavic insurrectionist movement exploded. Postwar Istria became Yugoslavia in 1947, but was flipped back in 1954 with an agreement that made the region part of Italy. Finally, in 1964, the autonomous region of Friuli-Venezia Giulia, with its main city Trieste, was born.

This has one of the most complex ethno-linguistic histories in Italy because remote areas speak dialects derived from a neo-Latin language called Ladino, while other dialects have Venetian influences. Other dialects are derived from ancient Slavic languages as in the town of Resia.

Despite producing only 2 per cent of Italy's wines, the whites are remarkable for their quality and the number of native and introduced varieties, including the Tocai Friulano. *See* **Italy Today**, 'Wine', pp.95–6, for more details.

Liguria

Napolean entered Italy, but never Genoa. His troops froze in their tracks when they heard the rumours of Genoa's supposed cannibals protecting the city fiercely from invaders. Today, the same coast holds stretches of beaches where Torinese and Milanese go to frolic at weekends and in the summer; it has become home to Italian retirees in the same way that Florida is home to aged Americans. And the Ligurians who once had a reputation for being wicked and inhospitable fling open the doors to a substantial source of income.

One of Italy's smallest regions, Liguria stretches west in a narrow ribbon along the coast from France. Mountains separate it from Piemonte to the north, Emilia-Romagna to the east and Tuscany to the south. Even if you've never been there, you've probably seen its northeastern border in all those movies where glamorous jet-setters hop into their sports cars and motor from Monte Carlo to Rome; the quaint customs booths any foreign film lover knows well are just outside **Ventimiglia**, the first town on the Italian side of the French border.

Known as the Italian Riviera, Liguria, with seaside resort towns but also the country's largest commercial and naval ports, is a close relative of Cannes and Monaco. The Ligurian coast with its lush forests of lemon trees, herbs, flowers, almonds and pines with heady sweet-smelling breezes, terraced hillsides and stretches of beaches is separated from the French Côte d'Azur by a few kilometres and a border. Its dissecting road, the Aurelia, runs up the coast all the way from Rome to Spain. Most people come to Liguria for its seashore, which is a virtually uninterrupted string of resorts that have been a mecca for Italian tourists for a hundred years. An Italian pop music festival takes place annually in glamorous San Remo. Ligurians have two names for the boomerang-shaped coastline – from France to Genoa it is called the **Riviera di Ponente** and from Genoa southwards the **Riviera di Levante**. The latter is where you will find Liguria's famous **Cinque Terre**.

The capital city of **Genoa**, birthplace of Christopher Columbus, is a typical bustling seaport with a maritime empire once rivalling Venice. Its steep, narrow alleys stretch from the picturesque medieval town centre to the hills crowding directly behind it. The city has a European elegance with herringbone brick roads and a royal palace that holds it own against Versailles for its extravagant trappings.

Emilia-Romagna

Industrious yet fun-loving, Emiliani and Romagnoli exemplify the art of being able to work hard and play hard. Long, foggy winters are no dampener for the exuberant, brash personalities that snap open lounge chairs and sun umbrellas as soon as the first warm day hits the Riviera Adriatico. Home of the deliciously ironic and larger-than-life film director Federico Fellini, scenes of exaggerated enjoyment, in winter and in summer, are this region's claim to fame.

The capital is **Bologna**, dubbed *la Grassa*, or Fatso, which lays the most credible claim to being the gastronomic capital of Italy, and its specialities have indeed conquered the world, albeit often in dubious versions. Fine eating is hardly confined to Bologna. Even the fast-food stands, with hand-rolled, flat *piadina* bread stuffed with cheese, meat, pumpkin and other yummies, offer cheap and delectable sustenance for those on the run. Parma ham (*prosciutto*) has made it on to top menus everywhere; *parmigiano* cheese from Reggio is sprinkled on pasta around the world and the indigenous regional red wine, Sangiovese, is produced throughout the country, but nowhere like in Romagna.

The region is known for its heavy fog, created by the Adriatic sea, marshes and underground springs. In the area near **Modena** the locals have as many ways of describing the different types of fog as the Inuit do for snow. One especially deadly, but beautiful, fog is the *galaverna*, which descends when temperatures hit zero and looks deceptively like snow.

Despite its industrial demeanour and play-hard attitude, the region is known for its strong socialist-leaning traditions and is dubbed the red heart of the land. Roads are named after famous communist leaders, like Via Stalin, and a generation of children has Russian names such as Yuri and Mirko. And Europe's oldest university, in Bologna, churns out political minds, economists and thinkers, keeping the city buzzing with coffee-shop debates and lively conversation.

The Islands

A smattering of islands surrounding mainland Italy have the mixed blessing of being isolated. Sicily and Sardinia, the largest offshore territories, are seeped in culture and speak a language barely comprehensible to the rest of the country. Divided by more than just water, centuries of visitors and invaders have left a linguistic, culinary and artistic heritage which locals preserve out of obstinacy as much as anything else.

Sicily

Sicily is one place that won't let you forget its past. Just try and remember that you are on Italian territory as you order a plate of local *cuscus*. Walk through Palermo's Vucciaria market with stalls of gleaming swordfish heads, dangling chilli peppers, roaming children with midnight-black eyes and raven hair, and you feel as if you have dropped into an Italian souk.

The island also possesses some of the best-preserved Greek ruins in the Mediterranean, as well as a riotous overflow of Baroque monuments, and the Greek and Spanish influences are still felt in the local dialects as well as in the culinary tradition.

This triangular land mass is represented by a three-legged figure superimposed with knowing eyes and a grin, a familiar motif on walls as well as the decorative ceramic plates sold in roadside stands. The restless volcano **Mount Etna**, whose fertile soil grows some of the world's best oranges, dominates the east above the port of Catania, and its snow-capped bulk is clearly visible from the chic resort of Taormina to the north. **Palermo**, to the northwest, has been the island's capital since the Arabs and Frederick II.

The island boasts spectacular and largely unspoiled beaches. Cool and buoyant waters lap against the northern shores from **Messina** to Palermo where high salt levels enable snorkellers to float without effort.

From Palermo westwards and around the corner, the currents grow colder and nourish the teeming schools of tuna, which finish bloodily in the nets of the fishermen during the annual *mattanza*, or tuna-kill, a term that is also used to describe particularly bad episodes in the endemic mafia wars. The word 'mafia' derives from Arabic, and began as a simple resistance to the occupying Normans. Sicilians have ever since been wary of foreigners, and still often refer to their excursions to the mainland as 'going to Italy'.

Sardinia

Glitzy yacht-set, resort-saturated coastlines are a relatively new addition to the island of Sardinia. The development of **Porto Cervo** and the **Costa Smeralda**, or Emerald Coast, started in the 1960s and 1970s much to the surprise of the locals, who historically avoided the sea and all the dangers it brought with it. Instead, crafty business entrepreneurs saw it as the new alternative to the Côte d'Azur, snapped up dirt-cheap coastal property and started building. The result today is a stretch of harbours and bays that begins pulsating with activity in early summer, swarmed over by actors, royalty and other tabloid-worthy personalities willing to drop immense amounts of money to rub elbows with others like themselves.

Thankfully, the rest of the island is sparsely populated and astonishingly beautiful, with enough fascinating architecture, ruins and towns to keep the

Long Live Sardinia

The fountain of youth may be just around the corner on the island of Sardinia. At least that's why scientists are digging around searching for the magic formula that gives the island the world's highest percentage of centenarians.

Perhaps it is wrapped up in the inhabitants' genetics, or the result of high-quality nutrition and the fresh sea air on the island. There is no doubt that the slower lifestyle of *i Sardi*, who have ample time for relaxation, much influenced the doctors' case studies.

The project, dubbed '*Kent'Annos*' after an old Sardinian salute meaning 'May you live to be 100', confirmed that the island has the world's highest documented percentage of people who reach 100. Of 1.6 million Sardinians, there are at least 220 who have reached 100, twice the typical ratio elsewhere. Five of the world's 40 oldest people live on the island, and until the death of Antonio Todde at 112 Sardinia boasted the oldest of them all.

island from being turned into a jet-set fun park. Lovers of prehistoric ruins are enthralled by the remains of the ancient nuraghe, cone-shaped tower buildings built with rough-hewn boulders, some of which are rumoured to have mystical fertility powers.

Pulled by the island's mineral wealth, eastern Mediterranean peoples such as Mycenaeans and Cypriots crossed the seas to trade with and raid Sardinia. The Phoenicians left permanent settlements starting in the 8th century BC, mostly around coastal areas. Carthaginians dominated the island from around 500 to 200 BC, and their influence can be seen on the Sardinian flag known as *I Quattro Mori*, with its white background, dark cross and four black heads with bands around them, looking as if they could conquer any islands on earth. All of these, combined with hundreds of years of Spanish domination, set the ethnic backdrop of Sardinians; it is claimed that they have a physiognomy all their own. Caricatured as stout and stubborn, *i Sardi* have a perilous reputation, so much so that people with names ending in the letter 'u', something typical to Sardinia, are said to be checked more thoroughly than other Italians at airports and borders.

Sardinia is divided into four provinces: **Cágliari** at its southern tip, which is also the capital city of the region; **Sássari** on the northwest coast; **Núoro** in the centre and **Oristano** on the west coast south of Sássari. Most of the region's dialects come from the Spanish domination of the Castilians, except for **Alghero**, where a 15th-century form of Catalan is spoken and poets sing of their city as Barcellonetta – little Barcelona.

Italy: The Ancient Cities

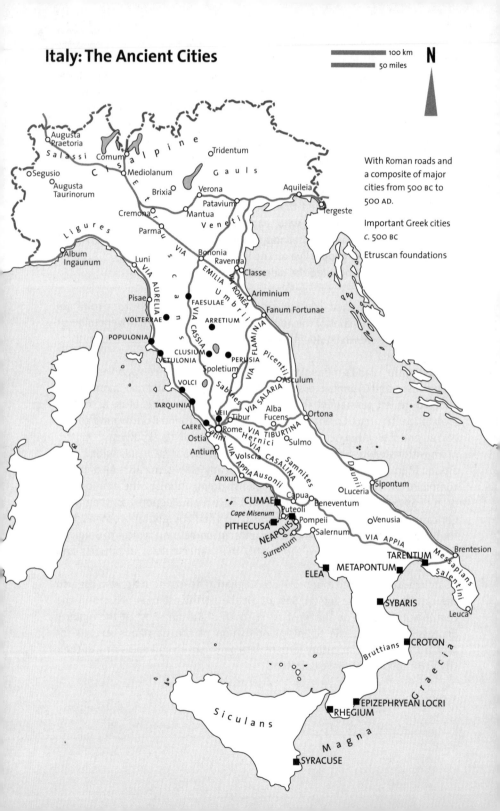

100 km
50 miles

N

With Roman roads and
a composite of major
cities from 500 BC to
500 AD.

Important Greek cities
c. 500 BC

Etruscan foundations

Augusta
Praetoria
Comum
Tridentum
Salassi
Segusio
Mediolanum
Cisalpine
Gauls
Augusta
Taurinorum
Brixia
Verona
Aquileia
Patavium
Cremona
Mantua
Tergeste
Parma
Veneti
Ligures
VIA
Bononia
Album
Ingaunum
Luni
Ravenna
Classe
VIA AURELIA
Etruscans
EMILIA
ROMEA
Umbri
Ariminium
Pisae
FAESULAE
Fanum Fortunae
VIA CASSIA
ARRETIUM
VOLTERRAE
VIA FLAMINIA
POPULONIA
CLUSIUM
PERUSIA
Picentii
VETULONIA
Spoletium
VOLCI
Sabines
Asculum
VIA SALARIA
TARQUINIA
VEII
Alba
Fucens
Ortona
CAERE
Tibur
Rome
VIA TIBURTINA
Daunii
Ostia
Latini
Hernici
Sulmo
VIA
Antium
Volscia
CASALINA
VIA
Samnites
Anxur
APPIA
Ausonii
Sipontum
Luceria
CUMAE
Capua
Beneventum
Cape Misenum
Puteoli
PITHECUSA
Pompeii
Venusia
NEAPOLIS
Salernum
Surrentum
VIA APPIA
Brentesion
TARENTUM
Messapians
ELEA
METAPONTUM
Salentini
Leuca
SYBARIS
Bruttians
CROTON
Graecia
EPIZEPHRYEAN LOCRI
RHEGIUM
Siculans
Magna
SYRACUSE

Italy touring atlas

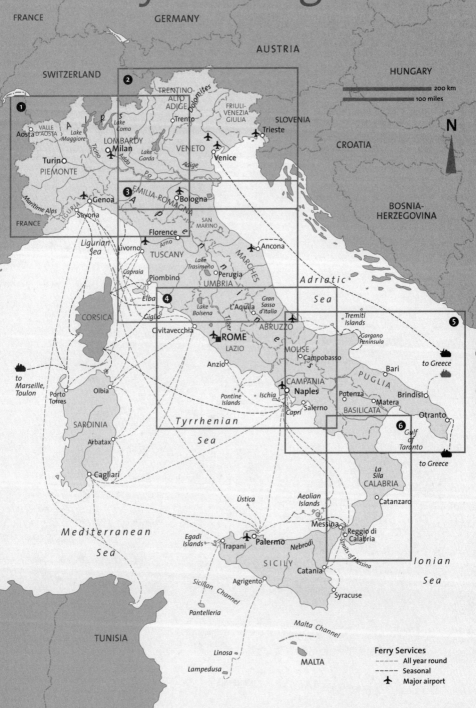

FRANCE

GERMANY

AUSTRIA

HUNGARY

SWITZERLAND

CROATIA

①

VALLE
D'AOSTA
Aosta ○

A L P S

Lake
Maggiore

Lake
Como

②

TRENTINO-
ALTO
ADIGE

DOLOMITES

Trento ○

FRIULI-
VENEZIA
GIULIA

SLOVENIA

Trieste ✈

200 km

100 miles

N

LOMBARDY

Milan ○ ✈

Ticino

Adda

Lake
Garda

VENETO

Venice ✈

Turin ○

PIEMONTE

Po

Adige

BOSNIA-
HERZEGOVINA

Maritime Alps

LIGURIA

Genoa ✈ ○

③

EMILIA-ROMAGNA

A
P
P

Bologna ✈ ○

SAN
MARINO

FRANCE

Savona ○

Ligurian
Sea

Livorno ○

Arno

Florence ✈ ○

TUSCANY

Lake
Trasimeno

e
n
n
i

MARCHES

Ancona ○

Adriatic

Sea

Capraia

Piombino ○

Perugia ○

UMBRIA

CORSICA

Elba

Lake
Bolsena

④

Lake
Trasimeno

L'Aquila ○

Gran
Sasso
d'Italia

Tremiti
Islands

⑤

Giglio

Tiber

ABRUZZO

Gargano
Peninsula

to Greece ⛴

Civitavecchia ○

✈ **ROME**

LAZIO

MOLISE

Campobasso ○

PUGLIA

Bari ○

to
Marseille,
Toulon ⛴

Anzio ○

CAMPANIA

Ischia

Naples ○

Potenza ○

Brindisi ○

Porto
Torres ○

Olbia ○

Pontine
Islands

Salerno ○

Matera ○

BASILICATA

Otranto ○

SARDINIA

Capri

⑥

Gulf
of
Taranto

to Greece ⛴

Arbatax ○

Tyrrhenian

Sea

Mediterranean

Sea

Cagliari ○

Ùstica

Aeolian
Islands

La
Sila

CALABRIA

Catanzaro ○

Egadi
Islands

Messina ○

Reggio di
Calabria ○

Straits of Messina

Ionian

Sea

Trapani ○

✈ **Palermo** ○

Nebrodi

Sicilian Channel

S I C I L Y

Catania ○

Agrigento ○

Syracuse ○

Pantelleria ○

Malta Channel

TUNISIA

Linosa ○

MALTA

Lampedusa ○

Ferry Services

- – – – All year round
- – – – Seasonal
- ✈ Major airport

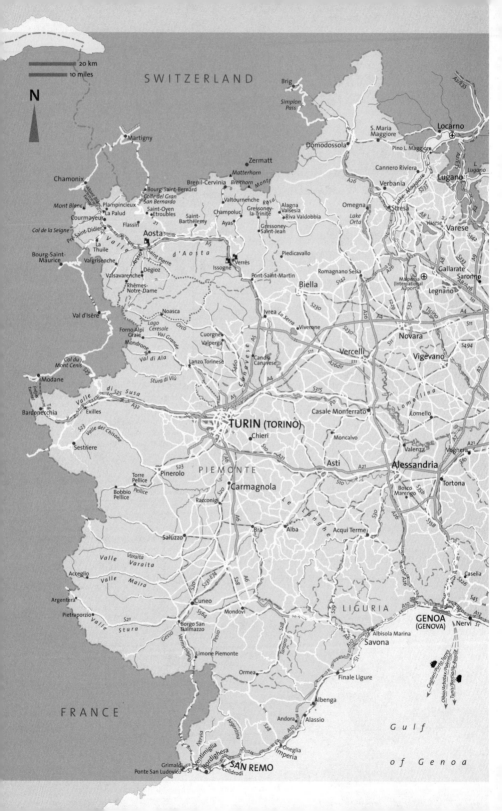

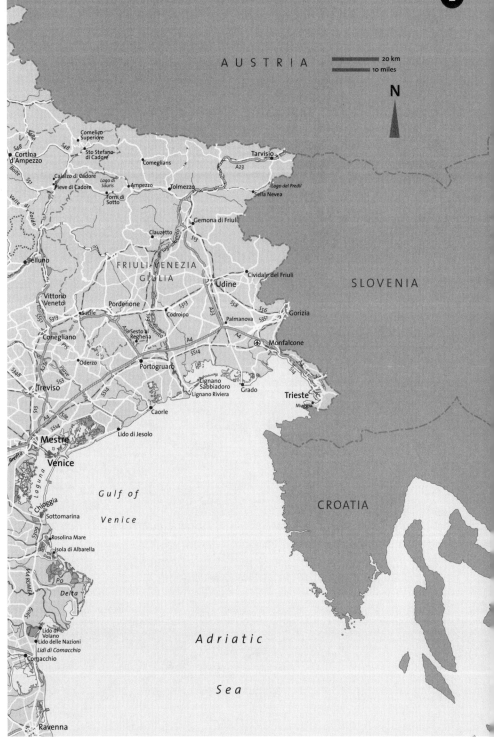

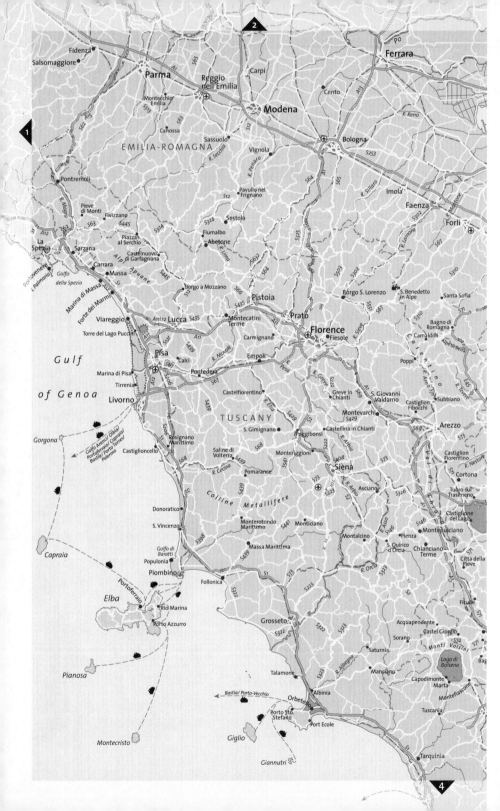

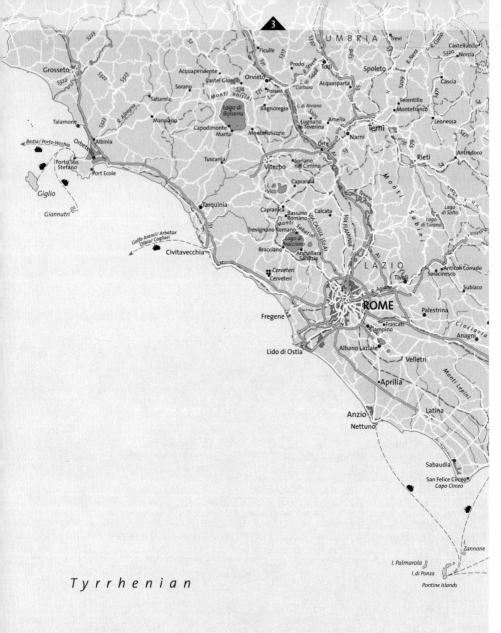

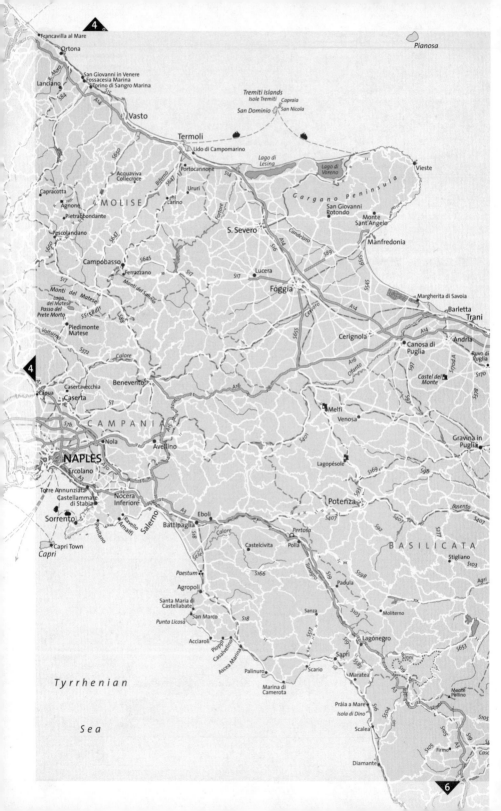

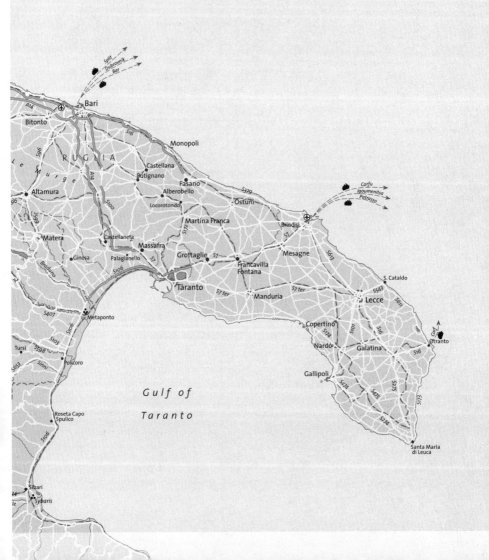

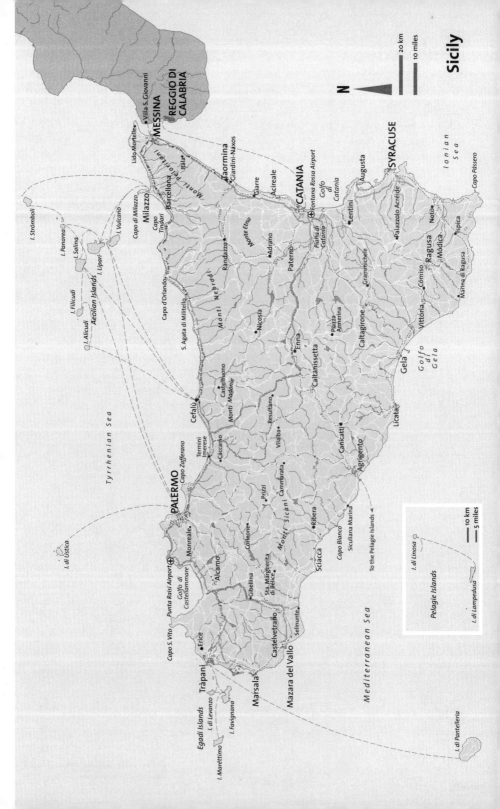

Sicily

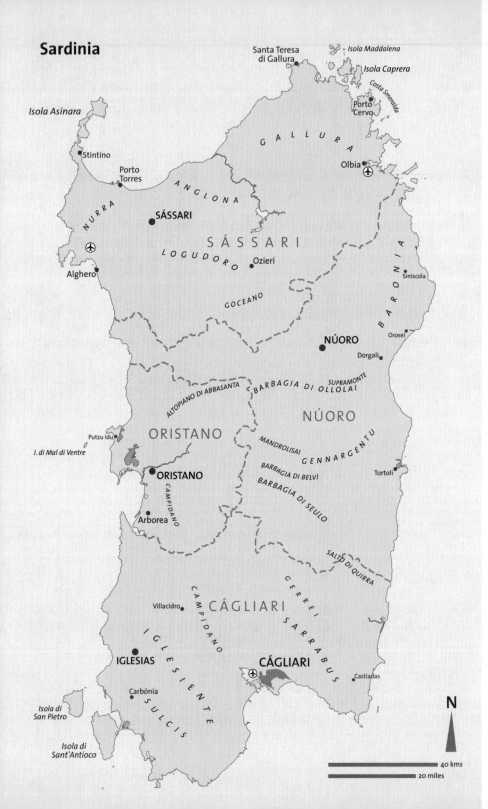

Italy Today

Italy of the 21st century clings tightly to its past, while stretching out some-times eagerly, at other times hesitantly, towards the future. Modernized public services, online payment systems, telephone technology like WiFi, GPRS and WAP, and highway toll machines accepting credit cards are more and more common, especially in the central and northern regions. Home-grown companies are beginning to operate under international rules and regulations, as the old-school cronies are replaced by a younger, more worldly-wise generation. Even labour laws are being shaken up – much to the dismay of those who believed that this would never happen – with reforms proposed that will change the protectionist system, allowing for layoffs as in the rest of Europe.

But don't be fooled. For every new convenience, another tradition remains in place. Politics remain vaguely Machiavellian as the economy struggles to keep pace with European standards. It is a country that carries the weight of its past on its shoulders when it comes to regional differences and the need to strengthen the infrastructure. After more than a century of unification the country's regions are still deeply divided. After hundreds of years, old wounds and defeats can still open up into terrific brawls and shouting matches.

By the same token there is a resistance to change that seeps from the Italians' very pores. Festivals and celebrations go on without alteration as they have for centuries. Mothers cook dishes that their grandmothers' great-grandmothers prepared, true to the original recipe. Security comes through familiarity for most Italians ... as well as for visitors who are sure to take that same photo on Piazza San Marco that their grandparents did, and not see a shred of evidence that all those years have passed.

Major Political Parties, Alliances and Elections

The Italian political system is in some respects comparable to the British two-party system. L'Ulivo, the Olive Tree coalition, corresponds roughly to the Labour party and the centre-right Casa della Libertà, the House of Liberties, is similar to the Conservatives. The Italian parliament is split into two chambers, the Senate and the House. The premier is the leader of the alliance that commands a majority in both. General elections are held every 5 years. This neat and rather simplistic breakdown neglects some of the finer intrigues of Italian politics, however.

When Italy was united by the Risorgimento, the three main characters of the movement – Giuseppe Garibaldi, Vittorio Emmanuele II and Camillo Cavour – all had overlapping ideas and ambitions. Piemontese admirer of the French

Revolution, Camillo Cavour, was a liberal who dreamt of modernizing Italy politically and technologically. Garibaldi was driven by his undying desire to unite a disjointed and factional Italy that had been disunited for 1,400 years, since the fall of the Roman Empire. He was also seething over the cessation of his birth town, Nice, to the French in 1860. And, naturally, the king had his kingly interests to protect. Garibaldi and his *Mille* – thousand – soldiers had stormed through and stitched the peninsula into one by March 1861, all except for Venice and Rome, which were added in 1866 and 1870. Cavour died before Venice and Rome were incorporated into Italy.

In the country's first 15 years of life there were eight different prime ministers and 13 different governments. By 1876 a series of left-wing governments came into power under Agostino Depretis. It is during this period that the Italian phenomenon of the transformation of political character by groups or deputies in order to survive in the government (*trasformismo*) took hold.

Today *trasformismo* is played out in the many senators who were once members of another party, but have converted to the current, more powerful majority. Mussolini himself was an avid socialist before consolidating the Italian fascist movement.

Years of constant humpty-dumpty tumbling of governments and prime ministers paved the way for Mussolini's assertive charisma; he took over in 1922 and ruled for 21 years – this was the longest rule of any government in Italy. After the Second World War ended, the first Italian republic was finally established, and the royal family headed by King Umberto II was sent packing off into exile; his son Vittorio Emmanuel returned for the first time in 2003 (*see* 'Rex non Grata', p.63).

Today's bipolar set-up of the government is relatively new. In the 1990s the Bribesville (*Tangentopoli*) investigations revealed widespread corruption among Italy's ruling élite, and the current system known as the 'second republic' emerged from this. *Tangentopoli* swept aside the 'first republic', a consensus-based system, which the Christian Democrats controlled with a string of revolving coalitions. The second republic, meanwhile, is about confrontational politics, and mud-slinging matches prevail.

Poles are not parties but coalitions – a fact that has been identified as important in reducing any incentive to toe the line. In fact, coalition partners seem to spend as much time undermining and spitting venom at each other as they do attacking the opposition. When legislators set about reforming the electoral system in the early 1990s they didn't do the job thoroughly. Rather than simply switching from proportional representation to a first-past-the-post system, they devised a complicated arrangement whereby 25 per cent of parliamentary seats are still elected according to proportional representation. This means the reform was a little half-baked and the system is still highly fragmented.

Parties and Coalitions – Past and Present

The ruling coalition is the **Casa della Libertà** – House of Liberties. Composed of Forza Italia, Lega Nord and Alleanza Nazionale, the coalition was elected in 2000 and remains in office until 2005. Its leading party **Forza Italia** (FI, reminiscent of a football cheer 'Come On Italy') was set up as a platform for Silvio Berlusconi's political ambitions in January 1994, and found itself – briefly – in government 2 months later, filling the vacuum on the centre-right side of Italy's political spectrum caused by the disintegration of the Christian Democrats (DC) after *Tangentopoli*. Having no real ideological roots, the party is blatantly populist, reflected in its name. Initially the parliamentary party was crammed with top members of Berlusconi's business empire, but over the years a number of former Christian Democrats (*see* discussion of *trasformismo*, p.61) still hungry for power have also joined its ranks.

Lega Nord (LN) or Northern League leader Umberto Bossi has stopped demanding independence for northern Italy, but still indulges in the 'Roma Ladrona' (Rome Robber) rant to keep his supporters happy. Much of his appeal comes from promises to prise power from alleged parasites in southern Italy and return it to the hard-working, wealth-generating north. Euro-sceptic Bossi hardly raises eyebrows when he makes his outrageously xenophobic statements, such as his suggestion to fire at boats carrying illegal immigrants.

Alleanza Nazionale (AN) or the National Alliance has its roots in the neofascist Movimento Sociale Italiano (MSI). In 1995 leader Gianfranco Fini started nudging the party towards the mainstream by dropping the name MSI, which carried the lingering aroma of Mussolini's regime. In 2003, during a trip to Israel, Fini said anti-Semitic racial laws passed by Mussolini were an 'absolute evil', further pulling the party away from its fascist roots. Some AN members felt betrayed, including the dictator's granddaughter Alessandra Mussolini, who left the party. Fini's party usually adopts hard-line stances on law and order, and immigration. It often champions the south and so finds itself at odds with the Lega.

The **Unione dei Democratici Cristiani e Democratici di Centro** (UDC), the Christian Democrats, is essentially a group of former Christian Democrats. Its presence in the House of Liberties brings a vital chunk of political credibility to an alliance that features Bossi, a band of reformed fascists and, in Berlusconi, a leader who has had a number of scrapes with the law.

L'Ulivo, the Olive Tree coalition, is led by the **Democratici di Sinistra** (DS) or Left Democrats, and is in essence a renamed version of what was western Europe's largest Communist party for some 40 years. With the fall of the Berlin Wall the party changed its name to soften its appearance. Since then, chairman Massimo d'Alema has tried to embark on a New Labour-style transformation, with mixed success. In October 1998 d'Alema became the first former Communist ever to head an Italian government, but his time at the helm only

Rex non Grata

The royal hot potato was finally dropped on the 23 October 2002 when the President of the Italian Republic, Ciampi, signed a law repealing the constitutional prohibition against male members of the House of Savoy entering Italy. After 57 years in exile, thousands of words and euros, and an appeal to the European Court of Human Rights, Crown Prince Victor Emmanuel and his family were finally allowed to return to Italy.

A visit to Naples by the 65-year-old head of the House of Savoy, his wife, Marina Doria, and their motorcycle-loving son, Emmanuel Filiberto, aged 30, was supposed to be a homecoming. Victor Emmanuel sailed away from the port of Naples when he was only 9 years old, when the royal family abandoned the country amid chaos. His father, King Umberto, pined away in Portugal during the 1950s until he retired to Switzerland and died, leaving the dynasty to his son.

As Communism fell throughout eastern Europe and the Balkans, exiled monarchs began to visit their beloved homelands. All except for the Savoys who were *persone non grate* – something that perturbed the easily annoyed Victor. Known as impulsive, the present-day Victor Emmanuel has renounced all claims to the throne, but his description of Mussolini's racial laws as 'not all that bad' didn't win him any support in Italy. Nor did his 'accidental' shooting of a fellow member of the yacht-set in an exclusive harbour in the 1970s (he was acquitted of manslaughter shortly afterwards).

All that is over now. Emmanuel has had the pizza he dreamt of eating, Victor has seen the shores of his departure and his wife has graced the shopping scene with her presence. And the family has returned to Naples where Alessandra Mussolini, granddaughter of *il Duce*, has lived undisturbed all these years. That is, when she is not sitting in the Italian parliament where she serves as a senator.

lasted 18 months. Although DS is the largest member of l'Ulivo, pundits say that it is unlikely that a coalition headed by a DS candidate will be elected in the near future, as the party still suffers from the legacy of its Communist past.

La Margherita, the Daisy, was formed shortly before the 2001 general elections through a merger between four centrist parties including the Partito Popolare, another gang of ex-DC politicians. La Margherita proved to be more than the sum of its parts, almost outdoing DS the first time it went to the polls. It is moderate on most matters, although the group's Catholic heritage sometimes shows over issues like divorce and artificial insemination. La Margherita is led by the centre-left's nominal head, former Rome mayor Francesco Rutelli.

Communisti Italiani, the Italian Communists, is one of two parties still proud of its red credentials well into the 21st century. They are vocal opponents of almost any form of military intervention and of the reforms of Italy's labour market and pension system.

Federazione dei Verdi, the Greens, tend to adopt positions close to those of the Italian Communists and are led by Alfonso Pecoraro Scanio.

A small clutch of independent parties remain. **Rifondazione Comunista**, the Communist Refoundation, parted company with the other communists in 1998 when its leader Fausto Bertinotti brought down Romano Prodi's l'Ulivo government by withdrawing support for the government over a matter so trivial hardly anyone can now remember what it was. The Italian Communists, meanwhile, decided to stay in l'Ulivo and formed a new party. Bertinotti is often accused of splitting the left's share of the vote and thus aiding the right. He does not seem concerned about this, as his street-cred is enhanced by his refusal to compromise, which means he gets to pose at anti-globalization protests. Nevertheless, Rifondazione and l'Ulivo regularly flirt with the idea of jumping back into bed with each other.

Last, and perhaps least, the **Unione Democratici per l'Europa** (UDEUR) is primarily a vehicle for its leader, another former DC man, Clemente Mastella. Whenever there is talk of someone walking out of the ruling coalition, UDEUR is mentioned as a potential replacement. Mastella only seems to make an impact when issues that directly affect the party are on the agenda, such as changes to the electoral system. In 2002 Mastella threatened to go on a hunger strike if a wrangle over party funding wasn't solved to his satisfaction. Some opponents suggested the protest might do Mastella, who has eaten his fair share of pizza and pasta in his days, more good than harm.

Religion

A giant roar wailed through the bastion of Roman Catholicism when it was announced that the largest mosque in all of Europe would be built in Rome – in spitting distance of the Vatican. That was in 1995. Six years after the final stone was laid and the Muslim temple opened, September 11 struck, upsetting the delicate balance that was painstakingly being built by Muslim and Catholic leaders. But efforts are again being made to promote tolerance, re-establishing an acceptable degree of cohabitation between the two religions rather than an understanding.

Roman Catholics

Though 96 per cent of Italians are Roman Catholic, most do not practise. Many Italians define themselves as 'culturally' Catholic, meaning their attitude and celebrations are rooted in Catholicism, but they live secular lives. Baptized at birth, and led through catechism and first communion by their families, the majority of Italians stop there until it is time to get married or buried. Recently a 45-year-old man sent ripples through the Vatican by asking to be 'unbaptized', stating that he did not want to be considered Roman Catholic when statistics were taken about church membership since he had never regularly participated in services. Once a powerful political body, the Vatican is now simply a spiritual magnet for Catholics worldwide. It is the world's smallest country with the largest basilica, St Peter's.

Jews

Jewish history in Italy goes back nearly two thousand years, to 161 BC, and the 'Romanim' Jews constitute the oldest uninterrupted community in Europe. The enslavement of the Jews by Titus after the destruction of the temple in Jerusalem in AD 70 is frozen in stone on the façade of the arch in Rome named after the emperor. The word 'ghetto' is an Italian–Jewish word originating from the historical community in Venice, where traditional artisans would *gettare* – throw – unused materials into the neighbourhood in which the Jews lived. Traces of Jewish heritage are embedded throughout Rome. Ruins of Roman-era synagogues, ancient catacombs and the turn-of-the-century Great Synagogue on the banks of the Tiber map reveal a continuous and vibrant presence of Italian Jews (*Ebrei di Italia*) in the city.

Waldensians

A small, thriving community of Waldensians (Valdesi) has been present in Italy since medieval times. Mostly concentrated in the Waldensian valleys, an area of the Cozie Alps in northern Italy, this nucleus constitutes the vanguard of European Protestantism in Catholic territory. Methodists have been around since the 19th century, and there are other more recent Protestant arrivals like Baptists, Episcopalians and Jehovah's Witnesses. Every major city has an Anglican congregation, usually composed mainly of UK citizens transplanted to Italy, but they also have some Italian members.

Other Religions

When Muslim Turks invaded and conquered Albania in 1431, the opposing Albanian Christians migrated to Italy. Towns along the Adriatic coastline, especially in Sicily, have sizeable Eastern or Greek Orthodox communities, which have seen a boost in attendance with immigration into Italy from parts of the Balkans and Romania.

In recent years there has been an increasing interest in Buddhism, especially but not only among artists, musicians and actors. The most popular branch, Nichiren Daishonin's Buddhism or SGI, has a widespread following and holds regular conferences throughout the country.

Italy's pagan mysticism has often been transformed into Christian ritual. Wild festivals and celebrations using snakes, music, fruit or chants are scattered throughout Italy and not only make for mind-boggling spectacles, but also keep ancient traditions alive, even if under the guise of a saint's or religious holiday.

The Family and the Role of Women

Italian women have some tough archetypal images to live up to. Icons of the Madonna (virgin mother, not singer) sit side by side with provocative advertisements using scantily clad or nude bombshells on city streets. At times it seems that Italian women are expected to be one or the other.

It would oversimplify to sing the overused refrain that Italy is 'the land that feminism forgot', and there needs to be a clear understanding that feminism for one woman is not the same as for another. Indeed, a strong feminist movement in the 1960s and 1970s left women feeling confident that the foundation had been laid for an equal and non-discriminatory society.

But it is a fact that women's issues are rarely the topic of open debate in Italy. In fact, the word *feminismo* has taken on an unattractive undertone, and is almost exclusively associated with homosexuality. The women's association Arcidonna agrees that most women simply feel that their rights were secured years ago and, with the fight won, there is no longer a need to debate. Also, younger women have not taken the torch of the previous generation, and rest confident that all is equal. Often that image is shaken when women enter the workforce for the first time.

Arcidonna maintains that many Italian women still have a relatively low quality of life, pay discrepancies are rampant and Italy has the lowest number of women in political office of all the EU countries. Redefinition of the rape laws in 1996 (making rape a felony for which proof of premeditation is no longer required to obtain a conviction) came relatively late in Italy. Before the rape law came into force it was considered a crime against 'morality' and not against an individual. Since conviction rarely led to punishment of any kind, women feared suffering the humiliation of court and the risks of retribution afterwards. Even after the laws were passed on divorce and abortion, the Catholic Church, in attempting to defend families as untouchable, was hesitant to recognize that sexual violence often occurs in families. Those days are gone, and women are filing more cases.

Younger women are also experiencing life in a more liberal society. Conservative views on morality, clothing and relationships are fading fast. Indeed, the revealing way many Italian women dress may seem shockingly unfeminist at first. But it is imperative to remember that this is hard-earned exhibitionism. For as casually as women of all ages strip off bikini tops on the beach today, 30 years ago that wasn't the story.

Another sign of the relaxing of strict societal rules is that women are marrying less, and couples are more often choosing to live together before tying the knot. New mothers are also working instead of staying at home, and fathers are no longer just breadwinners, but child caretakers and cookers of pasta.

But *la mamma* remains the hub of the Italian family and the family is still sacred. Meals together are respected and even children who no longer live at home return frequently to eat with their parents. Pensioners' homes and retirement villages are almost non-existent as children look after their parents as they age, knowing that their children will do the same for them. The family unit is an unshakeable part of Italian society.

Major Media

Television

Television is the most common form of media in Italy. Adults watch an average of four hours of TV per day, gleaning most of their news coverage and information from this source. Ninety per cent of Italian television is analogue terrestrial, the rest satellite.

Television is composed of two main groups with various channels. **Rai**, the public television and radio service, is the state broadcaster. There are three Rai channels – Raiuno, Raidue and Raitre (Rai One, Two and Three). **Mediaset** is the largest private group created by current prime minister Silvio Berlusconi in 1993. The group has three commercial TV channels – Italia 1, Rete 4 and Canale 5. These two broadcasting groups corner nearly the entire viewing population of the nation. Fine local broadcasting fills the gap in the regions with approximately 600 private channels, but very few viewers. **La7**, a newcomer, is the only channel free of state or Mediaset influence. It covers general topics and is also the music channel that hosts MTV.

Public television is financed by revenues from the annual TV subscription paid by citizens and from advertising. Rai faces more legal restrictions on advertising than the private networks.

Most Italians will tell you themselves that content is not the strong point of national TV. Singing and dancing are part of almost every programme and even some news shows. Topless and bikini-clad showgirls (*veline*) wiggle around announcers as part of a tried-and-tested ploy to increase viewership. There are more spectators who ask 'why not' than 'why'. It seems that television is the antithesis of the Italian cinema created by Passolini, Fellini, Rossellini and other of the world's finest directors.

A new, single-platform satellite called Sky Italia has thankfully brought alternative programming to Italy. It shows sport, history and nature programmes, documentaries and more, by national and international producers, usually in a choice of English or Italian. Sky news is a CNN-style presentation and other Sky programmes have a clear and comprehensible format.

Newspapers and Magazines

Italy has almost 200 different newspapers, of which *Il Corriere della Sera* and *La Repubblica* have the widest national circulation. Sports journals like the panther-pink *La Gazzetta dello Sport* and *Il Corriere dello Sport* are popular in the land of football enthusiasts. Economic and financial papers are *Il Sole 24 Ore* and *Milano Finanza*.

In the case of the two major weekly magazines, *Panorama* and *L'Espresso*, it is best not to judge the magazine by its cover. Despite a disproportionate number of t-and-a cover photos, briefs and articles inside are competently written by serious investigative journalists. *Panorama* has more right-wing coverage, as it is produced and published by Mondidori, part of Berlusconi's print empire.

Specialized and general periodicals are abundant, and many UK and US magazines now have an Italian version, like *Vanity Fair* and *Rolling Stone*. The Italian media also has a strong presence on the internet. More than 100 daily newspapers and 1,400 magazines have complete or partial sites. The main Italian press agencies are Adn-Kronos, AGI, ANSA, Ap-com and ASCA, and Il Sole 24 ore Radiocor for excellent economic coverage.

Major international papers, magazines and publications can be found at news stands in major cities. Getting them in smaller towns can be a problem. If you want to keep up with world news in English, you have several choices. You could ask your local newsagent (*edicola*) to make a special order and put aside the publication you want. Or you could subscribe and have it delivered to your home, but the problem with subscriptions is that delivery agencies, despite what they tell you, have difficulty delivering daily papers on the publication date. Often the paper will arrive one, if not two, days after the publication date. Another option, for those with internet access, is to subscribe to the online version of your favourite paper. If you subscribe to a magazine, there will be a delay while the magazine reaches you in the post. If you don't mind getting your *Economist* a week after publication date, a subscription saves money and the effort of tracking one down.

Reading publications in English is a way to keep abreast of domestic affairs without picking through the sometimes difficult Italian coverage. Two English language magazines available in Italy are *Wanted in Rome*, a biweekly publication available on international newsstands in and around Rome, and *Talk aBOut* in Bologna. News blogs and internet sites can help you keep up with Italian affairs. An excellent source is **http://italpolblog.blogspot.com** started and run by James Waltson of the American University in Rome. Zoomata (**www.zoomata.com**) has current affairs coverage and breaking news.

Radio

Around 2,500 commercial radio stations broadcast in Italy. A few of them have national coverage, such as Radiouno, the first of the three Rai radio channels, and Radio Deejay. They share the airwaves with public broadcaster Rai's radio stations, like Rai's Radiodue. Many of the remaining stations are local. Music radio attracts the majority of listeners, especially during the morning, but discussion programmes, football coverage and commentary and Radio Vaticano are also permanent fixtures on the airwaves.

Economic Background and the EU

Italy is one of the six founding member states of the EU and has a mixed industrial economy that has changed dramatically since the end of the Second World War, when it had an agriculturally based economy. Ranked as the world's twelfth-largest industrial economy, it has a total and per capita output slightly less than that of France and the UK. Up until the mid-1990s Italy risked not meeting the criteria to join the European Union's single currency area, even though the first agreement to create the union was signed in Rome way back in 1952. But stringent austerity measures shaped up the economy for its 1999 entry. Despite the occasional cold shoulder the country receives for economic sluggishness and recent diplomatic blunders, Eurosceptic or not, Italy is a major player in the European arena and worldwide.

After the Second World War Italy was swept away in rapid industrial development that peaked between 1958 and 1963, the years known as the 'economic miracle'. In 1961 the growth in the GDP reached a dizzying 8.3 per cent. Yet with the start of the 1973 oil crisis there was a significant pullback in economic performance.

Italy lacks natural resources and has to import most raw materials for industrial needs. More than 80 per cent of the country's energy sources are imported. Over 60 per cent of imports come from EU states, mostly from Germany. Of Italy's exports, 56 per cent go to the European Union and, again, Germany is the main export destination. Notable exports include industrial equipment, cars, aircraft, chemical products and artefacts of the highly developed textile and clothing industry.

When compared with the 11 founding nations of the Economic Monetary Union the inflation rate is within acceptable limits, according to the national statistics agency ISTAT. Nevertheless, the gross domestic product (GDP, *PIL* in Italian) growth rate of 0.4 per cent is the slowest of the 11 founding nations.

While the government maintains that inflation rose only 3 per cent in 2003, consumer associations maintain that spending power has dropped by 50 per cent. Overall, despite the economic slowdown in 2003, the OECD believes that signs of recovery are slowly appearing in 2004. The fact is that in the aftermath of September 11 and the global economic downturn, Italy – like the rest of the EU – saw its economy stumble. But in Italy imports decelerated faster than exports. Italy's inflation rate has just managed to keep within the norms specified by the Economic and Monetary Union – a major achievement for this historically inflation-prone country. However, a grim GDP growth rate of 0.4 per cent (2002 figures) shows that there is work to be done.

The North–South Divide

High unemployment and low participation in the labour force give Italy one of the lowest employment rates in the OECD area. Low employment (despite highly productive individual employees) suppresses per capita income. It is often noted that Italy is a two-speed country.

One of the aims of the unification (*risorgimento*) of Italy in 1861 was to bridge the gap between the impoverished, underdeveloped south (the *Mezzogiorno*) and the more prosperous north. With one currency and set of tax and labour regulations, the process was supposed to be under way towards allowing unencumbered trade and providing social laws that protected workers, enabling them to move to wherever they could find employment. In the late 1950s a concerted effort was initiated once again to bring the backward south to a level comparable with the richer north. Southerners' lives had improved as centurylong maladies such as malaria, malnutrition and illiteracy were beginning to disappear. Yet the differences between north and south remained, indomitable.

Perhaps southerners have tired of hearing promises of unification. And with good reason. EU averages still reflect a deeply divided country. If the percentage of the labour force working in agriculture is taken as an indication of the rate of industrialization and wealth, in Italy's case the figures clearly illustrate the grave imbalance between north and south. Against an EC average of 9.6 per cent in 1988, Lombardy compared favourably, with only 3.5 percent of the population working on the land, but in Molise 26.2 per cent were still engaged in agricultural work. Some 15 to 27 per cent of the GDP comes from the underground economy.

Privatization

One of the main culprits for lack of competitiveness in the Italian economy, the state-owned enterprise, is coming to an end. However, privatization has not been as widespread as was first foreseen in the early 1990s. The process was under way with the breakup of Credito Italiano in 1993. Another seven landmark state sell-offs, including the €2.6 billion Ente Nazionale Idrocarburi SpA (ENI) sale, have gone through, but other privatizations have been shelved for now. Another desperately needed privatization of the state telecommunications

One to One

Of all the European countries to go into the euro, Italy has been squeezed the tightest. What was supposed to be a fixed exchange conversions of €1 for 1.936 lire has become nearly a one-for-one rollover. Thus consumer associations claim that prices have practically doubled since the euro became the common currency of Europe on 1 January 2002. Using a national icon as a measuring stick could be helpful. Before the switchover, a small jar of the yummy chocolate-hazelnut spread Nutella cost 2,450 lire, or €1.26. Today, the same jar costs €2.18. Adding insult to injury, prices for Nutella are the highest in all of Europe in Italy.

company, Telecom Italia, ended in a €26.5 billion hostile takeover of by Olivetti. Enel, the state electricity provider, experienced a vertical integration that has left a quasi-monopoly, with a residual, majority government shareholding. Enel management has been permitted to engage in questionable acquisitions, to delay mandated divestiture of generation and transmission assets and to impede competition. While attempts at privatization yielded an average of €12.5 billion annually between 1996 and 2000, industry surveys estimate that only 30 per cent of privatization assets sold were actually removed from government control. Companies such as ENI, Enel and Alitalia, the country's flagship airline, all have nominated CEOs who have not been voted for.

By the same token, reducing public employment has so far proved an elusive goal. Public sector wages have risen faster than those in the private sector in recent years, and the preliminary wage agreement of early 2002 is difficult to reconcile with goals of fiscal consolidation. The promised labour market reforms have failed to materialize, and proposals have been met with staunch labour union opposition.

The Industrial Sector

Italy's industrial sector comprises 30 per cent of the economy and is composed of large corporations along with an immense number of small- and medium-sized companies (SMEs). These SMEs are seen as the vital sustainers of the Italian economy. Larger corporations and SMEs both play a role on the international market. Farming, the manufacturing sector, trade, services, building and tourism also contribute greatly to Italy's economy.

Large public companies are visible international players. They are often family-owned – such as Fiat of the Agnelli family; Pirelli, run by the Pirelli family; and Mediaset, operated by the prime minister, Silvio Berlusconi – control is wielded through holding companies and cross-shareholdings with industrial and financial allies. This allows families to maintain ownership with a small shareholding. However, with legislation that now requires listed companies to be more transparent and seeks to protect the rights of minority shareholders, this insiders' situation is beginning to break down.

The real driving forces of the economy are the clusters of small- and medium-sized, family-owned companies in so-called industrial districts, mostly in the northeast and the centre of the country. They generally employ between three and eight workers, compared with an EU average of about 15. Indeed, 99 per cent of Italian companies have fewer than 250 employees. With the exception of firms in the machine tool industry, most SMEs produce high-quality consumer goods, including clothing, furniture, kitchen equipment and white goods. Despite being traditionally export-orientated, SMEs face the serious challenge of global economic integration and increased competition. In particular, their unwillingness to go public to finance expansion has hindered growth

Bridge This

The Sisyphus-like project to build a bridge over the Messina Strait connecting the Italian mainland to Sicily was dubbed a national priority as far back as 1971 but, though progress is being made, the first stone won't be laid until 2005, if all goes well. The bridge itself will not officially open until 2010.

At a cost of US$4.6 billion for construction (plus another $1 billion in financing costs), the suspension bridge will be 3.25km (2 miles) long. Strung between two towers each measuring 366m (1,200ft), the Ponte Sullo Stretto, as it is known, will hover almost 64m (210ft) above sea level and measure 61m (200ft) across, with 12 traffic lanes and two railway lines carrying an estimated 9,000 vehicles an hour and 200 trains a day. According to officials the structure will be able to withstand an earthquake of 7.1 on the Richter scale – similar to the quake that flattened Messina in 1908. Destined to be the longest suspension bridge between two fixed points ever, the structure, three times the length of San Francisco's Golden Gate, will solve the centuries-long dilemma of how to link Sicily with the continent.

So, with all the benefits this bridge over troubled waters could bring, what are the drawbacks? 'Crime and environmental destruction,' says one of Italy's leading environmental groups, Legambiente. 'Not only are there no guarantees that state contracts won't be infiltrated by the Mafia and organized criminal gangs, but a huge stretch of coastline will be obliterated to make room for construction.' It is also maintained by opponents that the bridge is a waste of money at a time when many homes in Sicily are without running water during the summer and road and rail networks are substandard or nonexistent.

In many ways, the failure to get the bridge built has become a symbol of the country's inability to solve southern Italy's woeful transportation infrastructure malaise. Investment will only make sense if it is accompanied by overdue completion of highways and rail networks, together with an extensive overhaul of Catania Airport to create a freight hub for the Mediterranean area. Many political analysts contend that it's not a question of engineering, environment or scarce island infrastructure, it's a question of political will.

and has left some vulnerable to acquisition by larger foreign firms seeking to obtain established Italian brands. These brands are considered to be advantageous in the global marketplace, where the 'made in Italy' stamp is synonymous with quality and style. A further reason for acquiring Italian firms has been to gain a foothold in the domestic market, the sixth largest in the world.

The Service Sector

Italy's economic structure is similar to that of most European countries. Two-thirds of the GDP (68 per cent) is generated by the services sector. Some 62 per cent of the labour force is employed in service sector industries. Financial services and banking, insurance and tourism are its three brightest stars.

Infrastructure

A national agency for infrastructure, Infrastrutture Spa (Ispa), was set up in 2002 filling the 20-year-old infrastructure development gap in Italy. Sporadic development of the nation's infrastructure, such as building rail tracks and highways, has left the country with a deficit vis-à-vis competing countries, and has created a sizeable barrier in the south. A high-speed rail project will extend the Naples line further south, and a bridge planned to connect Sicily and the mainland would assist economic exchange with the Mediterranean, Africa and Europe. Bottlenecks in the tunnels beneath the mountains connecting France and Italy, and the highway around Venice where trucks are forced to wait in queues for hours, are further projects the national agency vows to resolve. Until Italy's rail network is expanded, industry remains dependent on the country's highways and roads for transportation of goods and products.

Internal Issues in Italy

Two burning internal issues gnaw at the soul of the country today. One is the unshakeable presence of the Mafia and the other is the newer upheaval caused by immigration, and a backlash of racism partly relating to it. These are not clear-cut areas, but anyone in Italy for any length of time will come across them at one time or another.

Immigration and Racism

A UK citizen of Jamaican origin once explained to me why she was moving back to London after 6 years in Italy. 'I am a woman of colour, and not unattractive. The overriding feeling I have had over these last years is that I am often

Call Me Italiana

With the crowning of Denny Mendez as Miss Italy in 1996 the floodgates were opened for lively debate on being Italian and an Italian citizen. Ms Mendez, a Caribbean immigrant, was hailed by some as Italy's new road towards ethnic diversification while others, including showgirl Alba Parietti, a judge in the contest, cried that being Italian had less to do with citizenship than with blood. In fact Ms Parietti left the judges' board in protest.

Italian law does not foresee automatic citizenship for those born on Italian soil. *Jus sanguinis* or bloodright wins over *jus soli* or birthright (literally law of the soil). But Denny's case is not unique and Italy is slowly becoming a more multi-ethnic nation. Tuscan textile town Prato has a well-established Chinese community with second-generation children speaking as elegantly as Dante himself. In the streets of Rome, second- and sometimes third-generation Italians of African origin have created their own slang that modern hip-hoppers are copying. A recent study of primary school enrolments showed that the national average of non-Italian students has risen by 15 per cent in the last 5 years. Seven years ago, the first obviously non-Mediterranean broadcaster, Fidel Mbanga-Bauna, a 52-year-old born in what is now the Democratic Republic of Congo, became the only non-Italian anchor at state television network Rai for Rome's local evening news.

While what it means to be ethnically Italian remains debatable, the national physiognomy is in transformation. And with a crown-winning smile like Denny's, it is hard to resist when she pleads, 'Just call me Italian.'

seen in one of two categories – a catwalk model or a hooker. It is only when someone finds out that I am British that their attitude softens. Whatever the reason, I was rarely made to feel as if I could integrate and be treated as an Italian. I will always be the *stranieria* in the best and worst ways. Yet I have experienced incredible moments of human warmth and compassion, hospitality and welcome – maybe more than in my own home country.'

One of the aspects of society that catches the attention of UK citizens (as well as other Europeans and Americans) is that there are very few non-Italians in the public sphere, working in shops, interviewed on TV, doing anything besides vending on the streets or in a store confined to one of the few ethnic areas of the country's urban hubs. This is an inescapable reality in modern-day Italy. Post-colonial policies did little to encourage immigration from the very few African countries Italy occupied. Italians themselves have emigrated off and on for the last 150 years in search of a better life and to escape from the extreme poverty they suffered during stretches of their history. And, despite centuries of being a cultural crossroads, Italy is just beginning to become a modern melting pot.

Immigration en masse is a relatively new phenomenon and has brought the country face to face with victims of wars in the Balkans, struggling eastern

Europeans and minorities escaping persecution. However, Italians who are caught unprepared will often expound on the dangers and difficulties of immigration. This discussion can be very basic and revolve around the argument that immigrants are likely to bring criminality, but can also lead to a consideration of the already difficult economic situation in Italy and a questioning of whether the country has the proper economic conditions for accepting immigrants. This argument is difficult to withstand, even by explaining that Italy has the lowest number of immigrants of the entire EU, or by citing the amount of Italian emigration there has been to America, the UK and Australia over the last century. Hostility to immigrants is the unfortunate flipside to an otherwise warm and welcoming nation, and is mostly born of fear and unfamiliarity, much of which could be resolved with assertive government measures to promote

Case Study: Where is Home?

Like many visitors to Italy, Ruf dreamed of staying during his 1981 trip to the *bel'paese*. Unlike many travellers, he did. And he has lived here ever since. A UK citizen of West Indian origin, Ruf has noticed some changes since the events of that fateful September 11.

Good-natured and amicable, Ruf has worked refining interiors, teaching English and in the tourism industry. With a distinctly Muslim second name, his UK passport doesn't always remove him from suspicion. 'Not too long ago,' says the easy-going 42-year-old, 'a group of tourists that I was to accompany around Italy asked my agency if they could change tour directors. I knew what it was all about.' In fact, when questioned, the group leader, a US citizen, said that he did not feel comfortable travelling with anyone who might be Arab.

However, Ruf's open attitude and distinct English accent helped him put the group leader's worries to rest. 'Anyway, I am used to it here. Italians don't know what to make of me half the time. When they ask me where I am from and I say the UK they always respond with "Where are you really from?",' he chuckles. 'They just aren't used to the multicultural society we have in the UK.'

After living for 10 years in Rome, Ruf chose to live in the serenity of the countryside. He now rents a home in a tiny mountain town in the far removed region of Abruzzo, where being a foreigner means less, and more. 'I know everyone, and they know me. That is the nature of a small town. So I feel comfortable that most people accept me as I am.' He recalls one recent, humorous incident that underlines the Italian's lack of exposure to different cultures. 'A man that I have known for four years now came up to me the other day, waving a small jar. He told me that he had something from my country ... you know, there.' What his friend had picked up was a small jar of the Chinese tiger balm. 'What could I say? Anyway, I wasn't sure if he was referring to Guyana, or England as "my country", so I just let it rest. After all, it was a mistake made in good faith, and with naïve enthusiasm.'

Comedy Routine

As well as the north–south divide, there is also an east–west divide in Italy. In fact, in any area there is a tendency to look at neighbouring regions with suspicion. Comedians from the north will affect a Neapolitan accent in order to feign ignorance; Sicilians are the criminals. On the other hand, Milanese are uptight and cold, according to southerners. Women from Bologna are wanton, and Genovese in general are stingy and greedy. As part of a stand-up routine or comedy show, these portrayals can bring out shrieks of laughter. In the wrong situation, they can bring on riots and violence. Nobel Prize winner Dario Fo uses a routine that plays on accents, while never actually using one. His potpourri of words, mixing medieval dialects in a way intelligible to all Italians, beautifully illustrates just how easy it can be to understand, and laugh about it at the same time.

affirmative action programmes, or at least provide education about integration. In 2004 the latest immigration law passed by Parliament, the Bossi-Fini, does more to criminalize immigrants and hinder integration than tackle the very difficult social problems surrounding the matter.

Yet UK citizens have no more obstacles in their way than other Europeans moving to the country. Learning Italian helps to break the ice but more and more Italians are picking up English and are anxious to chat with native speakers. It is often difficult to avoid being seen as the Inglese, but this can undoubtedly be advantageous.

La Mafia

Anti-Mafia magistrate Ilda Boccassini once said, 'You can make fish soup out of an aquarium, but not an aquarium out of fish soup.' What the powerhouse crusader against the Mafia and corruption in Italy was trying to explain was how the strong anti-Mafia laws of the late 1980s early 1990s have become weakened over the years by amendments and exceptions.

Boccassini's mentor was Giovanni Falcone, one of the driving forces against the Mafia, who was brutally murdered in May 1992. Shortly after Falcone's assassination his colleague Paolo Borsellino was blown up in July of the same year, with five of his security guards, while driving across a bridge in Sicily – warnings that the Mafia's power was not to be tampered with.

Shaken but determined, anti-Mafia investigations continued and unprecedented arrests of Mafia bosses took place. During a visit to the island, Pope John Paul II invited Sicilians to stand up against intimidation. And then more bombs followed – Florence was awoken one May night in 1993 to an explosion that blew open the Uffizi Gallery and left five dead and 40 injured. That same month another bomb exploded in Rome, supposedly planted to silence an outspoken television personality named Maurizio Costanzo, and his condemnation of the

Cosa Nostra, another name for the Sicilian Mafia. And as if even the Pope had stepped over the limit, in July 1993 three car bombs blasted through Rome and Milan, the worst damaging the Vatican cathedral of San Giovanni in Laterano.

Mani Pulite (Clean Hands) investigations encouraged informants to squeal on the organization's members and their political connections, and it looked as if it was the beginning of the end for the beast known as the Mafia. But despite the absence of shoot-outs and exploding bombs in the 21st century, it is unlikely that the Mafia has been eradicated. It has just become quieter and gets on with business as usual.

'Mafia', probably coming from the Arabic word meaning refuge or safety, is actually an umbrella term that describes four organized crime groups in Italy: the Cosa Nostra in Sicily, the Camorra in Naples, 'Ndrangheta in Calabria and, the least important faction, the Sacra Corona in Puglia. Outsiders notice the Mafia when there is a flurry of violence or murders, but the real hold of the Mafia is the shackles it puts on people's daily lives. Loan sharks continue to operate in much of the south and bribery still exists. Shopkeepers pay because they know that there is no state capable of protecting them. In Sicily many towns lack pizza-by-the-slice stands and instant photo booths – because there is no way for organized crime to pull in a profit since a booth can't cost less and can't pay bribes. The danger of the Mafia lies less in the chance of being caught in a shoot-out than in its capacity to stifle potential development and progress in southern regions.

Culture and Art

Italian culture and art does not begin with ancient Rome. The Etruscans and other tribes that preceded the Roman Empire, as well as the Greeks that they shared with and copied from, had a major impact on the roots of the art, architecture, literature and philosophy of the early Romans. But ancient Rome continues to have an enduring presence today.

The Classical Writers and Ancient Rome

Virgil is one of the first recorded, and probably the greatest, Roman author. His masterpiece the *Aeneid* spliced history and mythology together for the Emperor Augustus, who needed to win some favour as he emerged from the conflict surrounding the death of Julius Caesar. Virgil also immortalized the sufferance of rural Rome in *Georgics*, completed in 30 BC and, a farmer himself, captured the tranquil charm of farm life that he longed to see restored with the Golden Age. So beloved was Virgil that he would later reappear to guide Dante through *Inferno* and *Purgatorio*, even though pagan Virgil would not be allowed into Dante's *Paradiso*.

Ovid wasn't as lucky as Virgil, since he fell out of imperial favour and ended his writing life in exile. *Metamorphoses*, another epic poem blending history and myth, described the Roman world from its creation to the reign of Tiberius. One of the cornerstones of Roman literature, and one of the most influential poems in European literary history, was written by a depressed and dejected Ovid pining away on the shores of the Black Sea. Exile was also in the cards for the stoic philosopher Seneca, a proponent of universal humanity and opponent of the uncontrolled power that so many suffered under. He wrote philosophy and dramatic tragedies, ten of which still survive, providing a vivid illustration of theatrical tastes during his lifetime. He was inevitably called back to Rome as the tutor for a young, despotic Nero – the emperor who eventually ordered his death. Seneca accepted his sentence and committed a suicide that could not have been more tragic if written by his own hand.

Satirist and contemporary of Seneca, Petronius lived a life of luxury, while glee-fully jeering at the Roman nouveaux riches in his writings. In *Satyricon* Petronius depicts a vulgar dinner party witnessed by a fictional guest. He too fell from the fickle, if not psychotic, Emperor Nero's graces. Nero ordered his execution and he died by cutting his wrists (in front of dinner guests who watched him slowly bleed to death), but not before writing to Nero listing the Emperor's orgies and affairs. Legendary film director Federico Fellini released his own *Satyricon*, recalling the self-indulgent land of ancient Rome as a scan-dalous, modern apocalyptic anecdote that shocked the mainstream film industry in 1969.

In 30 BC Philo of Alexandria, a Jewish philosopher and scholar, documented and described the Jewish communities throughout the territories of the Roman Empire and in Rome before and after the turn of the 1st century. He wrote of the large Jewish neighbourhood on the Tiber and the treatment of the Jews under the Emperor Augustus whereby Jews were allowed to follow their traditions and ceremonies freely. That tolerance disappeared with Augustus' death, under Caligula and during the violence in Alexandria and subsequently in Rome. Philo's diplomatic visit to Caligula was recorded in *Embassy to Gaius* and his complaints against Flaccus, the Roman prefect of Egypt, in *Against Flaccus*.

A plethora of writers continued to chronicle events as the 1st century AD was drawing to a close. Tacitus, an orator and statesman, wrote the *Annals*, depicting the reign of Tiberius and Claudius and added his own moral judge-ments for good keeping. Other biographers and historians blended information from the imperial archives and first-person accounts with rumours and gossip, painting a detailed picture of the 1st century AD. All of these works resurfaced in philosophy, literature and art throughout Italian and European history.

As the philosophers and writers preserved ancient Rome in text, architects designed the Colosseum, the Pantheon (two of the most copied monuments in history) and other buildings, ensuring that ancient Rome would also be preserved in architecture. The amphitheatre in Taormina, Sicily, is one of the first examples of Romans improving on Greek design. The Romans kept the Greek temple as a base and built from there; many other buildings such as those at Pompeii, Paestum and Verona were also based on Greek models.

The Byzantine Empire

The western Roman Empire fell in AD 476, but the Byzantine Empire in the east, with its seat at Constantinople (modern Istanbul), survived for almost another millennium. Byzantine art and architecture dominated Italy for hundreds of years. While northern Europe sank deeper into the Dark Ages, extravagant churches, palaces, tombs and mausoleums were being built by Byzantine rulers throughout Venice, Ravenna, Palermo and other southern Italian cities. Local styles across Italy were strongly influenced by the art exported from the imperial capital.

Byzantine art was predominantly religious. Flat, timeless and static figures of the Madonna and Jesus, lacking any natural context, were produced by the thousand in Italy; European artists studied the closest examples they could find that displayed eastern technical expertise in art – in Italy. Mosaic art, too, experienced a renaissance: whereas in ancient Rome mosaics were floor decorations, in the Middle Ages mosaics were used on the walls and became a glittering new medium for the transmission of ideas about religion and power. The mosaics in the basilica and baptistry of Ravenna show the imperial court with Justinian and Theodora, emperor and empress, as equal to the apostles; other masterpieces in mosaic are the stunning Monreale cathedral outside Palermo and the unparalleled genius of St Mark's Basilica in Venice.

The Middle Ages

Nearly all culture in the Middle Ages was based on religion. The Church was, after all, the principal custodian of knowledge. In a world where few people could read and write, the Church provided rulers with clerks and chief ministers; monastery libraries were the unique repositories of what remained of ancient literature. The Church was sufficiently rich to be one of the chief sponsors of art. Medieval writings, too, were almost exclusively religious. The growth of universities such as those in Bologna and Pisa resulted from the preoccupation with theology and law. The greatest poet of the Middle Ages in Italy, the Florentine Dante Alighieri, in his *Divine Comedy* used a theological framework to comment on present-day events as well as his concept of heaven, purgatory and hell.

Change in art occurred only slowly. In the 13th century the new religious order of St Francis of Assisi, the Franciscans, was established; in the same century cracks in the Byzantine dominance of art began to appear. The Florentine painter Giotto began to make human figures three-dimensional with light and shadow. The stylistic change can be charted in the great basilica of St Francis in Assisi, where Giotto's influential fresco cycles caused a sensation. His followers dispersed his style across Italy. In Rome, the painter and mosaicist Pietro Cavallini made startlingly naturalistic figures and representations of ordinary life; whether he influenced Giotto or was influenced by him remains open.

The Renaissance

The rise of independent city-states in the Middle Ages, and of oligarchical government, began to affect art and literature. The new republic of Florence required a new philosophy to justify its existence: rather than the medieval idea that monarchy was a microcosm of God's rule over the universe, Florentines developed the idea of civic humanism, which looked back to the Roman republic as a model. Whereas medieval Europe rejected the life of this world in favour of the next, humanists made man the measure of all things. Architecture was measured in multiples of a human's height, art became increasingly natura-listic, and civic virtue supplemented piety. Humanism took its inspiration from the classical world, looking back to the ancient Greeks and Romans as literary models for a new and purer Latin style.

Initial developments centred on Tuscany, where Filippo Brunelleschi, consid-ered the first Renaissance architect, revived the Roman style of architecture and began incorporating arches, columns and other elements of classic architecture in his designs. The painter Masaccio followed Brunelleschi's techniques in a series of frescoes designed for the Church of Santa Maria del Carmine in Florence, where Biblical scenes are portrayed realistically, and with unprece-dented, intense emotion. Change was in the air, with a new interest in earthly rather than purely spiritual values.

In literature, a new spirit was bubbling forth. The 14th-century writers Petrarch and Giovanni Boccaccio told stories in familiar settings with real characters, a striking change from the traditional martyrologies and pious legends of saints' lives. The new cult of antiquity began to catch on across Italy during the 15th century, to the extent that authors became aware of themselves as partici-pating in a 'rebirth', or Renaissance, of the classical world, rejecting the period of decadence that they scornfully referred to as the Middle Ages, that depressing 'thousand years without a bath' that interrupted artistic purity.

Though many geniuses contributed to the development of Italian Renaissance art, three figures stand out: Michelangelo, Leonardo da Vinci and Raphael. Michelangelo is known as probably the greatest artist of the Renaissance, excelling in painting, poetry, sculpture and architecture. Leonardo – artist, philosopher, intellectual, inventor and scientist – was the bridge between Renaissance and the modern world with his motto *la sapienza e figliola della sperienza* – knowledge is the child of experience. Raphael's experi-ments with classical form and pure colour made him the model for centuries of followers. As always, art and literature went hand in hand with political devel-opments. As the central Italian republics one by one became monarchies, the idea of civic virtue mutated into the concept of service to the prince, as exemplified in Baldassarre Castiglione's 1518 handbook *The Courtier*. As the changing world of politics slipped from the grasp of the educated middle classes, perfecting the self became the new ideal. At the same time, Niccolò Macchiavelli's pragmatic manual of power, *The Prince*, laid out clear rules for the domination of a territory and the suppression of dissent.

The princes of Italy had to bow, in their turn, to the great powers of Spain and France. The Italian Wars, which began in the late 15th century, saw the peninsula become a vast theatre of struggle between Europe's two giants. Spain achieved dominance in the end, conquering the duchy of Milan in the north and the kingdom of Naples in the south and from the mid-16th century onwards Italian political life was forced to submit, with ill grace, to this foreign overlord. Literature was not the only thing to turn inward: Renaissance art, with its focus on naturalism, became distorted, mannered and academic. The 16th century limped out, having exhausted the style established by the great Renaissance artists. A new rebirth, however, was at hand.

Baroque

The turn of the 17th century brought the explosive birth of a new style. This time the artistic powerhouse was Rome and the style was Baroque. Early exponents like Annibale Carracci from Bologna re-established a Raphaelesque sense of colour, while the darkly brilliant Caravaggio painted with his trademark, brutally realistic use of *chiaroscuro*.

The great genius of the age was Gianlorenzo Bernini, who came to rule over the Roman artistic scene for most of the 17th century, and who stamped the city with his creations, like the Fountain of Four Rivers in Rome's Piazza Navona, the Baldacchino or Canopy in St Peter's, and many other churches, fountains and sculptures. Francesco Borromini, Bernini's rival, made curvaceous walls part of his architecture and scorned the banality of a strict adherence to a classical vocabulary in building.

The Enlightenment

Inching out slowly from its inward turn, the Age of Enlightenment in Italy began to find its way into a tight circle of narrow, avant-garde intellectuals in Naples and Milan. Illuminism and neoclassicism were promoted by writers such as Carlo Goldoni, who drew from the *commedia dell'arte* depicted by the thespian masks on characters such as Pantaloon, Harlequin and Columbine. He wrote drama and popular fairy-tales that inspired operatic works such as *Turandot*, by Puccini. The backlash against foreign influence exploded in the works of Giuseppe Parini and Vittorio Alfieri, as they stirred national pride in a way similar to the French writings that led to the French Revolution.

Revolutionary rumblings started to nudge Romanticism further aside, and writers like Ugo Foscolo witnessed and suffered the mutation. During that time journalism appeared with the periodical *Caffè*. Lyrical poet Giacomo Leopardi's was pumping out patriotic compositions seeped in Classicism and the true political writer of the *risorgimento* (*see* **Getting to Know Italy**, p.19), Alessandro Manzoni wrote the pinnacle masterpiece of Italian romantic fiction *I Promessi Sposi* (The Betrothed), as an attack on foreign oppression; it was the first literary work written in modern Italian.

Everyday speech and a simple style took over during the second half of the 19th century and beginning of the 20th with realism (*verismo*). Humorous, biting and sometimes raunchy poetry was dashed out in dialect by Roman sonnet grumbler Giuseppe Gioacchin Belli, whose dandy statue stands near the Tiber river in the capital, the Neapolitan Giambattista Basile and Milanese writer Porta.

20th-century Literature

Another decisive chunk of Italian 20th-century literature revolves around the fascist experience and the years of Mussolini's rule. Gabriele D'Annunzio, poet, novelist and dramatist, was also a military hero and supporter of fascist political ideas. Yet many openly opposed fascism, and suffered for voicing their opinion. Writer and scholar Giuseppe Antonio Borgese wrote *Goliath, The March of Fascism* in English in 1937, but did not see it translated into Italian until 10 years later. Novelist Ignazio Silone went into exile, gaining more notoriety abroad than in Italy for his political novels such as *Fontamara* and *Pane e Vino*.

The same post-war neorealism that exploded in cinema took hold of literature. Carlo Levi exposed the plight of impoverished, everyday people in malaria-ridden southern Italy in *Cristo si è Fermato a Eboli* (*Christ Stopped at Eboli*), and Elio Vittorini, the author of *Conversazione in Sicilia*, revealed the inner sadness of Sicilian abandonment.

One of the best-known historical Italian works, *Il Gattopardo* (*The Leopard*), written by Giuseppe Tomasi di Lampedusa and set against the background of Sicilian life, was made into an acclaimed film by director Luchino Visconti. It depicts an Italy ready for change and the Risorgimento but unable to let go of its traditions.

There are many internationally recognized modern Italian authors. One of the best-known contemporary writers, Alberto Moravia, portrays the moral dilemmas and trappings of various social and emotional circumstances. Natalia Ginzburg, a poet and novelist, won renown for her sensitive, spare treatment of modern Italian children and women, isolated within the family setting, and for her memoirs of her early life in Turin during the war. Primo Levi, a chemist by profession, began writing in 1977 and was immediately applauded for his memoirs of imprisonment in Auschwitz during the Second World War, such as

Survival at Auschwitz, Se Questo e un Uomo (If This Is a Man) and the follow-up book *La Tregua* about his voyage back to Italy after his liberation from the death camp. A brilliant collection of autobiographical essays using chemistry as life's metaphor was published in 1984, *Il Sistema Periodico (The Periodic Table)*.

Opera

Think of opera, and think of Italy. Though opera as we hear it today took its shape during the Italian Renaissance, Rome was already a centre of operatic composition from about 1620 until the late 1630s. Venice boasted the first public opera house, opened in 1637. At the end of the 19th century, *verisimo* opera started telling us stories about the seamier side of life among the lower classes, and the singing became more conversational. Puccini wrote *La Bohème*, *Madama Butterfly* and *Turandot* during this time. Verdi, the composer who dominated Italian opera for half of the 19th century, had a nationalistic drum to beat. His career unfolded during the period in which Italy finally achieved independence and unification, with many of his operas dramatizing the struggle against tyranny and oppression. The best known Verdi operas include *La Traviata*, *Aïda* and *Otello*. Italy is home to some of the world's most beautiful opera houses from la Scala in Milan to the Teatro Massimo in Palermo.

Cinema

The first film to ever be shot in Italy was Umberto and Margherita of Savoy's *Walking in a Park* (1886), by Vittorio Calcina. And it was just that – a realistic documentary of a stroll.

In contrast to the weepy sentimentalism of literary romanticism that the country was coming out of, Futurism was born in Italy in 1909. Though it was mostly a visual arts movement, Italian poet Filippo Tommaso Marinetti set the movement on its way with his manifesto celebrating the dynamism of the machine age. It was a movement that was to be characterized by the issuing of manifestos, something that fascist leaders later found to their liking.

The economic crisis that followed the First World War stunted the growth of Italian cinema, despite the introduction of sound. Near the end of the 1920s a few innovative films were directed by Alessandro Blasetti, Mario Camerini and his cousin Augusto Genina, one of which, *Nero*, was a satirical poke at Mussolini. Formal, heavily moral films called *telefoni bianchi* (white telephones, which had a fixed presence in each and every film) did little to advance the cultural level of the film industry or to depict Italy as a modern nation, but they introduced upcoming stars such as Vittorio de Sica.

Cinecittà, the fascist answer to MGM, was conceived by the dictator Benito Mussolini mostly as a vehicle for fascist propaganda. Built in 475 days, it was inaugurated in 1937 and reborn after the war as the cradle of Europe's best talent. It was during the war, between propaganda films, that the first neo-realist film, *Quattro Passi tra le Nuvole* (*Four Steps in the Clouds*), was filmed by Blasetti in 1942.

Italy found its true cinematographic soul in neorealism, poetically cruel, realistic and hauntingly unforgettable, with extraordinary actors and actresses playing out the difficult economical and moral conditions of post-war Italy.

Directors like Rossellini shot films outdoors on the devastated roads of a defeated country. *Roma Città Aperta* (*Rome Open City*) was begun no more than one year after the war had ended, with society's wounds still gaping. Some shots were also taken during the war. It is said that Rossellini collected loose ends of 35mm film and spliced them together to capture live images that would have otherwise been lost.

A demoralized and defeated nation cried to De Sica's *Sciuscià* (*Shoeshine*) written out to be pronounced as the bedraggled street children in bomb-flattened Naples would call out their services. There were heart-sickening stories of poverty and violated dignity, such as *Ladri di Biciclette* (*The Bicycle Thief*) and *Umberto D*, the name of an old, poor man left lonely and impoverished with his little dog in the midst of the new society. Many of Pier Paolo Pasolini's 1970s films are considered part of a new neorealist sub-genre, as he documented elements of common life in Italy during and after the so-called economic boom of the 1960s.

Many war-generation Italians still cannot bear to watch these tear-wrenching films. The atmosphere lightened up with what came to be known as 'pink neorealism'. Divas of the screen like Sophia Loren, Gina Lollobrigida, Silvana Mangano and Claudia Cardinale flourished in these more welcoming but equally challenging roles, giving Italy a star system and making Italian sex appeal world famous. The *commedia all'Italiana* was a bittersweet way of touching on serious social themes, while poking fun. Commercial production increased fourfold and actors like the Neapolitan genius Totó created an inimitable personage beloved throughout the country. Films like *La Dolce Vita* (*The Sweet Life*) by Fellini exported Italian glamour and absurdity throughout the world, and made the actor Marcello Mastroianni's sultry stare and sculpted face as recognizable as Rudolf Valentino's had been decades before. Fellini staunchly criticized modern Italy and its struggle to define its identity during the economic boom years.

In the 21st century Italian movies must compete against splashier, more expensive Hollywood fare. Of the ten top-grossing movies in Italy each year, usually only one is Italian. But production is picking up after years of B-grade movies filmed for national audiences. When it was released, *Pinocchio* by Roberto Begnini was expected to become the first real Italian blockbuster, and *La Vita e Bella* won the Tuscan actor and director an academy award. *Il Postino* tugged at the world's tear ducts, as did *Cinema Paradiso* before it. Italian cinema, from its beginnings to the present day, is an invaluable window to understanding and appreciating *la vita italiana*. A renaissance of regional films, such as the 1999 film *La Capa Gira*, recited in tight Pugliese dialect with Italian subtitles, have received plaudits at international film festivals, while other films like *L'America*, by Gianni Amelio, exposed the human side of the immigration issue from Albania to Italy. This inward-looking trend focusing on the internal aspects of Italy has begun to take off with state financing and a warm public welcome that heralds the movement as a sort of second neorealism.

Food and Wine

Italian cuisine, like other facets of the culture, speaks with highly inflected regional accents. There are certain self-consciously national constants: you can find spaghetti with tomato sauce and pizza pretty much everywhere from the Dolomites to Sicily, but this nationalization of culinary identity didn't really take hold until after the Second World War, when southern immigrants flooded to the north in search of work, and even those classics vary from place to place; small enclaves still hold fast to their unique local forms of pasta and particular preparations. Classics such as pasta and *fagioli*, while found everywhere, are prepared differently according to local traditions. Gastronomic explorations of Italy are best undertaken by knowing the local traditions and savouring the local foods on the spot.

There is a great deal of lively innovation at the level of haute cuisine. Low-temperature cooking methods, jellies, hot and cold foams and highly engineered multi-layer compositions with contrasting textures are all the rage these days. The Italian magazine *Gambero Rosso*, which publishes an English edition, is the best place to follow the latest trends in the culinary world (it also has a cooking school in Rome).

But by and large Italians are traditionalists when it comes to food, which evokes powerful connotations of family and roots. First of all, don't expect Italian food in Italy to resemble the 'genuine' Italian food you find in the UK. 'Genuine' in this case generally means northern Italian food, as opposed to the southern-influenced Anglo-Italian cuisine of yesteryear, which unfortunately culminated in such industrial horrors as spaghetti hoops in a can. It was the publication of the Venetian Marcella Hazan's admittedly superb and seminal work *The Classic Italian Cookbook* that etched in stone the northern culinary prejudice. Since then, a number of pretentious, arbitrary and quite un-Italian judgements have been imposed with Stalinist determination: that northern Italian food is more refined than southern (people who dismiss southern cuisine have, as a rule, never tasted the real thing in Naples or Catania); that fresh pasta is inherently superior to dried; and that 'in Italy, they dip the bread in olive oil before the meal' – no, they don't, at least Italians don't. Some restaurants in Florence have started indulging this curious whim for their American clientele, but it's generally seen as a cheapskate way to fill up for free, and you can raise eyebrows if you stuff yourself on bread and oil and then order just a single dish, while showing signs of affluence. The great majority of Italians I've asked about this presumed custom in the last 10 years had never heard of it anywhere, except as a Tuscan peasant tradition, caused by having little else to eat. As a restaurant tradition, however, it probably began in Malibu in the 1980s. And creamy polenta (made so by the addition of lots of heavy cream, whose butterfat prevents the cornstarch from congealing properly) is an incomprehensible aberration where cornmeal was a poor man's staple and cream non-existent.

The Traditional Italian Meal

A traditional Italian meal is not to be taken lightly or out of order. A full meal begins with an appetizer course, the *antipasto* (a masculine word indicating the course before the meal, or *pasto*, nothing to do with pasta), and although one often has a single dish, the ideal is to have a smorgasbord ranging from fresh shellfish and squid to cold cuts and a variety of (usually marinated) vegetables, especially the ubiquitous aubergine (eggplant), olives, artichokes and peppers. The first course is almost always some form of starch – either pasta, risotto or polenta – although a soup will do as well. But where most Americans would stop there, the Italians don't consider the meal complete without a proper main course of meat (*carne*) or fish (*pesce*) with vegetables (*contorni*) as the side. Dessert is often bypassed for fruit, and the entire affair is capped off with an *espresso* and an *amaro* or *grappa* to help with the digestion and provide an excuse to stay longer at the table. *Cappuccino* or any kind of coffee with milk is, according to Italians, bad for the liver and should not be drunk after a meal.

Lunch used to be the principal daily meal, although modern work schedules have impeded that tradition, and pizza, on the other hand, is considered a light evening meal; most pizzerias that make the archetypal hand-tossed variety of pizza aren't even open at lunchtime.

Pasta Shapes

While to most foreigners the endless variety of pasta shapes seems gratuitously picturesque, Italians obsess over the appropriateness of shape to condiment. As a rule, finer, smoother shapes go with similar sauces, while chunkier shapes marry well with a more textured meat sauce (*ragù*), or vegetables such as broccoli, although it would be misleading to search for a consistently rational pattern in the various couplings; glaring exceptions, such as *tagliolini* or *fettuccine* with porcini mushrooms, abound. Still, *penne* with pesto is just plain barbaric to most Italians; Ligurians, inventors of pesto, insist on serving it with *trenette*, a slightly plumper sister of *linguini*. *Penne* (quills), on the other hand, traditionally accompany the *pepperoncino*-laced *arrabbiata*

To Each His Starch

Fad diets forgo starch. Italian culinary genius transforms the lowly staple into high art. Never forget that the typical Italian meal revolves around a plate of starch in one of three forms – pasta, polenta or rice. Substantially grain-based carbohydrates dressed with vegetables have fed the Italian peninsula for centuries and form the staple of the Mediterranean diet.

Legend has it that Marco Polo brought back pasta on his return from China, but the ancient Etruscans ate a form of pasta in the 4th century BC, as did the ancient Romans. *Macaroni* is recorded in 1279 in Genoa – 20 years before Marco Polo's return. Indeed, Polo more than likely just introduced spaghetti, a pasta treasured by the Chinese as symbolic of longevity. Even today Italians never cut spaghetti as it brings bad luck.

Fresh pasta is made from wheat flour, water and sometimes egg, and dried pasta from hard durum wheat, with its stiffening, high gluten content. The dough should have a slight roughness to the surface, helping sauces to adhere. Fresh pasta is not more chic, as assumed by many outsiders. To Italians it is a matter of regional taste. Rich, fresh egg pasta belongs to the north, while the southern Italians prize the toothier character of the dried variety.

Polenta, from the Latin *pulmentum*, once meant anything served with meat or sauce. Now it is almost exclusively the corn porridge eaten predominantly in northern regions. Corn, called *grano turco*, meaning Turkish grain, actually arrived from the New World through the Spaniards, who controlled Milan in the mid-17th century. Creamy when freshly cooked, it quickly sets and hardens. Italians eat it mushy, but often let it set, and fry slices in various ways – with sugar as a snack for children or layered lasagne-style with a sauce and cheese.

Venetians claim that they introduced rice in the form of risotto. It's more likely that rice, cultivated by the Arabs in medieval Spain, arrived through the Aragonese in their kingdom of Naples, and from there they sent diplomatic samples of this useful wet-climate plant to their allies in Milan.

Risotto, meaning 'fat rice', uses short-grain and starchy rice, lightly sautéed in oil or butter, cooked over a low flame while spooning in hot broth until it swells into a creamy, unctuous sort of dry soup. Grains remain slightly *al dente* and never lose their identity. The dish is enriched with liberal helpings of butter and grated cheese, called the *mantecata*. Flavourings depend on the region and time of year, and include wild asparagus or white truffle, *radicchio* around Treviso, pumpkin in Mantova, and of course saffron in the most famous version of all, *risotto Milanese*.

sauce, and so on. A Neapolitan friend once tried to explain to me why flat pasta was absolutely incompatible with seafood, a process made more difficult in that the proposition had only the most tenuous of logical holds on my uninitiated mind, while for her its truth was simply self-evident. When I tried to counter by bringing up the national standard *linguini* with clams, she correctly retorted that *linguini* were not flat but ovoid in cross-section. Now, hers is, I think, a personal rather than canonical view, as one does often find *fettuccine* with shrimp, but to be fair this is the only real exception to her taboo that I've come across (the exception that proves the rule?), and anyway, the point is not so much the rule per se but the passionate intransigence with which she held her opinion: passionate intransigence is a canonically Italian approach to food.

Olive Oils

Olive oil has been produced in pretty much every region of the peninsula except the frigid Alps since ancient times, and if you ask 20 Italians from different regions which one produces the best, you'll get 20 different answers. The Tuscans have been by far the most successful at international marketing and have managed to convince the world that Tuscan oil has no rivals, but a fraud was uncovered several years ago in England. Brands that presented themselves as 'bottled in Tuscany' and priced themselves by Tuscan standards were found actually to be blends of cheaper oil from other regions or even countries, and sometimes entirely lacking in Tuscan origin.

Tuscan oil, in particular that of the areas of Chianti and Lucca, does have a rich and somewhat peppery flavour, but there are quite good reasons other than regional chauvinism to prefer an oil from another region. Break it down with a wine analogy: some connoisseurs prefer Bordeaux, others Burgundy; and oils from the various regions, themselves blended from different varietals, have their own distinct personalities and greatly affect the tenor of the local cuisines. The strong Tuscan oil, while perfect for steaks, can quite easily over-power a grilled fish or buffalo mozzarella. The Lago di Garda area in the north produces a delicate, lemony oil which goes perfectly with seafood, and gives Venetian and Friulian cuisine a good deal of its delicacy. The Italian Riviera on the west coast of Liguria also prides itself on the *gentile* variety of trees, which cling to the seaside cliffs and inhale the salty air, and locals have a good case when they insist that pesto should be made only from the light and fruity nectar, with a mild scent of almond undertones, that they yield. Umbria produces a suave and less expensive cousin of Tuscan oil, and then the real bargains are in the long-maligned oils of the south. While the macro-climates there still encourage industrial production, a swarm of small producers are pressing exceptional and quite underpriced oils in Lazio (particularly the Sabine country northeast of Rome), Campania (notably in the peculiar conditions on the Amalfi coast), Puglia, Basilicata, Calabria and Sicily. One chef swears that the most memorable oils he ever tasted were from the island of Pantelleria between Sicily and Tunisia: bright and innocent and redolent of fresh-snipped chives, is how he described it.

Wineries now strive to produce single-estate vintages from their olive groves as well as their vineyards, which has led to a plethora of upmarket designer

Taking it Slowly

When the Slow Food movement ratified its 1989 manifesto in Paris, representatives from 20 countries agreed to protect humanity from the 'fast life, which disrupts our habits, pervades the privacy of our homes and forces us to eat fast food'. The movement, founded by Italian journalist and president Carlo Petrini, was a backlash against the first McDonald's opening on the Piazza di Spagna in Rome. It quickly became a call to arms for European food enthusiasts. Now this bugle call has an army of chefs, cooks, producers and professors who form a daunting body of knowledge with the capacity for action worldwide.

The Slow Food movement aims to protect foods, and a way of life, that is getting run over in the fast lane. Biennial food fests held in Piemonte, such as Cheese and Salone del Gusto, promote all that is good and fair in the culinary eyes of president Carlo Petrini. The movement encourages farms that produce small-scale, higher-quality yields, and fights mass-production methods in the food industry.

bottles at expected prices. Italian pantries often stock at least three different oils: a strong one for meats, a delicate one for fish, and a cheaper one for basic cooking. Look for oil labelled extra-virgin, marked by its low acidity: so-called 'pure' oil is not pure, by even the most indulgent interpretation of the word, and even oil that lays claim to being 'virgin' can in fact legally have its honour compromised by the addition of other oils such as corn or safflower oil. Keep in mind that, in contrast to wine, olive oil does not mature with age but rather oxidizes and goes rancid, so it is best consumed within a year of its production and keeps better if kept out of sunlight and in a cool place, rather than on aesthetically pleasing display over your stove.

Regional Cuisines and Specialities

Regional cuisines developed out of local products at a time when transport was not easy and refrigeration was virtually nonexistent (the wealthy could have things packed in snow), and still focus heavily on the local heritage. While nowadays the peninsula's restaurants pride themselves on the fresh seafood available from the surrounding waters, Fernand Braudel, in his classic *History of the Mediterranean*, reminds us that before the refrigerator the only seafood widely available off the immediate coastline (and indeed, for the non-wealthy in the coast towns) was dried salted cod (*baccalà*) from the north Atlantic, which still turns up as an important speciality in important ports such as Genoa, Venice and Messina.

The tendency to emphasize local products and tradition has been encouraged lately by the organization Slow Food, which is intent on taking Italian local cuisine back to its roots.

The mellow, austere *prosciutto* cured in the Parma area is the most famous ham cured worldwide, but I follow a number of Italian connoisseurs in preferring the sweeter, silkier version from San Daniele in Friulia; and Norcia in Umbria also puts out some stellar hams with an elegantly rustic tang. In fact, you'll find that cured and smoked pork products, which lasted the winter well and did not require ownership of land, turn up in local varieties, from the suave *mortadella* of Bologna to the spicy *pepperoni* of Calabria or the classic *salame* of Milan.

The North

Crossbreeding from a large variety of cultural influences contributed to the peninsula's complicated gastronomic heritage. In the Tyrol region abutting Austria you will find typically Austrian food: *spaetzle*, *canederli* (dumplings in broth) and lots of cabbage; the frugal cuisine of Friulia next door also speaks the language of Mitteleuropa, with Hungarian paprika, lots of soups and strudel.

In the Valle d'Aosta, next to France, Swiss-style cheese is close to the French cheeses, as it is in Piemonte, not surprising for the former kingdom of Savoy. They are possibly the only two regions not averse to – God forbid! – putting butter on their pasta. There is a rich selection of cheeses in the northwest, such as the famous gorgonzola and a variety of creamy *toma*. Polenta, one of the region's specialities, is ladled on to long wooden trays and covered with meat sauce or rich gorgonzola cheese, and lots of butter, an ingredient rarely seen in olive-oil-dependent Italy. Castelmagno from the mountains in the west is a mellow, aged cheese from Cuneo, a town that, along with Turin, also boasts Italy's most developed chocolate tradition.

The area around Alba, known as the Langhe, is renowned for its exquisite and rare white truffles, best shaved over a plate of fresh buttered *tagliolini* or a delicately cheesy risotto, as well as for its powerful Barolo and Barbaresco wines, perhaps the best reds in Italy. Piedmont also produces superb beef, and the Venetian *carpaccio* is really just a personal interpretation by Harry Cipriani of a traditional Langhe raw beef dish.

Venetian cuisine is a world apart, making the most of the unique seafood from the brackish lagoon. This is where you'll find the best fried *calamari* (if the restaurant offers *moscardini*, or baby octopus, by all means take them), and the pasta courses advertise Neptune's treasure-trove with panache. Venice's long maritime contact with the Byzantine empire can be seen in the sweet-and-sour sardines *al saôr*, served cold as an appetizer. The Veneto is also the homeland of polenta, served with stewed cod, sautéed porcini mushrooms, or a meat *ragù*.

The immense stretch of Lombardy plains produces mostly rice, and the region's cuisine counts heavily on it. The Milanese risotto with saffron is traditionally served with braised veal shank (*osso buco* or in dialect *os büs*) and shows up in the most modest of restaurants as it does in Milan's more upmarket restaurants. Crushed amaretti cookies, graced with a sage butter, are one of Mantua's unexpected treasures. Sturgeon and caviar are specialties from Lombardy's lake region and, as in much of the north, polenta is a mainstay.

Parma and Modena, between Milan and Bologna, are the powerhouse towns of Italian food production, abounding in spectacular hams, the quintessential grating cheese *parmigiano* (parmesan), and the succulent balsamic vinegar produced from the charming and callow local wines. The Bolognese unabashedly draw on the wealth of nearby ingredients. This is ground zero for fresh egg pasta, which many restaurants, humble and grand, still insist on rolling out by hand on un-sanded wooden boards to give just the right irregularity in the surface texture for maximum sauce adhesion. Of course they love to show off their handiwork in ribbons of *fettuccine* adorned with the famous meat *ragù* (aka Bolognese sauce, here a surprisingly delicate combination of beef and veal). But they'd just as soon stuff the pasta with various mixtures of meat and parmesan in *tortellini* and serve them in a rich capon broth, or make larger packages of *tortelloni*, stuffed with meat or ricotta combinations and served with any number of sauces (often more than one at a time). What has been called boloney, and sometimes more appropriately *bologna*, is actually the melt-in-your-mouth *mortadella* cold cut, a regional delicacy. Locals and other Italian men like to refer to women of the region as *mortadellone*, by analogy with the ham's soft shape and sweet flavour.

There is no counting the number of variations on *ravioli*, and then, of course, the famous *lasagne*: typically a lavish dozen layers of fresh spinach pasta with *ragù* and béchamel (not ricotta). In fact, béchamel sauce, while apparently French and quite un-Italian in character, seems to have been indigenous to the city since at least the Renaissance and turns up everywhere; apart from the *lasagne*, especially on meat-stuffed *cannelloni* rolls. With first courses so rich, the main course tends to the simple: the classic is *bollito*, literally mixed boiled meats, which also features heavily in Lombardy, but perhaps receives its most exalted expression here, accented with a pungent fruit *mostarda di Cremona* or a herbal green sauce.

Central Italy

Tuscany, oddly enough, has one of the more limited culinary traditions. Its ruggedly picturesque hills are splendid for growing wine and olive oil as well as grazing cattle, but rather stubbornly resist most other agriculture. The Florentines and Sienese have always made the most of their superb Chianina beef, though – together with that of Piedmont it is the best in Italy – which they grill in an ostentatious multi-portion slab of enhanced T-bone called the *fiorentina* and drizzle with their peppery olive oil, accompanied by a robust Chianti or Brunello. Game is still bountiful in the hills and predominates on the menu, not only as a main course but also in hearty *ragùs* of duck or wild boar (*cinghiale*), which often resemble a brown stew more than a tomato sauce. The

Case Study: The Accidental Cook

One of the best-known culinary schools in Italy is run not by an Italian chef but by Englishwoman Diane Seed. 'I had always loved cooking and collecting personal recipes,' says the cheerful, world-renowned author, 'but for 15 years I taught English literature at a big international school in Rome.' Diane's flair for noting down scrumptious recipes proved providential. 'When my daughter went off to university in the UK I wrote down five foolproof, classic Italian pasta recipes for her – a real labour of love for me since I have always despised measuring.' Those five recipes not only nourished her daughter through the slim first days of university, they also caught the eye of a publisher who eventually convinced Diane to write her first cookbook, *The Top One Hundred Pasta Sauces*, which sold more than a million copies and has been translated into 12 languages.

Following this stunning success, she cooked, wrote, travelled, gave lessons as a visiting expert, gave classes to tourists in Puglia, Sicily, and on the Amalfi Coast, and started being called to speak at conferences about olive oil and culinary traditions in Italy and the Mediterranean. She works frequently for the International Olive Oil Council, and counselled Marks and Spencer for many years as their Italian food consultant. Nine books later, Diane imparts her 30 years of accumulated expertise in intimate classes in a noble attic in the Doria Pamphili palace on Piazza Venezia with a window looking towards the Colosseum. A passionate defender and inspired exponent of southern Italian cuisine, Diane teaches cooks to enrich their repertoire with authentic regional dishes, and her enthusiasm, lively delivery and amusing anecdotes bring out the sheer pleasure of Italian life as expressed in its food.

unsalted Tuscan bread dates back to when citizens preferred to go without salt than to pay the tax levied on it. As it is rather tasteless on its own, it serves to sop up sauces, and also gets recycled into the delicious *panzanella* salad or the comforting *ribollita*: a poor man's winter feast scrabbled together from a handful of beans and some weeds from the garden. In contrast, the wealthy resort coast from Livorno to Grosseto boasts a number of Italy's finest seafood restaurants. Umbrian cuisine is the wealthier cousin of Tuscan cuisine, lacking the beef, perhaps, but making up for it in black truffles and a more subtle olive oil. Much is made of *farro*, the ancient Romans' wheat, either in pasta or savoury porridges spiked with sausage. Wines range from the most basic, hearty, by-the-barrel variety to the most sophisticated, award-winning vintages. With a Tuscan wine, it is hard to go wrong.

The South

The tomato and dried pasta hold sway from Lazio southwards. Roman food also features a wide variety of greens, most notably chicory or Swiss chard (*bieta*), often sautéed with garlic and red pepper, and its bold, simple sauces are set off by the local ewes'-milk grating cheese, *pecorino romano*, which is more piquant than the cow's-milk *parmigiano*. Ancient Roman dishes such as sweet-and-sour *baccalà* still survive in the local Jewish cuisine, and much is made of the 'fifth quarter' from butchered animals: offal such as ox-tail (braised in tomato sauce), brains (fried with zucchini) and the notorious *pajata* (intestine of milk-fed lamb or veal, served with *rigatoni*).

The bay around Naples produces some of the most stunning vegetables in the world, shouting with colour and flavour, and these combine with a wealth of seafood into a lusty and hedonistic joyride. When Neapolitans say *al dente*, they mean that the pasta still has a noticeable crunch, and the fresh soft-wheat pasta of the north just seems to lack character for them (also, pasta has its longest tradition here, and dried industrial pasta, when introduced in the 19th century, was and remains a sign of affluence, since it meant that the housewife could free herself from the daily pasta-making grind – interestingly enough, precisely the contrary of the present view in the United States). The poor and adventurous Neapolitans discovered the new and doubtful tomato (thought to be toxic) before their fellow Italians, and pasta with *ragù* here has perhaps its purest expression, as well as the Caprese salad of tomato, mozzarella and basil, so often banal but so brilliant when made with the right stuff. Naples is, of course, the home of pizza, and Neapolitans still insist that the rest of Italy can never do it right.

The fresh, sunny, healthy cuisine of Puglia and Basilicata also abounds in vegetables, and its most characteristic pasta shape, *orecchiette* ('little ears'), is usually graced with turnip greens or shoots of the local broccoli. Meat other than lamb or goat is in short supply, but plentiful seafood fills the gap nicely, as does the famous Lucanian sausage rolled up in gently spiced coils, just as it was in ancient times with its earliest inhabitants the Lucani.

Raw fish and sea urchins (*ricci*) are eaten in abundance at roadside restaurants with long tables set up to serve them fresh. Ingredients such as almonds, almond milk, fresh whey, honey, quince and dried fruit are used as they are in Greece. Cheeses range from creamy soft *burrata* to smoked *fagottini*, a speciality of Foggia. One local success story, the red wine Cirò, is now exported worldwide. Calabria, the toe of the boot, possesses a rugged, mountainous terrain, and a cuisine where aubergine in its various guises, the sun-dried tomato and spicy red pepper hold pride of place.

The Islands

Sicily has collected culinary influences from the Greeks, Arabs and Spaniards over the centuries of its history as crossroads of the Mediterranean, and its stunning food can be the greatest surprise of all for Americans. Unexpected flavours turn up in the signature dish of Palermo, *pasta con le sarde* (with sardines, wild fennel, raisins and pine nuts), or a plate of pasta with shrimp and orange, as well as in *caponata*, a slightly sweet-and-sour stew of aubergine, onion and celery smoothed out with sun-dried tomato paste and a dusting of cocoa. The island produces superb citrus fruit (notably the unique blood-orange), almonds and perhaps the best pistachios in the world, and these find their way into a heavily Arab-influenced tradition of sweets including the famous *cannoli* and *cassata*. Marsala is famous for its sweet fortified wines, Agrigento for its almonds, and the sun-drenched southeast for its cherry toma-toes, called *pacchino*, and luscious melons.

Finally, Sardinia holds its own island tradition somewhat aloof, with its paper-thin *carta di musica* bread and hard-won pastoral riches combining with the bounty of the sea. The island cuisine has been inspired, first, by its shepherds, then by its fishermen. *Mirto* (myrtle) is paired with meat, and the bitter berry is fermented into a tasty after-dinner drink. Sardinia produces a cheese so 'aged' that live worms wiggle inside. Enzymes inside the creatures are said to improve the taste. and die-hard cheese fans wouldn't think of pulling them out. *Merca* is small fish wrapped in herbs and left to 'ripen' for several days, and *spaghetti alla bottarga* is pasta served with female lobster eggs that have been pressed and dried in the sun like raisins. The bark from a special oak, called *sughero*, makes the world's best wine corks.

Quality is Important

Although the daily local market is facing serious competition from the onrush of large supermarkets with their more flexible hours, many Italians still insist on making the small pilgrimage for better-quality vegetables and fruit, and you can find a number of stall owners who now conveniently offer vegetables cleaned and ready to cook: trimmed artichokes and green beans, shelled peas and fresh *borlotti* beans and packaged of pre-cut minestrone veggies.

Another good place for good-quality convenience is at your local *rosticceria*, which offers not only roast chickens but also prepared side dishes and other main courses.

In spite of the three-hour lunch-and-siesta tradition, Italians are masters of fast food, with bars vying to put out the most interesting sandwiches (the *panino* on a bread roll, stuffed *focaccia*, or the *trammezzino* on sliced white loaf-bread) and a dazzling variety of pizza by the slice (*pizza rustica*). As for sit-down service, a *trattoria* or *osteria* was once a simple locale where a *ristorante* meant something more upmarket, but these terms have now lost a great deal of distinction with the advent of expensive, shabby-chic establishments bearing humble names. Likewise, wine bars (*vinerie*) can serve simple cheese-and-cold-cut platters with their wine selections, or full and very trendy menus.

Wine

Wine is undergoing an exciting if hard-to-follow burst of experimentation, where the implantation of international varietals such as Chardonnay, Cabernet and Syrah interacts with the rediscovery or revaluation of ancient indigenous varietals; this phenomenon is especially intense in more traditionally underrated areas, and once again this means the south. The real hotspots of Italian wine-making these days are Campania, Puglia and Sicily, and it's not just due to the abundant sun any more. Here again, the *Gambero Rosso* wine guide, produced in tandem with Slow Food, provides the best overview of the subject. In particular, the Nero d'Avola grape, happy from Campania to Sicily, is turning up in both surprisingly good pure varietal form as well as softer blends with Cabernet, Merlot or Syrah. The viticulturers of Puglia have awakened to the success of Zinfandel in California and responded by concentrating on its ancestor, their Primitivo, in complex wines with 12 to 18 degrees alcohol content. Piedmont is famous for its Barolo and Barbaresco wines, still the most consistently expensive, but also puts out the delightful Dolcetto; the Veneto has long prided itself on the voluptuous Amarone produced by leaving the grapes to dry slightly, concentrating their sugar, and crisp white Soave.

Tuscany boasts the world-conquering blend known as Chianti as well as its 'purer' cousin Brunello, though Tuscan viticulturers also started to introduce French varietals with the cultivation of Cabernet, which now features prominently in some of its most famous and expensive wines, such as Sassicaia or Ornellaia.

The northeast (Trentino-Alto Adige and Friuli) is best known for its delicate and aromatic whites. Because of confusion between the Hungarian grape called Tokaj and the French Tokay, the European Community has ordered the names of the French and Friuli grapes to be changed by 2006, allowing Hungary to keep the original Tokaj name. Other local whites include Chardonnay, Müller-Thurgau, Pinot Bianco, Pinot Grigio, Ribolla Gialla, Riesling Italiaco and Riesling Renano, Sauvignon Blanc, Traminer Aromatico, Verduzzo and Malvasia Istriana, a somewhat metallic wine that accompanies Adriatic seafood recipes and is completely unrelated to the Malvasia produced in Sicily. Among the red produced in Friuli-Venezia Giulia are Cabernet Franc, Cabernet Sauvignon, Collio and Collio Cabernet, Merlot, Pignolo, Pinot Nero, Refosco dal Peduncolo Rosso, Schioppettino, Tazzelenghe and Terrano. The Terrano is made with the Refosco grape grown in characteristic red soil. Also, the region is a powerhouse of small furniture factories; it is said that every third chair in the world originates in Friuli-Venezia Giulia.

Liguria's best wines are the whites from the terraced slopes of the Cinque Terre. Emilia produces the light and fizzy Lambrusco to set off its rich cuisine, and Romagna is valiantly trying to compete with Tuscany and Umbria with its admittedly less corpulent versions of Sangiovese. The Marche has made inroads recently with its high-quality, reasonably priced Montepulciano-based reds, and whites from the Trebbiano grape. Umbria produces excellent Sangiovese and Trebbiano as well, but look out especially for its own rich red, the Sagrantino of Montefalco. The area south of Rome is famous for its Trebbiano and Grechetto-based white from Frascati, but one of the peninsula's best Merlots hails from north Lazio, and vintners in the Frascati area are contributing some innovative and prize-winning red varietal blends. Again, taste around, starting with the local jug (the local house wine is a consistently good bet in most Italian restaurants) and make friends with a good wine-dealer; the march of progress is such that it's a full-time occupation to keep up with what's good. But what bliss to try.

First Steps

This is it – the time for arrival has descended like a hungry vulture or a soaring seagull. Happy or sad, willing or dispatched, the eagle has landed. You are going to Italy, a country affectionately called by many who live here the Golden Cage. With its breathtaking beauty and diversity, *bell'Italia* is truly eye candy for the aesthetically wanton. Artists, poets, tourists and sojourners of all types have not only sung the praises but have let the mesmerizing allure of the country seep into their pores.

Enduring customs refuse to loosen their grip on a country very much based on family and tradition. Town festivals (*sagras*) are in abundance throughout the country year round, each one playing out a piece of the country's history. There's no better way of understanding the importance of an orange harvest to Ligurians than by having townsmen on wagons loaded to the brim with citrus cannon balls hurl them at you at 160km per hour (100mph), or of understanding the deep significance of the New Year than to dodge objects tossed out of windows on to the street below at the strike of midnight in the age-old tradition of making room for the new. Whether religious or not, many gaze in awe as a jewel-clad Madonna is sent drifting out to sea

Italian Pride

A popular joke goes that in a speech to the Italian National Team before World Cup 2000 matches began, one of the head trainers supposedly chided players to make a *bella figura* (good impression) and sing the national anthem before the match. To which one player responded, 'Do we have to learn the words, or can we just move our lips?' The truth is, the everyday Italian is hard put to it to sing more than two lines of their national anthem, the Mameli hymn. More than that, they just aren't terribly patriotic.

Patriotism aside, Italian pride knows no limits. *Mamma, pizza* and *casa* hang on the lips of the average Italian like baseball, hotdogs and apple pie for Americans. And a veritable smorgasbord of delicacies, like *parmigiano* cheese, *prosciutto*, Parma and *mozzarella* cling to the national heart. Though *mamma* and *casa* may be tough to patent, *prosciutto* and co. are basking in a new wave of attention and a push to keep them Italian. Some 2,171 food products have been presented to an EU committee that is doling out a new protective certification that would guarantee their 'Made in Italy' glory. Basically, any of the products on the list, if made outside Italy, cannot be called by their proper name. Kind of like Champagne not from Champagne.

Italians have long known the meaning of slicing real Parma ham, made in one of the town's historical curing establishments. And if anyone has ever tasted authentic 'fresh' (not aged) *parmigiano* from the Emilia-Romagna region, something that can only be bought there owing to export restrictions even within the country, they will have a deeper understanding of the ferocious desire to make sure Italy gets the credit it deserves for these masterpieces.

surrounded by candles on a moonlit summer night. Some say that Italy is for the mystical and passionate rather than the logical.

Certainly Italy is a land of the more ethereal professions – Italians themselves proclaim it is a country of poets, artists and navigators. Yet Italy is also one of the European Community founding members and Europe's fourth largest economy. Some predict that it is the country most on the verge of an economic power surge, despite strong bouts of sluggishness and its retro-industrial atmosphere. Whether this transformation will come about remains to be seen but, in any case, Italy has something for everyone and if the objective of being in Italy is to catch the wave or ride one, study art or just appreciate it, get immersed in an industrial crunch or blissfully avoid it, you've made it to the right place. *Benvenuti* and *buon divertimento.*

Why Live and Work in Italy?

What's so unique about Italy that drives flocks of expats to relocate, temporarily or permanently, or at least dream of it? If the approximately 28,000 UK nationals living in Italy were asked why they had come, or stayed, undoubtedly they would come out with a discussion of what is different, and at times superior, about living there! Pull out those stereotypes once again because, well known though many may be, they still have validity.

Living the Expected and Unexpected Beauties

Anyone moved by Audrey Hepburn clinging to Gregory Peck while being charioted around Rome on the back of a Vespa 150, or by Sophia Loren provocatively hanging laundry from a Neapolitan balcony singing 'O Sole Mio', is not being misled. All those sparkling travel programmes and glossy coffee-table picture books that look suspiciously airbrushed aren't building sandcastles for marketing. They tell the truth. Fasten your seat belts and get ready. Italy really is as gloriously beautiful as in picture books and it is surprisingly easy to live moments as magical as those you see on the silver screen.

Character

This will touch dangerously close to stereotyping, but there's no doubt that the Italian personality has certain archetypes: a heart-splitting smile flashed out of nowhere, pharmacists striking up small talk, storekeepers holding up queues to finish a conversation, policemen ready to hear your side of the story when they pull you over (and, sorry men, being more lenient on women depending on skirt length) and small gifts juxtaposed by genuine ripoffs are just some examples.

A foreigner in Italy, with a kind word and a bit of patience, can move mountains. Belligerent insistence can seal shut doors. Italians can be extremely expansive, at times naively so. Even after uncountable years in the country, if they have been lucky enough to stay that long, expats are singled out by their accents and asked if they like living in Italy. Frustrating as it may be to be questioned about personal happiness while queuing up to pay exorbitant electricity bills or put petrol into the car, in Italy a foreigner will always remain *straniera*. This can sometimes be to your advantage (*see* **Red Tape**) but at others it is a downright nuisance.

Safety

In 2001 more than one million muggings were reported in Italy but fewer than 3,000 murders, as recorded by the national statistics institute ISTAT. But that number was slightly down from 1999 figures, and dropped again in a September 2003 government report (only the figure for murders in families rose slightly). Though not free of the one-off weirdo crime, Italy's crime rates often rank below European counterparts and fall into very acceptable limits.

And rest assured, Italians are not the kind to turn their backs – a scream or cry for help is almost always met with concerned neighbours running to the rescue and street crime during the day rarely lacks witnesses to assist in filing the police report. This is the upswing of an overdeveloped sense of curiosity and a total challenge to the 'rigid ... privacies of an Anglo-Saxon mind', as writer Eleanor Clark admitted. Unsettling stares and a complete failure to keep at arm's-length is as notable in tight spaces as it is when there is room enough to do jumping jacks. But there is a certain sense of security in being watched.

As for the Mafia, note that it has not been defeated, and figures relating to the activities of the organization are not included in the discussion above.

See also **Italy Today**, '*La Mafia*', pp.76–7.

Taste: Fashion

Fashion geeks, beware. This is not the country for the stylishly weak at heart. It is a country where self is shamelessly at the centre of attention. Italians spend approximately one-third of their income each year on clothing, and devote an average of 3hrs a week to cosmetic treatments. Even men are inching up the vanity poll, dishing out one-quarter of their annual income at the hairdresser, aesthetician and plastic surgeon. Throwing on some grubby duds for a dash down to pick up milk just doesn't exist. And even casual Sunday gear is usually designer-labelled and well pressed.

Following the rule of supply and demand, certain areas of Italy, especially around Florence and Prato, are teaming with wholesale designer outlets. Cosmetics are standard European prices, but the average sales attendant won't hesitate to toss in a handful of samplers and give out small but appreciable *sconti* (discounts) to faithful customers. Along the same lines, hairdressers are truly artists in Italy. Many women find themselves following along the Italian coiffeur road and going regularly simply to *mettere in piega* (have their hair set) – a wickedly lavish proclivity, but amazingly affordable in the country of cured locks.

Taste: Food and Drink

Dieters, hang it up. Recipes will not be altered for a low-fat version and sugar-free drinks are still a slow-growing phenomenon. For anyone who may not want to eat Italian every day, tough luck. Despite there being the occasional ethnic restaurant (some Indian, perhaps Thai, an overabundance of Chinese), Italians eat Italian. Regional, local, upscale or greasy spoon style, a meal will rarely be without pasta (risotto and polenta in the north can substitute for pasta, though noodles rarely get more than a two-day holiday even there). Vegetarian meals are less than creative unless sampled at one of the rare, specialized restaurants. But Italian food is scrumptious and based on singularly superior ingredients, which become flavourful masterpieces, even on the most modest of tables. And the Mediterranean diet, with its worldwide fame, seems to work for most Italians; obesity is not the problem it is in many other developed countries.

The creed that two are better than one doesn't apply when choosing produce, wine and drink. A pre-dinner drink (*aperitivo*) is had after work, a glass or two of wine at dinner and a digestive liqueur (*amaro*) after dinner. Extra cash flows into the *enoteca* tills to ensure a finer vintage. Quality always wins over quantity.

Guiltless Lounging

In the healthiest sense, Italians have 13 national holidays and approximately 30 days of vacation days each year. This is 10 more than the European average and 20 more then the US standard. Lounging and socializing can be experienced in full living colour if you pop in to the local bar. *Il bar* is not a pub, but an establishment open from morning until late afternoon where one has morning cappuccino and afternoon *aperitivo* with snacky things. One glance at the guys hanging, smoking and chatting says it all. *Piazza* or life on the square is just as revealing as observing *il bar*, and the standard lunch closing time (shops close at lunch, yes) is two hours. 'Sunshine and leisure and conversation', as Henry James said, provides the greater part of the Venetian, but we'll say Italian, diet.

Work Can Wait

Going to the office with a fever, or even the sniffles, brings gasps of concern and horror – and often the cold shoulder for fear of infection. Italian workers have unlimited sick leave with a doctor's note and protective labour laws make it nearly impossible to lay off employees – a reality in hot debate following the proposed reforms by the Berlusconi government. New mammas recuperate fully during their 3–6-month maternity leave since there is no rushing through those crucial first months of *bambino*'s life. But, then again, aren't they all so very important (*see* **Living in Italy**, 'Living with Children', pp.216–18)? Sick leave and convalescence is not seen as slacking off, but a fundamental part of the Italian character that places life, *la vita*, before *la fatica* (which directly translated means exhaustion) or work in Neapolitan and other southern dialects.

Getting to Italy

Trains, planes or automobiles – whatever the choice, the logistics of moving to Italy have simplified greatly over the years. Whatever the choice of getting there is, double, triple and quadruple checking and confirming details should be the rule of thumb. The blessing of a strong labour rights mentality also means that Italy is plagued by strikes, not least by Alitalia and airport workers. In one single day in 2003 more than three hundred flights were cancelled, inconveniencing tens of thousands of passengers.

Having said that, Italy has two major international hubs and 30 smaller but also international airports; most have national train connections, sometimes no further than a 10min walk from the exit gate. Numerous charter flights have pushed down ticket prices and advance bookings on major airlines can bring absurdly low rates. Major highways with scrumptiously supplied *Autogrill* snack bars set the background for a comfortable drive through the country. And modern Eurostar trains that speed through Italy have slashed travel-time by days.

By Road

Once on French soil there are approximately 24hrs (including an overnight stay) and 1,045km (650 miles) between you and the Italian border. The choice is between the fastest route (Calais, down to Nancy, Lucerne and entering Italy at Lugano) totalling 1,045km (650 miles) or the more scenic Alpine way through Switzerland. Note that in Switzerland there are higher motorway tolls and mandatory supplementary car insurance. Motorists may buy the stickers in the UK (call the Swiss Centre on freephone **t** 00 800 100 20030 from anywhere in Europe for information) or in Switzerland from customs offices at the border or service stations, garages and post offices throughout the country. Caravans pay a fixed tax for periods of 1 day, 10 days, 1 month or 1 year. In France and Italy there are tolls as well to be calculated into the total cost of the trip.

Before leaving, make sure you have these items:

- **vehicle registration documents**

- **a driving licence and an International Driving Permit (IDP) – although Italian police are familiar with UK permits, an IDP (essentially a translation**

Italy's Road Network

of your licence) is still recommended, though not essential; they can be obtained at one of the major motoring associations before leaving and local outlets supply you with the appropriate application forms; IDPs cost approximately £4, are valid for 1 year and require a recent passport-type photograph. Check with the AA (**www.theaa.com**), the RAC (**www.rac. co.uk**) or Green Flag (**www.greenflag.co.uk**)

• minimum insurance (third party), though full coverage is optimum; insurance companies provide a green card (*carta verde*), valid throughout most of Europe, as proof of coverage

• if the vehicle is not registered in your name, a letter from the registered owner giving you permission to drive

And we recommend strongly that you also take with you:

• a list of emergency numbers for each country you are travelling through

• any local road assistance numbers that your insurance company may be able to give you

• a detailed map, if possible including all the countries you'll be passing through (saves paper shuffling at borders)

• a copy of a European Accident Statement form, which is available from your insurer or online from the Automobile Club of Italy (**www.aci.it**)

• small change for calls, tips and so on

Numerous passes and tunnels connect continental Europe to the peninsula. Choosing your entry point should depend on your final destination in Italy, or the amount of time and sense of adventure you have as you shape the trip. Check the weather forecast as most passes and tunnels are at dizzying altitudes and may lead to altitude sickness. Most major tunnels have a website, or check weather conditions on **www.travel-italy.com**.

• The longest tunnel, **St Gotthard Tunnel** (**www.gottardtunnel.ch**), runs for 16km (10 miles) between Switzerland and Italy. On the Italian side is Airolo, on the northern Goschenen. Once on Italian soil, the A3 motorway leads directly down to Milan. There is no fee.

• The next longest tunnel, **Fréjus** (**www.tunneldufrejus.com**), is 13km (8 miles) long, and joins southern France with the Piedmont region. From there it is a straight shot to Turin, passing the San Michele Monastery, which Umberto Eco immortalized in *The Name of the Rose*.

• The **San Bernardo Tunnel**, 5.8km (3.6 miles) long (**www.grandsaintbernard. ch**) is open all year long, the southern end opening into the autonomous region of Valle d'Aosta near the mountain town of Aosta, where the A5 motorway leads down to Turin.

• The **Mont Blanc Tunnel**, 11.5km (7 miles) long, was reopened in 2002 after a tragic fire. Newly equipped with cutting-edge safety features, it spills out on to Valle d'Aosta soil like St Bernardo and connects to the motorway leading to Turin or Milan.

- There are two major passes. The **Brenner Pass** (Brennero) is open all year long; the pass is at 1,370m (4,500ft) in altitude and links Innsbruck and Vipiteno, from where the A22 runs to Bolzano, Trento, Verona and easy connections with the A4 highway transversing the great Padania plains. Another option between June and October is the **Monte Croce Carnico Pass**. Of spectacular beauty, it runs into the Dolomite mountains and to Tolmezzo from Lienz.

If you are going by car for the thrill of a cross-continent trip, there are numerous sites to see on the way and landscape to admire. Keep in mind the length of the journey, time of year you are travelling (roads in and around Italy in August are traditionally clogged to the maximum with as many as 13 million vehicles circulating at the same time, as the entire country goes on holiday), unexpected costs like road tolls and fluctuations in petrol prices (though coming from the UK should work in your favour) and take into account the cost of overnight expenses and meals. But driving right up to your new home in Italy, with your own car loaded with precious possessions, does give a sense of belonging.

By Air

Hurrah for the open skies. With the splintering of flagship carrier Alitalia, space was made for alternative airlines flying into and around Italy. Subsequently, still-existent Alitalia has been forced to lower fares to keep up with the competition, but better fares are usually found elsewhere.

- **Ryanair** (**www.ryanair.com**; **t** 0871 246 0000): European travellers' little darling now flies to more than 10 locations in Italy from various UK gateways, always through Stansted. Rates vary greatly but can dip as low as €10, depending on last-minute or advance bookings, promotions and availability. On 1 April 2003, Ryanair took over the smaller budget airline Buzz, further expanding its range of destinations.

- **EasyJet** (**t** 0870 600 0000; **www.easyjet.com**): flies to Bologna, Milan, Naples, Rome and Venice.

- **British Airways** (**t** 0845 773 3377; **www.ba.com**): abundant flights daily from Heathrow and Gatwick, to Milan, Rome and Venice.

- **British Midland** (**t** 0870 607 0555; **www.flybmi.com**): flies to Milan Linate and Venice from Heathrow, and from East Midlands its budget **Bmibaby** picks up the Milan (Bergamo) and Pisa routes.

- **Alitalia** (**t** 0870 544 8259; **www.alitalia.it**): though they've slashed the number of flights from 30 to 12 a day, Alitalia still services Rome and Milan from Heathrow and Gatwick. Offers vary, and if you plan to travel by air as you travel to and from Italy be sure and sign up for their *Mille Miglia* (frequent flier) programme and earn those extra points, as well as an extra baggage allowance without penalties.

By Rail

It's no Orient Express trip, but getting there by train can be comfortable, if not pleasant, depending on time constraints and what flavour of motion sickness one is stricken by. A sleeping car, or couchette, is highly recommended for a good night's rest. Prices (and comfort) depend on sleeping quarters. Couchettes that sleep six are the least expensive, but there are also cosy double rooms complete with private bathroom. But before settling into a locomotive cradle, you have to get from London to Paris by Eurostar. Two options are to leave Waterloo at 11.53am and and arrive in Paris (Gare du Nord) at 3.59pm, or to leave at 12.53am (12.48 on Saturdays and Sundays) and arrive in Paris at 4.47pm. From there get the metro to Gare du Bercy for the overnight express.

There are four choices:

- **Palatino**: departs at 6pm, then runs down the Ligurian coast stopping at Genoa, La Spezia, Pisa and its final destination, Rome at 9.09am, 16hrs later.
- **Galilei**: departs at 7.09pm and travels through central Italy, stopping in Parma, Bologna and Florence; it arrives at Rome Termini station at 10.42am.
- **Rialto**: with a dead-giveaway name, the Rialto leaves daily at 8.01pm and drops you practically straight on to your gondola in Venice at 8.25, after stopping in Brescia at 6.05am, Verona 6.44 am and Padua 7.47am.
- **Stendhal**: chugs forth at 10.20pm, travelling through Turin then Milan.

Check with **europeanrailways@railpasseurope.com** for point-to-point tickets or call **t** 800 356 6711 for the best travel route based on your departure point and destination. To buy tickets online for London–Paris–Italy routes, contact **Rail Europe** (**t** 0870 584 8848; **www.raileurope.co.uk**). From London to Paris, check the **Eurostar** times and fares (**t** 020 7928 5163; **www.eurostar.com**). From Paris to Italy, or within Italy, go to **www.trenitalia.it**. This Italian site is also in English. And check all train times since they are susceptible to change.

There are other ways to make the journey. Some travel from London Waterloo by Eurostar to Lille and then from Lille to Lyon by high-speed French TGV, from where there is a train to Turin and Milan. Another option is to take an overnight train from Brussels to Milan.

By Coach

Travelling by coach is perhaps not worth the few pence saving compared with travel by train. The coach from London to Milan takes 21hrs, the coach to Rome

30hrs. However, adventurous landlubbers should contact National Express Eurolines (**t** 0870 580 8080; **www.gobycoach.com**).

By Sea

Unless planning a pleasure cruise, a sea voyage is best used for shipping boxes. *See* **Living in Italy**, 'Making the Move', pp.162–3.

Buon viaggio!

Red Tape

No matter what they say, bureaucracy continues to rule in Italy and anyone in the position to snap the red tape whip can and will. The degree of red tape varies greatly from region to region and the size of the town one is living in, but it is generally a national phenomenon with federal origins and therefore difficult to avoid. Grin and bear it is the only way to handle it without raising the blood pressure.

Upon arrival the logistical hurdles seem overwhelming. Interlinking bureaucratic requirements can get a person as nervous as a long-tailed cat in a room full of rocking chairs. Take all the necessary precautions and another stumbling block pops up. Not to fret, however, *per ogni porta chiusa si apre un portone* – for every door that closes, a larger gate opens. This Italian proverb, used to soothe over tragedies of life, like love, applies just as much to dealing with official procedures in Italy.

There are agencies for those moving to Italy, which can often take over some of the frustrating work of setting up utility bills, initiating the documentation process and helping with moving companies. But keep in mind that those agencies are subject to the same laws and regulations as everyone else, and can sometimes be expensive and ineffective.

Despite Italy's bureaucratic obsessing, the country still remains relatively inefficient: one can generally escape unnoticed until the niggling paperwork is sorted out. Generally, police will not be storming into your apartment and shipping you off.

Visas, Permits and other Paperwork

It has happened more than once that a short jaunt to Italy has ended in a heartfelt determination to make the country part of one's life. Entering Italy, for a UK passport holder, is not the problem. For those bitten by the 'want to live here' bug the difficulties arise when enterering the labyrinth of becoming a legal resident. Italian government departments and offices are well practised at ladling out contradictory information on how to get the correct working, studying or living permits. This is partly because every time the government changes new laws are passed, or old ones amended, and much is delegated to municipal discretion. Though often it is easiest to live on the verge of legality, there are benefits and civic reasons for getting both the required and the recommended permits.

Choosing to get the process going before departure from the UK or after arrival depends greatly on what one intends to do once in the country – study, work as a freelance, retire, or whatever. Remember, once the process is under way, shameless insistence and persistence pays.

Administrative Departments in Italy

The trinity of bureaucracy, the *questura*, the *comune* and the *anagrafe*, are where all paperwork in Italy comes from and must return. Here is an identikit of each to familiarize you with the offices that you will inevitably have to visit.

Hardly an official transaction slips by that doesn't call for a **carta bollata** or at least a **marca da bollo**. These are the vehicles by which the state taxes. The *carta da bollo* is lined paper with a pre-affixed stamp, and costs €7.50 per sheet. The *marca da bollo* comes in varying increments and is a stick-on stamp, which looks much like a postage stamp (*francobollo*). These can be purchased at any tobacconist (*tabbacci*) – look for the black or blue sign with a white T. Remnants of the old days still exist. Many tobacconist signs still have sale (salt) written on the bottom of them, left over from when salt was a state monopoly, like stamps, and could only be purchased through the tobacconist. Another commodity that the state used to have a monopoly on is the anti-malaria drug quinine. Cigarettes are still a state monopoly, though this is to be liberalized before long.

The *Questura*

Immigration of any kind – including applications for a *permesso di soggiorno* (*see* above) – is dealt with by the *questura* or police headquarters. The *questura* is also where a police report (*denuncia*) can be filed in case of accident, muggings, robbery or other crimes. Going to the *questura* is no pleasure cruise. But a *denuncia* can also be filed with the military police (*carabinieri*), who have the reputation for being better organized and friendlier. However, for the *permesso*, a trip (or two or three) to the *questura* is obligatory.

The *Comune*

The Chinese boxes are organized as follows – the *comune* or the municipality fits into the regions (*regione*). Within the *comune* there are districts (*circoscrizioni*), usually indicated with Roman numerals (*X circoscrizione* in Rome is the area near Piazza Navona, for example). The head of the *comune* is the mayor (*sindaco*). There is also a *presidente regionale*, or regional president, and it is not uncommon for the mayor and regional president to be from opposing political parties creating a tit-for-tat series of local laws and initiatives that can cancel each other out or at least cause a quagmire of misunderstanding.

The *Anagrafe*

Perhaps at the helm of the trinity is the *anagrafe* or bureau of vital statistics (census) – a Kafkaesque institution where all vital human data is documented and guarded. Births, deaths, marriages, residency, criminal records and family status all come from and return to the *anagrafe*.

Useful websites when dealing with red tape are:

- www.stranieriinitalia.com/inglese/page1/soggiorno.htm
- www.romebuddy.com/givesadvice/thepermesso.html
- www.uwrp.org/permesso.htm

Entering

There is no visa requirement for British passport holders or EU member country citizens entering Italy. Other nationalities exempt from visa requirements to enter are Andorra, Argentina, Australia, Bolivia, Brazil, Brunei, Bulgaria, Canada, Chile, Costa Rica, Croatia, Ecuador, El Salvador, Guatemala, Holy See, Honduras, Hong Kong, Israel, Japan, Macao, Malaysia, Mexico, Monaco, New Zealand, Nicaragua, Panama, Paraguay, Romania, San Marino, Singapore, South Korea, Switzerland, USA, Uruguay and Venezuela. A valid passport allows a 90-day stay. For more than that, you are legally required to obtain a *permesso di soggiorno* or stay permit.

Visas

For UK residents not holding a British passport who do not fall into the visa-exempt category, an Italian consulate or embassy in England issues the visa. The 24-hour hotline (**t** 0906 550 8984) or **emblondon@embitaly.org.uk** or **www.embitaly.org.uk** has up-to-date information on the requirements. You must have a permit issued by the Home Office that is valid for a minimum of six months after the requested date for Italian entry. If you have a passport with a stamped leave of entry to the UK of six months or less, your country of origin must grant you a visa, as the Italian consulate cannot.

There is no shortening the process, so start well in advance – at least three–four weeks before you need the visa. Remember that if it is around holiday times there may be further delays. You will have to visit the embassy or consulate at least twice, as visas cannot be issued the same day that the

Case Study: The Invisible Man

Here is an insight from an Italian-Australian on 'status' or slipping through the cracks. 'I am a 42-year-old, employed as an independent consultant for more than 13 years now. I earn approximately €32,000 annually, but have never paid taxes. I live in my now-deceased grandfather's flat, and all my utility bills still come in his name. Officially I am the unemployed son of a pensioner. In other words, I barely exist for the government. And I like it that way – I ask nothing from them, I get nothing from them, and they don't get anything from me. I am one of many who have slipped through the cracks.'

application is submitted and you cannot send in the paperwork by post. Make sure you book the appointment first and then confirm what paperwork and other documents you will need to provide before making the journey to the consulate.

Visa applications can be downloaded from the website **www.embitaly.org**. Within, the UK applications should be filed by appointment at the nearest consular office:

- **If you live in Scotland or Northern Ireland, you should apply for a visa at the Italian Consulate General in Edinburgh (t 0131 226 3631).**

- **If you live in Cheshire, Cleveland, Cumbria, Derby, Durham, Humberside, Lancashire, Leicester, Lincolnshire, Greater Manchester, Merseyside, Northumberland, Nottinghamshire, Staffordshire, Shropshire, Tyne and Wear, Yorkshire, Clwyd, Gwynedd, Powys (districts of Montgomery and Radnor) or the Isle of Man, you should apply for your visa at the Italian Consulate in Manchester (t (0161) 236 9024).**

- **If you live in Bedfordshire, Cambridgeshire, Norfolk, Northamptonshire, Suffolk or the northern part of Buckinghamshire, you should apply for your visa at the Italian Vice Consulate in Bedford (t (01234) 356647).**

- **If you live in Avon, Berkshire, Buckinghamshire, Channel Islands, Cornwall, Devon, Dorset, Dyfed, Essex, Gloucestershire, Glamorgan, Gwent, Hampshire, Hereford and Worcester, Hertfordshire, the Isle of White, Kent, London, Oxfordshire, Powys (Brecknock District), Somerset, Surrey, Sussex, Warwickshire, West Midlands or Wiltshire, you should apply to the Visa Section of the Italian Consulate General in London (t (020) 7235 9371). Appointments can be made by telephoning (Mon–Fri 3–4.30) or by e-mail (itconlond_visti@btconnect.com). You can go in person to make an appointment during office hours (Mon–Fri 9–12). Once the appointment has been arranged, applicants are required to submit their application using the form that can be downloaded from the website (www.embitaly.org.uk).**

For minors under 18 travelling without parents or legal guardians, an authorized affidavit (from parents or guardians) must:

- **authorize them to travel on their own**

- **appoint a responsible party at the Italian end**

If travelling to study, the rules covered by the Schengen short-stay entry visa apply (*see* 'The Schengen Visa', below). The school or college you are visiting should have up-to-date information about the requirements.

The cost, duration and type of visa varies depending on exchange rates and bilateral agreements between the applicants' country of origin and Italy. Expedia.com (**www.expedia.co.uk/daily/service/passport.asp**) updates the visa information on its site every three months.

The Schengen Visa

In 1995 Italy took the plunge and became a signatory to the Schengen Agreement. Passport and visa regulations within the Schengen area have been consolidated enormously with this accord. Nationals from Austria, Belgium, Finland, France, Germany, Greece, Italy, Liechtenstein, Luxembourg, Malta, Monaco, the Netherlands, Norway, Portugal, San Marino, Spain and Sweden can travel freely among Schengen countries with a valid passport or a national ID card. *Note that the ten new countries that joined the EU on 1st May 2004 (Cyprus, the Czech Republic, Estonia, Hungary, Latvia, Lithuania, Malta, Poland, Slovakia and Slovenia) do not yet have access to free border movement.*

But the Schengen Convention not only facilitates the movements of signatory-country nationals, it has its perks for non-Schengen nationals, too. For all countries recognized by Schengen member nations, a visa allowing freedom of movement across borders reduces the extra weight of stamps and individual visas. The validity of the visa is based on the recognition of your country by the relevant Schengen states. Check with each country you will be entering for information. Travellers visiting just one Schengen country should apply to the consulate of that country. For travellers visiting more than one Schengen country, apply to the consulate of the country chosen as the main destination or the first country of entry if there is no main destination.

A Schengen visa is not appropriate if you plan on staying in a Schengen member state, including Italy, for more than three months or wish to take up employment or establish a business, trade or profession.

You need a Schengen visa if you are:

- **from Afghanistan, Bangladesh, Congo (the Democratic Republic of), Eritrea, Ethiopia, Ghana, Iran, Iraq, Nigeria, Pakistan, Senegal, Somalia and Sri Lanka and in transit through a Schengen member state on an international flight**

- **passing through one or more Schengen state territories by land**

- **visiting for tourism, business or studies for up to three months**

The three types of Schengen visa are:

- an **airport transit visa**, which costs £6.40, and allows the visa holder to pass through international departures, without leaving the airport

- a **transit visa**, which also costs £6.40, and is for overland trips; it is valid for a maximum of five days per entry, including the day of arrival, and is available for single and multiple entries; note that the visas cannot be extended and a new application must be made each time

- a **short-stay visa for tourism, business and study purposes**, which costs £16.80 (up to 30 days), £23.50 (over 30 days); valid for six months from date of issue, it can be used for single and multiple entry with stays of maximum 90 days per entry.

Short-stay Visa for Tourism, Business and Study Purposes

When applying for the short-stay visa for tourism, business and study purposes there is a slightly different procedure depending on the purpose of the stay:

Tourism

For this visa, you will need the following:

- a passport or official travel document, valid for at least three months beyond the validity of the requested visa, with a blank page on which to affix the visa sticker.
- one application form, fully completed and signed by the applicant, with one passport-size photo.
- a residence permit issued in the UK valid for at least three months beyond the expiry date.
- proof of travel arrangements (evidence of accommodation such as hotel reservations, or a letter of invitation and a photocopy of the passport of the Italian citizen who invited you).
- evidence that you have sufficient funds to cover the cost of your stay. Credit cards and cash are not accepted as proof of financial means.
- evidence of occupation/student status. This should be an original letter from your employer, solicitor or a Chamber of Commerce.

Business

For this visa, you will need the following:

- a passport or official travel document, valid for at least three months beyond the validity of the requested visa, with a blank page on which to affix the visa sticker.
- one application form, fully completed and signed by the applicant, with one passport-size photo.
- a residence permit issued in the UK valid for at least three months beyond the expiry date.
- proof of the purpose of your visit. This proof should be in the form of an official work or professional presentation letter, addressed to the Italian Consulate General, explaining in detail the nature and dates of your trip to Italy. People who are self-employed should provide a letter from their accountant, solicitor, company secretary, bank manager or local Chamber of Commerce. Applicants should also arrange for an invitation to be faxed from the Italian company or firm. It should be faxed directly to the Italian Consulate General in London (t (020) 7823 1609), 48 hours prior to the application submission. The fax should specify the date of your visit and the nature of your business.

- Depending on individual circumstances, additional documents may be required.

Study

For this visa, you will need the following:

- A passport or official travel document, valid for at least three months beyond the validity of the requested visa, with a blank page on which to affix the visa sticker.

- One application form, fully completed and signed by the applicant, with one passport-size photo.

- a residence permit issued in the UK valid for at least three months beyond the expiry date.

- A letter (original plus a copy) from the Italian university, confirming acceptance of the application, which includes details on the course (duration, programme of study, etc.)

- A statement (original plus a copy) from the UK university.

- Proof of medical insurance for the entire period of stay.

- Proof of financial means to cover the cost of the intended stay.

It cannot be emphasized enough that prices fluctuate depending on exchange rates. Visitors are advised to check with the consulate (or consular section at the Embassy).

Spouses and children of EU nationals (a passport and the original marriage certificate are required), and nationals of some other countries, receive their visas free of charge (enquire at the embassy for details).

The *Permesso di Soggiorno*

What used to be a relatively 'live-and-let-live' practice, which persisted for years regarding the stay permit (*permesso di soggiorno*) is starting to tighten up. Whereas border guards would rarely stamp UK passports and British citizens could therefore comfortably overstay the 90-day limit without drawing attention, there have been recent cases of suspicion and questioning when UK nationals without the proper stay permit re-enter Italy. Perhaps it comes hand in hand with being part of the EU or the current government's trend of turning the screws on illegality. Whatever the case may be, if you plan to stay more than three months in Italy, start the process to obtain the required permits before the 90 days are up. It should technically be done within 8 days of arrival, but don't let that stop you should you decide to stay after already being in country for longer than that.

The *permesso di soggiorno* is also called a *carta di soggiorno*. They mean the same thing and the two names are sometimes used interchangeably.

The different main types of *permesso* include:

• The **permesso di soggiorno per turismo**: for extended tourism stays; if staying for more than a week, not in a hotel (or other paid lodging) this is required, though rarely obtained (one *questura* in the Umbrian town of Orvieto records that the last *permesso di soggiorno per turismo* that was issued was in 1976). When checking into a hotel you will be asked to provide identification because hotel guests are registered with the local police; the *permesso di soggiorno per turismo* replaces that gap if you are staying with friends or acquaintances.

• The **permesso di soggiorno per ricongiungimento familiare**: a permit allowing family unification for a husband or wife, dependent children or dependent parents of legalized immigrants in Italy.

• The **permesso di soggiorno per coesione familiare**: granted to non-Italians married to nationals and/or their dependent children.

• The **permesso di soggiorno per studio**: for international students of language schools, university exchange students or in some cases high school exchange students.

• The **permesso di soggiorno per dimora**: for retirees or anyone intending to move to live in the country who has no intention to work or study.

• The **permesso di soggiorno per lavoro**: a work permit for a company employee.

• The **permesso di soggiorno per lavoro autonomo/indipendente**: a work permit for the self-employed or freelance – probably the trickiest to obtain.

If all of the above seems daunting, never fear. Despite the fiery hoops, it is difficult for a UK citizen to be refused in the end, if all the requirements are met.

No matter which is applicable to your status, you'll have to start by going to the foreigners' office (*ufficio stranieri*) at the local police station (*questura*). This is a timely process and, if you are a visa holder, can only be based on the type of visa you have been issued.

You will need:

• **your passport (bring a photocopy of the page with your photo) and the applicable visa if necessary**

• **an application for the** *permesso* **(a blue or green form available at the** *questura***)**

• **a** *marca da bollo* **tax stamp for €10 (be sure to check the price at the time of application)**

• **three passport-size photos**

• **any expired** *permesso di soggiorno***, plus four photocopies, if you have come for a renewal (you should start the renewal process at least one month before the permit's expiration date**

• depending on the type of permit requested, you may also be asked to supply your birth certificate, marriage certificate, or proof of financial means; students are usually asked for proof of health insurance coverage. You will be required to authenticated or notarize some documents

Codice Fiscale and *Partita IVA* – Tax ID Numbers

One of the second most common pieces of bureaucracy to be asked for after your *permesso di soggiorno* is the *codice fiscale*, your personal tax identification number. This tax identification number is alphanumeric: it contains alphabetical letters and numbers based on your name, birth date and other inexplicable markings with which the Ministry of Finance identifies you.

Once you have a *permesso di soggiorno*, apply for your tax identification number at any local tax office (*ufficio imposte diretto*) to obtain the *codice fiscale*. With your tax number, you can:

- **enrol in the National Health Service**
- **be paid for dependent and contract work**
- **sign any type of contract (for instance to rent or sell a house)**
- **open a bank account**

The *codice fiscale* is free of charge. A paper document is issued immediately and the plastic, credit-card-sized one arrives at your home address.

The *partita IVA* (*imposta sul valore aggiunto*) is a value-added tax for the self-employed and owners of small businesses. Having a *partita IVA* has been likened to having a child minus the joy. It is nearly impossible to follow the rigmaroles entailed in providing the *registri* or special accounting registry with the information they require to keep track of your financial transactions. There is a hefty initial fee followed by annual renewal fees. It is advisable to hire a local accountant to manage the complicated procedure, which must be immaculate for the annual income tax return resulting from the *registri*'s entries. But with the *partita IVA* you can issue official invoices necessary for a small business.

Italian Residency

Leaping even further into the paperchase, once you have a *permesso di soggiorno* and have stayed in the country for five years, you can apply for a residency permit (*residenza*). This does not give you citizenship, but you will be issued an Italian identity card. Though this may seem a further bureaucratic performance and more trouble than it is worth, it may well be worth the hassle to obtain one. With a *residenza* one can:

- **stop renewing the *permesso* (you have to renew the *residenza*, but it doesn't expire like a *permesso*)**

- enter and leave Italy freely without visas or permits
- work for Italian or foreign companies unrestricted
- have access to public health care and administrative services
- get a national driver's licence
- get an identity card
- buy and register a car
- send children to public schools (those aged under 14 are placed on their parents residency card, 14–18-year-olds are given their own)
- benefit from almost all privileges allowed to Italians, apart from participating in the electoral process

This entire process teeters on one of Italy's peculiarities – the stagnant and booby-trap-laden housing market (*see* **Living in Italy**, 'Finding a Home', pp.125–61). To be a resident, you must have a *residenza*. Sounds easy enough, since you will surely be living somewhere, but think again. Italian property laws are almost absurdly tilted in favour of tenants and a renter with (or sometimes without) contract in hand can rest assured that it is almost impossible that they will be evicted. Therefore, the chance, as a foreigner, of signing a registered contract that can be used as your official residence is slim. The 'non-residents only' stipulation in contracts is standard.

However, with a suitable residence, a five-year sojourn under your belt, a *permesso di soggiorno* that allows an undetermined number of renewals, sufficient income for you and your family and a clean criminal record, you can head off to enrol in the general registry office (*anagrafe*). Each municipality (*comune*) has at least one and big cities have offices in each district.

Go armed with your passport and *permesso di soggiorno* and prepared to fill out a declaration of residence (*dichiarazione di residenza*). You may want to ask both the *anagrafe*, as well as your embassy, if you need a consular declaration (*dichiarazione consulare*). This is a document from your embassy certifying your personal data. The whole process takes approximately six months, and is likely to involve a visit by the police to your residence. While waiting, you will have a temporary card demonstrating that you have an application for a *residenza* in process. A notified letter will arrive when the residency card is ready and waiting at the same *anagrafe* where the application was submitted.

Italian Citizenship

Italians have spent so much of the last century seeking to become other nationalities that they have a hard time imagining why anyone would want to ask for Italian citizenship, despite the country's now well-established economic position. This sense of bafflement is undoubtedly underpinned by a sense of curiosity, if not a bit of suspicion. But the long road to cultural diversification and integration is underway, and Italy even has 1996 Miss Italia to prove it (*see* **Italy Today**, 'Call Me Italiana', p70).

Applicants no longer have to choose between their country of birth and adoptive country since the *doppia cittadinanza* became recognized. Young men should be aware that, until Italy's mandatory military service is completely phased out, they could be called to arms as an Italian citizen.

Italian citizenship is automatically given to the following:

- **a child of an Italian mother or father**
- **a child born in Italy to unknown or stateless parents**
- **a child born in Italy to non-Italian parents, as long as they are from a country where the law does not impose adopting the citizenship of the parents**
- **a child of unknown parents found in Italy with no proof of other citizenship**

If you do not qualify for automatic citizenship, you may acquire it if you fall into one of the following five categories:

- **one of your parents or one of your grandparents are or were citizens at birth**
- **you were born in Italy and have resided in the country legally without interruptions until the age of 18 and you declare your intention to acquire Italian citizenship within one year of reaching 18**
- **you marry an Italian citizen; you must be the spouse of an Italian citizen and have resided legally in Italy for at least six months or have been married for three years; you will not be considered if there has been a legal divorce or annulment, or if you are in the process of separating**
- **you are naturalized: EU citizens must live in Italy for at least four years before acquiring citizenship; naturalization is also considered if you have worked for the Italian State for at least five years, or if you are a non-EU citizen and have lived legally in Italy for at least ten years**
- **you are the minor son or daughter of someone who has acquired or re-acquired citizenship and you live with one of your parents at the time that he or she is granted or re-granted citizenship**

Although each case differs, you will be required to provide a truckload of documents. The process can take months, if not a whole year. The application must be presented (with five copies, and the original must have a *marca da bollo*) to either the Ministry of the Interior (Ministero degli Interni), or to your local *comune*, or to an Italian embassy abroad. You will need your birth certificate; your residency permit (if required); proof of how long you have lived in Italy; marriage certificates; a family status certificate; proof that you don't have a criminal record; your parents' or grandparents' citizenship (if required); your spouse's citizenship (if required); and, in some cases, a copy of your tax returns. All photocopies presented in lieu of originals must be notarized.

Living in Italy

06

Europeans will feel familiarity with many aspects of Italy. Many words are recognizable. City planning is not terribly different from that of other major urban hubs. Supermarkets (*supermercati*) are burgeoning, side by side with the traditional and (thankfully) ever-present one-off shops (butchers, those selling cheese, shoes, buttons, and so on). Petrol stations (*stazioni di servizi*) are run by many of the same companies as in the UK – the Italian Agip and IP and the non-Italian Q8, Shell, Fina, Esso and Tamoil. EU regulations have resulted in a standardization of what was left of erratic road signs and traffic laws (though driving in Italy can still be a grisly affair in cities like Rome and Naples) and car makes and models hold few surprises. There are more Benetton stores than you can shake a stick at, along with other well-known clothing shops such as Sisley and Max Mara, and fashion pinnacles like Gucci, Prada and Armani.

And yet, the homogeneity that plagues many European high streets is blessedly absent. Starbucks and the numerous copycat cafés haven't found their way into Italy. McDonald's exists on a much smaller scale than elsewhere, and Burger King has just a handful of joints throughout Italy. There are no chain pizzerias to speak of, but you'll find a pizza joint, either sit-down or by the slice, on almost every block. Cafés, the life blood of daily social life, have mostly the same goodies to offer, but are privately owned. There may be much monotony in what can be found, but it is an Italian standardization.

Living in Italy without becoming at least a little bit Italian inside is impossible. On arrival, what is familiar will be a comfort and the rest is unexplored territory ready to be discovered, appreciated, adopted or at least understood.

Learning Italian

Stephen, an Irish vacationer on holiday in Italy, stopped to chat with Senegalese vendors using the Wolaff he had mastered during his years as a relief worker in Senegal. In amazement, one of the hawkers turned around and, in Wolaff, said 'Why are you speaking French in Italy?' The point being that, for the African far from his home country, hearing his own language spoken was an unexpected treat that just didn't register. The same goes for Italians. They expect a mangled version of their *lingua* so anyone speaking proficiently is worshipped, though usually met with a dumbfounded expression.

A foreign accent will never pass unnoticed, no matter how fluently the Italian flows. As your accent seeps through in Italian (and it will, if you aren't perfectly bilingual), expect to be mimicked – something that can be unsettling. Italians are the masters of banter and any teasing should be taken as lightly as it is dished out. Put it down to national character differences – the reserve rather than the expansive nature or however you want to label it. It is usually all in good faith.

Fortunately, anyone who has studied a Latin language (including Latin) or even English (let's not forget how much Latin there is in English) can learn the basics quickly. One confidence-building trick is to go through the alphabet, letter by letter, and see if you know a word in Italian that begins with it. For example, A: You probably know *arrivederci*. B: Know what *bella* is? C? I bet *ciao!* hasn't slipped you by. And so on like that. Then start again.

Though many acquire the ability to stitch together sentences, order meals and make very small talk all on their own, learning to speak Italian fluently takes some effort. Many swear that nothing can take the place of real lessons. Whether private, one-on-one or in a classroom setting, structured learning not only boosts language ability, but also confidence.

If you have come to work for a company and do not speak Italian, request that your company provide language lessons. This is in its best interests, as well as yours. Private teachers will come to your office for personal instruction, and will give lessons focusing on your needs.

To find **private instructors**, look in classified listings of local English-language publications or ask at one of the numerous language schools (*scuole di lingua*). Companies often have a list of teachers to recommend. If the company does not foot the bill, keep in mind that private lessons cost about double that of class-room lessons. At that point, you may want to study in a classroom setting and socialize for language practice (among other things).

To begin, an intensive language course is not a bad idea for a limited time. **Universities for foreigners** such as the Università per Stranieri in Siena (**www. unistrasi.it**) and Perugia (**www.unistrapg.it**) are well known for their language schools, and are partially sponsored by the state and therefore less expensive. But nearly all public universities offer language programmes. See below for a selection of other Italian university links.

- Università degli Studi di Ancona, **www.unian.it**
- Universitá degli Studi di Bari, **www.uniba.it**
- Università degli Studi di Bergamo, **www.unibg.it**
- Università degli Studi di Bologna, **www.unibo.it**
- Università degli Studi di Brescia, **www.uniba.it**
- Università degli Studi di Cagliari, **www.unica.it**
- Università degli Studi della Calabria, **www.unicat.it**
- Università degli Studi di Catania, **www.unict.it**
- Università degli Studi di Catanzaro, **www.unicz.it**
- Università degli Studi di Ferrara, **www.unife.it**
- Università degli Studi di Firenze, **www.unifi.it**
- Università degli Studi di Genova, **www.unige.it**
- Università degli Studi di Lecce, **www.ulile.it**
- Università degli Studi di Messina, **www.unime.it**
- Politecnico di Milano, **www.poliml.it**
- Università di Milano-Bicocca, **www.unimib.it**

- Università degli Studi di Milano, **www.unimi.it**
- Università degli Studi di Modena, **www.unimo.it**
- Università degli Studi di Napoli 'Federico II', **www.unina.it**
- Seconda Università di Napoli, **www.unina2.it**
- Università degli Studi di Padova, **www.unipd.il**
- Università degli Studi di Palermo, **www.unipa.it**
- Università degli Studi di Parma, **www.uninr.it**
- Università degli Studi di Pavia, **www.unipv.it**
- Università degli Studi di Perugia, **www.unipg.it**
- Università degli Studi di Pisa, **www.unipi.it**
- Università degli Studi di Reggio Calabria, **www.unirc.it**
- Università degli Studi di Roma 'Tor Vergata', **www.uniroma2.it**
- Università Cattolica del Sacro Cuore di Roma, **www.unicatt.it**
- Università degli Studi di Salerno, **www.unisa.it**
- Università degli Studi di Torino, **www.unito.it**
- Università degli Studi di Trento, **www.unitn.it**
- Università degli Studi di Urbino, **www.uniurb.it**
- Università degli Studi di Varese, **www.vaibio.unimi.it**
- Università degli Studi di Verona, **www.univr.it**
- Università degli Studi di Venezia, **www.unive.it**
- Università degli Studi di Sassari, **www.uniss.it**
- Università degli Studi di Trieste, **www.univ.trieste.it**
- Università degli Studi di Udine, **www.uniud.it**

Every major city has and nearly all small towns have more than a handful of **language schools** to choose from. The Associazione Scuole di Italiano come Lingua Seconda (ASILS) is an independent regulatory body that sets and monitors standards of Italian language schools. About one-third of all schools are members, but some of the large and noteworthy are not. ASILS guarantees that there are regular inspections, classes of no more than 15 students, clean and modern facilities, and instructors with a university degree and five years' experience. Their website (**www.asils.it**) lists schools around the country.

Another source listing language schools is the English *Yellow Pages* or the Italian *Pagine Gialle* (look under '*Scuole di lingue*'). State-sponsored D**ante Alighieri**, with its head office in Rome (Via Aurelia 137, 00165 Roma, **t** 06 3937 5966, **f** 06 3937 5804, **www.languageinitaly.com**) has schools throughout the country, as do **Leonardo da Vinci** (Piazza dell'Orologio 7, 00186 Roma, **t** 06 6889 2513, **f** 06 6821 9084, **www.scuolaleonardo.com**, **scuola leonardo@scuolaleo nardo.com**; see website for other cities), **Galileo Galilei** (Via degli Alfani 68, 50121 Florence, **t** 055 294680, **f** 055 283481, **www.galilei.it**, **info@galilei.it**) and **Torre di Babele** (Via Bixio 74, 00185 Rome, **t** 06 700 8434, **f** 06 7049 7150, **www.torre dibabele.com**). Courses range from two weeks to three months in length and prices vary. An average price is generally €120 per 8hrs of classroom instruction, but this depends on the course package you choose.

Other possibilities for schools throughout Italy are:

- Accademia Italiana (Firenze), **www.accademiaitaliana.com**
- Accademia Leonardo (Salerno), **www.accademialeonardo.it**
- DILIT International House (Roma), **www.dilit.it**
- Linguaviva (Firenze), **www.linguaviva.it**
- Scuola Italia (Urbania), **www.scuola-italia.com**
- Tiberius International (Rimini), **www.infotel.it/tiberius-international**
- Accademia Italiana (Salerno), **www.accademia-italiana.it**
- Istituto Italiano (Firenze), **www.istitutoitaliano.it**
- I Maltesta: Centro di Lingua e Cultura Italiana (Rimini), **www.imaltesta. com**
- Il Sillabo: Centro Culturale per Stranieri (San Giovanni Valdarno, AR), **www. sillabo.it**

Usually schools will issue a certificate after completion of Italian courses, stating the level the student has obtained. The **Certification of Italian as a Foreign Language** (CILS) certifies linguistic competency and is the closest thing to an official rating that is awarded. Created by the University of Siena for Foreigners, it is recognized by the Italian state on the basis of an agreement with the Italian Ministry of Foreign Affairs, and can be taken throughout Italy and abroad at authorized Italian cultural institutes. Although it doesn't involve taking an exam, it holds some weight with paper-wielding Italian bureaucrats. See **www.unistrasi.it/inglese/certif/2003_04/Cils.htm** for up-to-date information on how and where to obtain the CILS rating.

The best way to learn any language is to immerse yourself in it. Just being surrounded by Italian – the daily paper, TV news, radio, neighbours, announcements, shopping, and so on – has a way of permeating the brain. Even making the smallest effort, like ordering at the local café every day in Italian, is an exercise that pays off. And with Italians' love of socializing, you'll never find yourself short of someone to lend you their ears.

Finding a Home

Casa mia, casa mia,
per piccina che tu sia,
tu mi sembri,
una badia

My home my home
Though tiny as a gnome
To me you seem
A grand dome
> Loose interpretation by author

Another popular saying in Italian, *'due cuore e una capanna'* or 'two hearts and a cabin', romantically suggests that even the most modest of hovels is transformed into a home when affairs of the heart are blazing. As sweet as that sounds, Italians are fastidious when it comes to setting up home. It is rare for young couples to make do with the bare necessities and many prefer to put off marriage until they can decorate their house perfectly before moving in. As with their own personal good looks, Italians do not leave details in their *casa* to chance. Fixtures, furniture, tiles and wall coatings are usually expensive and designer creations. A middle-aged man or woman would prefer to continue living with their parents than to sacrifice comfort for independence and a less-than-perfect place to live.

Moving into a place that needs fixing up is not the Italian way of approaching a living space. Before moving in, owners of a home will have every last detail finished to perfection and probably keep it that way for at least a generation. Italian interiors tend to be timelessly decorated and, all in all, hold up well over the years. And if cleanliness counts for anything, Italians are sticklers for sanitizing, polishing, dusting and disinfecting. You could eat off nearly any surface in an Italian home.

Renting

Housing shortages in big cities are no laughing matter. In Rome they have pushed up prices to dizzying heights, at least compared with Italian salaries. Homes and apartments are passed down in families, from parents to children, and even though a home owner or inheritor may live in another area of the city or country, the preference is to leave a home empty instead of risking renters who don't want to vacate, or damage family property.

Many British companies, well aware of the difficulties involved in finding accommodation in Italy, will have a list of preferred agents who specialize in speedy delivery, or even have company housing already arranged.

When looking for a house on your own, leave no stone unturned. One lucky writer, on a limited artist's budget, was offered a 'modest flat' by a semi-noble family that he interviewed for a book. It was only for a limited time (one year) but a place for him to lay his head at night and work during the day. I will leave Anthony to describe it: 'It was a fourth floor walk-up, [in a] 15th century building near the Tiber River, across from Castel Sant'Angelo. All I can say is that when I walked in, I came face to face with a Roman statue, and a postcard-perfect view of the city.' So asking around and networking on arrival are highly recommended.

Get to know the town you will be living in, and visit it before you begin hunting for accommodation, if possible, to narrow down the neighbourhoods you prefer. Don't exclude other areas if an interesting possibility pops up as most cities and towns have effective public transport and other means of getting around. Sometimes a zone that seems too far out can be better connected than a more central neighbourhood. Before moving, or on arrival, stroll the streets. Often owners who prefer not to go through agencies will hang a 'for rent' or '*affitasi*' sign outside a building. If the sign specifies no *agenzia* you can fairly be sure that the rental agreement will be made privately; if the sign says *agenzia*, an agency will be brokering the deal.

Despite the housing shortage there is no lack of **agencies** in Italy. Bars and shops often have free magazines that you can pick up and flip through, though they often aren't the most desirable of properties, and many are for sale instead of rent. A few large Italian estate agents are Tecnocasa (**www.tecnocasa.it**), Agenzia Toscana Immobiliare (**www.agenziatoscana.com**) and SoloCase (**www.solocase.it**). Go to their websites to find the office nearest to you or look in the phone book under *Agenzie immobilari*. Sites alone are numerous. One such site that has had success with foreigners looking for accommodation is Property in Italy (**www.propertyinitaly.com**), with properties to sell and rent, short and long-term accommodation, homes and apartments. Another is Live in Rome (**www.liveinrome.com**), which targets English-speaking foreigners.

Private agents are usually recommended by word of mouth. It is a small and vicious sector, in which transparency is never the rule. It's best to ask your colleagues, chamber of commerce, embassy or consul just who those local, private agents are.

Magazines and **listings** should be snatched up as soon as they come out. Individuals and craftier agencies know exactly when publications are hot off the press, and crouch in waiting to pounce before you can. In Rome, the *Porta Portese* bi-weekly listings paper comes out every Tuesday and Friday. Get it at your newsstand first thing in the morning and flip to the lets (*affiti*) or purchases and sales (*compri/vendite*) section. The *Secondo Mano* weekly magazine in Milan, Bologna and Florence has rental sections, and nearly all major Italian dailies (*see* **Italy Today**, 'Major Media', p.68) have extensive listings or weekly inserts. English publications, like the monthly *Wanted in Rome* (**www.wantedinrome.com**) and Easy Milano (**www.easymilano.it**) offer listings that, for good or bad, are usually geared towards foreigners.

In the UK there are news stand publications as well as agents to tap into. *Italy* (**www.italymag.co.uk**) has been out for more than a year now and has increased its listings, as well as the number of agencies that advertise. *World of Property* and *International Homes* both have extensive Italian classifieds.

Agencies in the UK can be found through the Federation of Overseas Property Developers and Consultants (FOPDAC), an umbrella organization representing select agents dealing with Italy (PO Box 3534, London NW5, **t** (020) 8941 588). It can also direct you towards agents and agencies selling properties.

Last, but not least, **short-term rentals** can help soothe the soul and be practical research while looking for your final destination. Centro Rustico Tuscany sells property, but also has holiday rentals and provides property management services once you have secured property in Tuscany (Matt or Heather Purse, **t** 055 836 1530, **mattpurse@tiscali.it**). A site strictly for rentals in Tuscany and Rome is **www.rentitalianvillas.com**. Accommodation tending towards the high end and exclusive in Rome, Siena, Florence and Venice can be found through Italian Homes (403 Parkway House, Sheen Lane, London SW14 8LS, UK, **t** (020) 8878 1130, brochures **t** (020) 8878 1991, **f** (020) 8878 0982, **enquiries@venice-rentals.com**, **www.italian-homes.com**). In Rome, **www.comfortitalia.com** has temporary housing solutions in and around the centre.

On rental properties, agentcies usually ask for one month's rent as a fee for their services. Alternatively, they ask for 10 or 20 per cent of the first year's rent. If you are renting for less than a year, make sure to negotiate a percentage, as paying one month's rent will not be cost-effective.

Under new laws, the standard **lease** in Italy is for four years and is renewable. Contracts lasting three months, six months, one year or any length of time you desire can be negotiated with the owner or the agent. A wise move is to include a 'diplomatic clause' in the contract. This lets you terminate the agreement if you must leave Italy sooner than you foresee. Many tenants are asked to produce proof of income such as a bank statement or pay slips showing monthly income to prove that they are solvent. You will be required to pay one or two months' rent up-front as a safety deposit, and some owners ask for three. If the property is found to be in good condition upon your departure, the deposit is refunded.

Rent is usually paidmonthly (or sometimes quarterly) by direct bank transfer (*bonifico bancario*), by cheque or cash. Most contracts call for six months' advance notice in writing prior to the termination of the lease agreement. It is called the *disdetta* and should be sent registered-return-receipt mail (*lettera raccomandata con ricevuta di ritorno*). Three months' notice is required on leases of one year. If you help the landlord find an another tenant to replace you, you can usually agree on your departure date with the owner without waiting.

Make sure you check all appliances well (especially the refrigerator and washing machine) before renting. The high calcium content in Italian water makes dishwashers and washing machines clog easily and you don't want to be burdened with the cost and inconvenience of repair if the damage was done by a previous tenant. Also make sure the *caldaia*, or water heater, functions well. Check all appliances with the owner before signing the lease agreement. As a rule of thumb, major repairs such as wiring, plumbing and blinds are the owner's responsibility. Minor repairs due to wear and tear are your responsibility.

It is a good idea to make a detailed list of all the furniture, cutlery, kitchen and bathroom items before you sign the contract. Itemize everything and make a note of its condition. If an inventory is given to you, you should check it and draw attention to any disparities.

Semi-furnished apartments usually include major appliances, like a cooker and refrigerator, but little or no furniture. Unfurnished apartments are usually bare, with tubing for water and gas protruding from the walls for you to connect your own appliances. If the house owner is willing, ask if you can buy a kitchen with their approval and subtract the cost from your rent.

Heating

Heating (*riscaldamento*) can be *autonomo* or *centralizzato*. *Autonomo* gives you the choice of turning it off and on, and *centralizzato* means that you are at the mercy of the predetermined hours of *accensione* when the heat is running throughout the building. Note that from central Italy southwards, homes can be quite chilly in the winter, as they are designed for long spells of hot weather. Check the window fixings and insulation for draughty areas and get them fixed before the first cold hits. Double-glazed windows are a blessing for both summer and winter extremes.

Home Owners' Fees

Home owners' fees (*condominio*) are the fees that all building inhabitants pay for communal electricity, cleaning and repairs in shared spaces of the apartment block. This may or may not be included in your rent, so be clear from the start with the agency or apartment owner. You may also have a porter (*portiere,*) in your building – a person who is posted in a booth at the entrance. This can be enormously helpful for packages that arrive and must be signed for, or don't fit in the post box, and saves hours of chasing missing parcels at the post office. The *portiere* expects tips for extra work and for the holidays (like Christmas and summer). It is advisable to do so and keep in the *portiere*'s good books.

Bills

Utility bills (*bollette*) will probably stay in the apartment owner's name, but know ahead of time in case you have to arrange for bills to be transferred to your name, and make sure you get the meter readings for all utilities before you move in. Also check if the electricity voltage has been raised. Standard Italian homes have 3kW but you can have it increased to 6kW.

Box Rooms

Many flats have a box room (*cantina*) or garage detached from the building or a cellar that you can use for storage. Since space is often in high demand, especially in cities, landlords may be hesitant to include this space, or won't offer it as available, but may be willing to include it if you ask.

Alterations

Painting and upgrading alterations (*modifiche*) are usually fine with owners, as long as no permanent changes are made. If you know straight off that the colour isn't for you, let them know that you will be painting, and ask if they would like it returned to its original colour when you leave.

Security

Security (*sicurezza*) is important. Get to know your neighbours and local store owners. Enquire if burglaries are a problem in your area and if most people have had alarms installed. Once you get to know the inhabitants of your building, people will feel more comfortable with you and know to keep an eye out for your home.

Buying and Leasing

Up until even a few years ago, a country manor or tiny farmhouse in Italy might have been a faraway dream. Prices were low enough, but access to the nearest airport from them could push them so far off the map that, unless one was moving to Italy permanently, they just weren't practical to live in if one wanted to get back and forth to and from the UK. Thanks to the recent boom of budget airlines and numerous new routes, some country homes are now more accessible from England than from parts of Italy. And, as many say, investing in property is always a sound move.

When considering renting or buying, it must be remembered that it is hard to avoid having an agent. Most Italians strive to do so, which brings benefits and handicaps. But for a non-Italian, trying to buy a home without an intermediary is near suicide. An estate agent (*agente immobilari*), as the liaison for the whole affair, can either answer all your questions or direct you to someone else who can deal with them. International agents (*agenti internazionali*), are more costly, but experienced in dealing with foreign clients. Italian agents probably won't have much international experience or the linguistic skills, but have more inside knowledge about the area they work in. *See* also p.134.

Searching for a Property

Agencies and agents can be national or local. Grimaldi (**www.grimaldi.net**, based in Turin), Gabetti (**www.gabetti.it**, with 300 branches) and Tecnocasa (**www.tecnocasa.it**) are dispersed nationwide and are well established. Otherwise, if you know the area you are interested in, look into local agents and agencies directly. Some local and international agencies divided by the region(s) they focus on are listed below.

• **Friuli-Venezia Giulia**: An agent for business and commercial properties in Venice is **www.netimmobiliare.com**.

• **Lombardy and Liguria**: For properties around breathtaking Lake Como, scan the list of realtors on **http://italianlakes.com**. The Swiss site **www.italimmo.ch** has properties throughout Lombardy, Liguria and some in Tuscany.

• **Emilia Romagna**: For properties in Emilia Romagna try La Casa Emilia (11 Westfield Avenue, Beverley, East Yorkshire HU17 7HA, **t** 0845 644 3763, **f** (07970) 703788, **info@lacasaemilia.com**, **www.lacasaemilia.com**).

• **Tuscany and Umbria**: Two experienced agents for properties in Umbria and Tuscany are Balducci Estate Agent (**www.casa4you.net**) and Casa Italia (**www.casait.it**). Properties in Umbria (**t** 075 850 4420, **jon@technet.it**) specializes in country properties.

• **Lazio**:The Rome-based agency Palladio ImmobilWeb (**www.palladioweb.com**) specializes in historic properties. It also deals with castles and palaces in Umbria, Tuscany, Marche, all of the Lazio countryside and Abruzzo, as do West Coast Properties (**t** 34 087 45330).

• **Marche**: Farmhouses and town homes in Le Marche (**www.lemarcheproperty management.com**, **LeMarchePropMan@libero.it**) are often affordable and some are predicting that this area will be the future Tuscany of Italy. Complete house buying service Marche Properties (**t** (07733) 445984 or **t** (01635) 269632, **www.marcheproperties.com**) from the UK can get you rolling, but you always need to visit the property before signing on the dotted line. Another is agent is Monica Bruni (**www.monicabruni.org**).

• **Abruzzo and Basilicata**: Specializing in the areas that are yet to be fully exploited, they say 'snap it up now' at **www.housearounditaly.com**.

• **Piedmont: Piedmont Properties** (4 Beechcroft Close, Ascot, Berkshire SL5 7DB, **t** (01344) 624096, **pp@smithgcb.demon.co.uk**) has villas and vineyards in the area of Asti. Local Knowledge (**www.itslocalknowledge.com**) has more than 100 estate agents specializing in the wine country of Piedmont.

• **Puglia**: Government incentives to restore old farmhouses and build B&Bs make Puglia interesting for investment. Sitidoltremare (**www.sitidoltremare.it**) is an agency run by an architect in Milan.

A UK portal offering hundreds of properties to buy in the popular destinations of Tuscany, Umbria, Marche, Lombardy and Liguria is Prestige Property (**www. prestigeproperty.co.uk**). Search the listings by keyword and price, or use the map-based menu system to specify a region, area and then the precise location.

Private vendors can advertise their property for sale and buyers can build up an online portfolio of properties in which they are interested. Another to try, Find a Property (**www.findaproperty.com**), has properties from selected agents for sale in locations throughout Italy. The site has a brief description and includes small pictures of properties, followed by the link to the full listing held on each individual agent's own site.

Listings of property and estate agents, personal finance information and property prices are on The Move Channel (**www.themovechannel.com**) and Buying Property in Italy (**www.buying-property-in-italy.com**). For a general look at property values, taxes, mortgages and updates on the latest changes in laws

Case Study: A Company Man

'This isn't the first time I've moved, but it has been one of the most obstacle-ridden ones,' says 42-year-old Tony, originally from Liverpool, with a smile revealing a saving sense of humour. 'Things really do move at a different pace here – it's no unjustified stereotype.' Tony Majakas is part of the upper management for a growing Italian company with an international ethos. 'But sometimes I have to downshift and realize that, as world-savvy as the company is, there are deeply entrenched Italian characteristics that are slow to shift and that I must adjust to, and help to transform.'

After five years in the company dashing around the globe but keeping his base in England, Majakas decided to give it whirl when the company president suggested he move to headquarters in northeast Italy. 'I wanted to maximize my time with my family while giving the most to the company as an employee.' So, as a test run, the Majakas family packed up and transplanted themselves to Italy in August – in the middle of one of the hottest European summers ever. He transferred to the seaside town of Cesenatico with his son, barely three years old, and his wife Debbie, not speaking a word of Italian.

Months down the road, Tony says that he has become wiser, but not as much as needed, in his opinion. 'That dream house I was sure I would find? Don't know if it exists. I have learned to expect less. And picking up Italian quickly – that's another expectation that I've had to adapt.' Laughingly, Tony admits, 'As much as I thought it through, part of me still says, "What? Are you daft moving just like that?"'

Real estate agents have taken the family from one unsuitable property to another. Rolling his eyes, Tony says, 'that is one waste of time I could do without. No matter how clear I am on what I am looking for, agents keep taking me to places so far from my needs that I wonder if they ever hear a thing I say.'

Italy, however, has its saving graces and Tony is a company man 100 per cent. 'This is all an experience,' he says, grinning over his pasta *penne all'arrabiata*, 'and I am sure that once we have a comfortable house where we feel at home, the worst will be over.' On being asked about the possibility of not finding decent lodging in the near future, he still insists that 'there wouldn't be much of a point in giving up now. Besides, I figure that I have seen 50 per cent of what is on the market. How many more possibilities can there be?'

and legislation affecting property purchases in Italy, go to **www.real-estate-european-union.com/english/italy.html**.

International agencies based in the UK with properties around Italy can be an immense help by taking you through the entire process once you have decided on the property you are going to buy. One of these, Casa Travella (**t** (01322) 660988, **www.casatravella.com**) handles nearly all aspects of the process, arranging insurance, surveys, translations, specialized lawyers and mortgage possibilities.

A general site with information about recommended agents, updates on law

changes and posted messages to consult is **www.arpnet.it**, the Italian Federation of Professional Real Estate Agents; for state offerings there is an online
auction site at **www.asteimmobili.it**.

What Preparation Should You Make?

Understand the System

The system of buying and selling property in Italy is, not surprisingly, different
from the system of buying property in England or Scotland. On balance, neither
better nor worse – just different. It has many superficial similarities, which can
lull you into a false sense of familiarity and overconfidence.

The general procedure seems, at first glance, similar to that in England: sign a
contract; do some checks; sign a deed of title. This is deceptive. The procedure is
very different and even the use of the familiar English vocabulary to describe
the very different steps in Italy can produce an undesirable sense of familiarity
with the procedure. This can lead to assumptions that things that have not
been discussed will be the same as they would in England. This is a wrong and
dangerous assumption. Work on the basis that the system is totally different.

The most important thing to remember is that buying a home in Italy is just as
safe as buying a home in Cardiff – providing that you take the right professional
advice and precautions when doing so. If you do not take such advice there are
many expensive traps for the unwary.

See a Lawyer

It will save you a lot of time and trouble if you see your lawyer *before* you find
a property. There are a number of preliminary issues that can best be discussed
in the relative calm before you find the house of your dreams rather than once
you are under pressure to sign some document to commit yourself to the
purchase. These issues will include:

- **who should own the property, bearing in mind the Italian and British tax
  consequences of ownership**
- **whether or not to consider mortgage finance and if so in which country**
- **what to do about buying the euros needed to pay for the property**
- **how to structure your purchase to minimize taxes and cost**
- **sorting out the tax and investment issues that will need to be dealt with
  before your move if you are to get the best out of both systems**

Only UK lawyers who specialize in dealing with Italy will be able to help you
fully. Your normal English solicitor will know little or nothing of the issues of
Italian law and an Italian lawyer is likely to know little or nothing about the
British tax system or the issues of English or Scots law that will affect the way
the transaction should be arranged. The lawyer may also recommend estate
agents, architects, surveyors, banks, mortgage lenders and other contacts.

A face-to-face meeting is still the best way to start an important relationship. It has a number of advantages. It allows you to show and be shown documents and to wander off more easily into related topics. Most importantly, it is usually easier to make certain that you have each understood the other in a personal meeting than it is by letter. But, these days, 'seeing' your lawyer does not need to involve an actual meeting. If it is more convenient to you it could be done by telephone conference call, by video-conference or over the internet.

Decide on Ownership

How should you officially structure the ownership of your new home? This is the most important decision you will have to make when buying a property. Because of the combination of the Italian and British tax systems, getting the ownership wrong can lead to totally unnecessary tax during your lifetime and on your death. This subject is dealt with more fully later, see pp.142–5.

Get an Offer of Mortgage/Finance

These days, with very low interest rates, more and more people borrow at least part of the money needed to buy their Italian home. Even if they don't need to do so, for many it makes good business or investment sense.

If you want to borrow money to finance your purchase it is better to get clearance *before* you start looking at property. Your lawyer should be able to get a preliminary mortgage offer within about 72 hours.

Estate Agents

The role of Italian estate agents (*agenzie immobiliari*) is similar to the role of the British estate agent. Their job is to find buyers for properties entrusted to them by a seller, but there the similarity ends.

In the UK a person can be a plumber today and, without any qualifications or experience, set up an estate agency tomorrow. They cannot do this in Italy. In Italy in order to practise as an estate agent you must be professionally qualified and hold a licence to practise. You must also have indemnity insurance. All this is partly an example of the generally greater paperwork and red tape prevalent in Italy and partly a useful consumer protection measure.

There are certain agents operating in Italy illegally without a licence. Many are foreigners servicing the foreign buyer: British selling to British, Germans to Germans, etc. Some of these 'illegals' are excellent, skilled people who offer a service at least as good as many of the legal agents. Despite this, you are better dealing with a 'proper' agent or his genuine employee as you will then be covered by the legislation and the codes of conduct.

An agent's fee is usually 3 per cent, but can sometimes swell to 8 per cent depending on the property. Often the fee is divided between buyer and seller so each may pay 3 per cent. Some agents prefer to negotiate a flat fee. Unfortunately, the cheaper the property, the higher the agent's fee usually is as a percentage of the final price.

Property Inspection (Surveys)

Whatever property you are thinking of buying, you should think about having it inspected before you commit yourself to the purchase. It costs just as much and causes just as much disruption to repair property in Italy as in the UK, so you don't want any surprises. In fact – foolishly – very few buyers of property in Italy do this. There is no substitute for a thorough survey, but other options are outlined below and the choice is yours.

A new property will be covered by a short guarantee running from the date of handover and covering minor but not trivial defects in a new property. The property will also benefit from a guarantee in respect of major structural defects that will last for 10 years. As a subsequent purchaser you assume the benefit of these guarantees. After 10 years you are on your own. For property more than 10 years old (and, arguably, for younger property too) you should consider a survey.

If you are buying a rural property that is being split off from a larger property you must use a surveyor to establish your boundaries.

Surveys

Most surveys can be done in 7–10 days. If you decide on a survey, there are several options available to you. Whichever report you opt for, its quality will depend in part on your input. Agree clearly and in writing the things you expect to be covered in the report. If you do not speak Italian (and the surveyor doesn't speak good English) you may have to ask someone to write on your behalf. Your lawyer would probably be the best bet. Some of the matters you may wish to think will involve you in additional cost. Ask what will be covered as part of the standard fee and get an estimate for the extras.

Do-it-yourself

Certain things about the general condition of the property will be apparent to you. These will help you decide when to instruct a surveyor to do a proper survey and help direct him or her to any specific points of interest.

Estate Agent's Valuation and 'Survey'

It may be possible to arrange for another local estate agent to give the property a quick 'once over' to comment on the price asked and any obvious problem areas. This is far short of a survey. It is likely to cost about €300.

Mortgage Lender's Survey

This is no substitute for a proper survey. Many lenders do not ask for one and, where they do, it is normally fairly peremptory, limited to a check on whether it is imminently about to fall over or not and if it is worth the money the bank is lending you.

Italian Builder

If you are going to do a virtual demolition and rebuild then it might make more sense to get a builder to do a report on the property. A reputable and experienced builder will also be able to comment on whether or not the price is reasonable for the property in its existing state. Make sure you ask for a written quotation for any building work proposed. As in any country it is as well to get several quotes, though this can be tricky. There is a lot of work for builders.

Italian Surveyor

The person doing the survey is usually the *geometra*. Your lawyer can put you in touch with the right people. In most rural areas there will be limited choice but if you prefer you can select 'blind' from a list of local members supplied by the surveyors' professional body. The cost of a structural survey (*perizia strutturale*) is typically €750–£2,000.

You will find that the report is different from the sort of report you would get from an English surveyor. Many people find it a little 'thin', with too much focus on issues that are not their primary concern. It will, hardly surprisingly, usually be in Italian. You will need to have it translated unless you speak very good Italian and have access to a technical dictionary. Translation costs amount to about €90–£150 per thousand words, depending on where you are located and the complexity of the document. Incidentally, always use an English person to translate documents from Italian into English. An alternative to translation of the full report would be to ask your lawyer to summarize the report in a letter to you and to have translated any areas of particular concern.

A few Italian surveyors, mainly in the popular areas, have geared themselves to the non-Italian market and will produce a report rather more like a British survey. They will, probably, also prepare it in bilingual form or at least supply a translation of the original Italian document.

UK-qualified Surveyor Based in Italy

A number of UK surveyors – usually those with a love of Italy – have seen a gap in the market and have registered and set themselves up in Italy to provide UK-style structural surveys. As in this country, they usually offer the brief 'Homebuyers' Report' or the fuller 'Full Structural Survey'.

This is not as simple as it would first appear. To do the job well they must learn about Italian building techniques and regulations, which are different from those in Britain. Without this knowledge the report will be of limited value. Prices are generally slightly more expensive than for an Italian report, but it will be in English and so avoid the need for translation costs. Your UK lawyer should be able to recommend a surveyor able to do a survey in your area. Alternatively, look for advertisers in the main Italian property magazines.

Check they have indemnity insurance covering the provision of reports in Italy. Check also on the person's qualifications and experience in providing reports on Italian property and get an estimate. The estimate will only be an estimate because they will not know for sure the scope of the task until they visit the property and because travelling time means that visits just to give estimates are not usually feasible.

UK-based Surveyor

Some UK surveyors provide reports from a base in the UK. These can be very good but travelling time often makes them impractical – especially in remote areas – and expensive. They also may not be as aware of local building conditins and regulations.

Contracts 'Subject to Survey'

This is unusual in Italy. Legally there is nothing to stop an Italian preliminary contract containing a 'get-out clause' (*clausola resolutoria*) stating that the sale is conditional upon a satisfactory survey being obtained. It is unlikely to meet with the approval of the seller or his agent unless the transaction is unusual. In an ordinary case the seller is likely to tell you to do your survey and then sign a contract.

Checklist – Things You May ask your Surveyor to Do

- electrical condition and continuity check
- drains check, including assessment of drains to point where they join mains sewers or septic tank
- water quality check if property uses a well
- septic tank check
- adequacy of foundations
- earthquake resistance if in an earthquake zone
- rot check
- check on cement quality in property constructed out of cement
- check of underfloor areas, where access cannot easily be obtained
- check on heating and air-conditioning
- check on pool and all pool-related equipment and heating
- wood-boring insect check
- evidence of asbestos
- evidence of radon gas – if it is in an affected area

Financing and Mortgages for Buying

With interest rates still fairly low, many choose to finance their home by taking out a mortgage or loan, even if they are perfectly capable of buying without doing so. If getting a loan or mortgage is paramount to the purchase, however, get clearance before you begin your search. Be sure that it is clear that the loan is for a home in Italy. While many agencies can help with mortgage possibilities, your lawyer should be able to confirm that you are eligible for a mortgage. There are also various sites with information and assistance, such as **www.loanweb.com**.

Mortgaging your UK Property

Because of fierce competition to lend money there are some excellent deals to be done, whether you choose to borrow at a variable rate, at a fixed rate or with one of the hybrid schemes now on offer. Read the Sunday papers or the specialist mortgage press to see what is available, or consult a mortgage broker. Perhaps most useful are mortgage brokers who can discuss the possibilities in both the UK and Italy.

Advantages

- **The loan will probably be very cheap to set up.**

  You will probably already have a mortgage. If you stay with the same lender there will be no legal fees or land registry fees for the additional loan. There may not even be an arrangement fee.

  If you go to a new lender, many special deals mean that the lender will pay all fees involved.

- **The loan repayments will be in sterling.**

  If the funds to repay the mortgage are coming from sterling earnings then the amount you have to pay will not be affected by fluctuations in exchange rates between the pound and the euro. Equally, if sterling falls in value then your debt as a percentage of the value of the property decreases. Your property will be worth more in sterling terms but your mortgage will remain the same.

- **You will be familiar with dealing with British mortgages and all correspondence and documentation will be in English.**

- **You can take out an endowment or PEP mortgage or pension mortgage or interest-only mortgage, none of which is available in Italy.**

  Normally only repayment mortgages are available in Italy, see below.

- **You will probably need no extra life insurance cover.**

  This can add considerably to the cost of the mortgage, especially if you are getting older.

Disadvantages

- **You will pay UK interest rates, which may at any time be higher than Italian rates.**

  Note, however, that Italian rates, over the last few years, have generally been higher than UK rates.

  Make sure you compare the overall cost of the two mortgages. Crude rates (which, in any case, may not be comparable as they are calculated differently in the two countries) do not tell the whole tale. What is the total monthly cost of each mortgage, including life insurance and all extras? What is the total amount required to repay the loan, including all fees and charges?

- **If sterling increases in value against the euro, a mortgage in euros would become cheaper to pay off.**

Your loan of €60,000 (now worth about £41,000 at €1 = £0.68) would only cost about £35,000 to pay off if the euro rose to about £0.58.

- If you ever need to let the property, it will be difficult or impossible to get Italian tax relief on the mortgage interest.

- Some academics argue that, in economic terms, debts incurred to buy assets should be secured against the asset bought and assets in one country should be funded by borrowings in that country.

Getting an Italian Mortgage

An Italian mortgage is one taken out on your Italian property. This will either be from an Italian bank or from a UK bank that is registered and does business in Italy. You cannot take a mortgage on your Italian property from your local branch of a UK building society or high street bank. The basic concept of a mortgage to buy property is the same in Italy as it is in England or Scotland. It is a loan secured against the land or buildings. Just as in England, if you don't keep up the payments the bank will repossess your property.

The Main Differences between an English and an Italian Mortgage

- It can be expensive to take out an Italian mortgage. Set-up fees, administrative costs, legal fees and taxes can easily amount to three to four per cent of the amount borrowed.

- An Italian mortgage (*mutuo ipotecario*) is almost always created on a repayment basis. That is to say, the loan and the interest on it are both gradually repaid by equal instalments over the period of the mortgage. Endowment, PEP, pension and interest-only mortgages are not known in Italy.

- There are often restrictions or penalties for early payment of the loan.

- The formalities involved in making the application, signing the contract subject to a mortgage and completing the transaction are more complex and stricter than in the UK.

- Most Italian mortgages are usually granted for 15 years, not 25 as in England. In fact the period can be anything from five to (in a few cases) 25 years. Normally the mortgage must have been repaid by your 70th (sometimes 65th) birthday.

- The maximum loan is generally 80 per cent of the value of the property and 60 per cent is more common. As a planning guide, you should think of borrowing no more than 60 per cent of the price you are paying.

- Fixed-rate loans (*tasso fisso*) – with the rate fixed for the whole duration of the loan – are more common than in England. They are very competitively priced.

- The way of calculating the amount the bank will lend you is different from in the UK. As you would expect, there are detailed differences from bank to bank, but most banks are not allowed to lend you more than an amount the monthly payments on which come to 30–33 per cent of your net disposable income. *See* below.

• There will usually be a minimum loan (say €30,000) and some banks will not lend at all on property less than a certain value. Some will not lend in rural areas.

• The way of dealing with stage payments on new property and property where money is needed for restoration is different from in England. *See* below.

• The paperwork on completion of the mortgage is different. There is often no separate mortgage deed. Instead the existence of the mortgage is mentioned in your purchase deed. It is prepared by and signed in front of a notary public (*notaio*).

How Much Can Be Borrowed?

Different banks have slightly different rules and different ways of interpreting the rules. Generally they will lend you an amount that will give rise to monthly payments of up to about 30–33 per cent of your net available monthly income.

The starting point is your net monthly salary. If there are two applicants the two salaries are taken into account. If you have investment income or a pension this will also be taken into account. If you are over 65 your earnings will not usually be taken into account, but your pension and investment income will be. If your circumstances are at all unusual, seek advice as approaching a different bank may produce a different result.

e.g.	Mr Smith – net salary per month	€4,500
	Mrs Smith – net salary per month	€3,000
	Investment income per month	€1,500
	Total income taken into account	€9,000 per month

The maximum loan repayments permitted will be 30 per cent of this sum, less your existing fixed commitments.

i.e. Maximum permitted loan repayment €9,000 x 30% = €2,700 per month

Regular monthly commitments would include mortgage payments on your main and other properties, any rent paid, HP commitments and maintenance (family financial provision) payments. Repayments on credit cards do not count. If there are two applicants, the commitments of both are taken into account.

e.g.	Mr and Mrs Smith – mortgage on main home	£750
	Mr and Mrs Smith – mortgage on house in Italy	£400 (€600)
	Mrs Smith – HP on car	£200 (€300)
	Total pre-existing outgoings	£1,350 per month

Maximum loan repayment = €2,700 (£1,800) – £1,350 = £450 per month.

Applications for an Italian Mortgage

Once again, the information needed will vary from bank to bank. It will also depend on whether you are employed or self-employed. Applications can receive preliminary approval (subject to survey of the property, confirmation of good title and confirmation of the information supplied) within a few days.

The Mortgage Offer

Allow four weeks from the date of your application to receiving a written mortgage offer as getting the information to them sometimes takes a while. It can take longer than four weeks. Once you receive the offer you will generally have 30 days from receipt in which to accept it, after which time it will lapse. Have the mortgage explained in detail by your lawyer.

Stage Payments for New Property

In Italy, when buying a new property one normally makes payments as the development progresses and takes title at the end. This can pose problems for banks as you do not own anything you can mortgage until you make the final payment and take title. In most cases the mortgage will therefore only be granted to cover the final payment. As this is often 60 or 70 per cent this is seldom a problem. In some cases if the earlier payments are more substantial the banks will offer a credit facility to make the earlier payments. Once the property has been delivered to you (and thus the full loan has been taken) the normal monthly payments will begin.

Property Needing Restoration

Not all banks will finance such property. If you have enough money to buy a property but need a mortgage to renovate it, you *must* apply for the mortgage before buying the property as it can otherwise be difficult to find a lender.

The Cost of Taking Out a Mortgage

This will normally involve charges amounting to about three to four per cent of the sum borrowed. These charges are in addition to the normal expenses incurred when buying a property, which normally amount to about 12 per cent of the price of the property.

You will probably be required to take out **life insurance** for the amount of the loan, though you may be allowed to use a suitable existing policy. You may be required to have a medical. You will be required to **insure the property** and produce proof of insurance – but you would probably have done this anyway.

The offer may be subject to **early redemption penalties**. Early payment penalties are of particular concern in the case of a fixed-rate mortgage.

Foreign Currency Mortgages

It is possible to mortgage your home in Italy and borrow, not in euros, but in sterling – or US dollars or Swiss francs or Japanese yen.

There may be some attractions to borrowing in sterling if you are repaying out of sterling income. The rates of interest will be sterling rates, not euro rates. This will currently mean paying more.

Usually the rates are not as competitive as you could obtain if you were remortgaging your property in the UK, as the market is less cut-throat. You will have all the same administrative and legal costs as you would if you borrowed in euros – i.e. about five per cent of the amount borrowed.

Who Should Own the Property?

There are many ways of structuring the purchase of a home in Italy. Each has significant advantages and disadvantages. The choice of the right structure will save you possibly many thousands of pounds in tax and expenses during your lifetime and on your death.

Because, in Italy, you do not have the total freedom that you have in the UK to deal with your assets as you please on your death the wrong choice of owner can also result in the wrong people being entitled to inherit from you when you die. This is a particular problem for people in second marriages and unmarried couples.

Sole Ownership

In some cases it could be sensible to put the property in the name of one person only. If your husband runs a high-risk business or, if he is 90 and you are 22, this could make sense. It is seldom a good idea from the point of view of tax or inheritance planning.

Joint Ownership

If two people are buying together they will normally buy in both their names. Your half is yours and your fellow owner's is his or hers. On your death your half will be disposed of in accordance with Italian law. A person who owns in this way, even if they own by virtue of inheritance, can usually insist on the sale of the property. So if your stepchildren inherit from your husband they could insist on the sale of your home.

If you decide to buy together then, in certain cases, it can make sense to split the ownership other than 50/50. If, for example, you have three children and your wife has two, then to secure each of those children an equal share on your death you might think about buying 60 per cent in your name and 40 per cent in your wife's name.

It is very important to seek clear advice from your lawyer about the form of ownership that will suit you best, with regard to the consequences both in Italy and in the UK.

Adding Your Children to the Title

If you give your children the money to buy part of the property and so put them on the title at once, you may save quite a lot of inheritance tax. On your death you will only own (say) one fifth of the property rather than one half. Only that part will be taxable. It may be such a small value as to result in a tax-free inheritance. This only works sensibly if your children are over 18.

Of course, there are drawbacks. For example, if the gift is not properly structured it could become subject to gift tax in Italy immediately. If the children fall out with you they can insist on the sale of the property and on receiving their share. If they divorce, their spouse may be able to claim part of the property. If you die within seven years then the gift of the money in the UK (which allows them to buy the property) will be taxed in whole or in part as part of your UK estate. If they die before you, then you may end up inheriting the property back from them and having to pay inheritance tax for the privilege of doing so.

Seek advice from your lawyer.

Putting the Property in the Name of Your Children Only

If you put the property only in the name of your children (possibly reserving for yourself a life interest – *see* below) then the property is theirs. On your death there will be little or no inheritance tax and there will be no need for them to incur the legal expenses involved in dealing with an inheritance. This sounds attractive. Remember, however, that you have lost control.

A life interest is the right to use the property for a lifetime. So, on your death, your rights would be extinguished *but* your second wife or partner, who still has a life interest, would still be able to use the property. Only on their death would the property pass in full to the people to whom you gave it years earlier.

This device can not only protect your right to use the property but also save large amounts of inheritance tax, particularly if you are young, the property is valuable and you survive for many years. As ever, there are also drawbacks, not least being the fact that after the gift you no longer own the property. If you wish to sell you need the agreement of the 'owners', who will be entitled to their share of the proceeds of sale and who would have to agree to buy you a new house. If you wish to do this you must structure the gift carefully, otherwise it could be taxable at once in Italy.

Limited Company

For some people owning a property via a limited company can be a very attractive option. You own the shares in a company, not a house in Italy. There are various types of company.

Italian Commercial Company

Ownership via a company can, in certain circumstances, reduce your tax bill. Ownership in the form of a company also gives rise to certain expenses: accountancy, filing tax returns, etc. Buying through an Italian company gives rise to a host of potential problems as well as benefits. The plan needs to be studied closely by your advisers so that you can decide whether or not it makes sense in the short, medium and long term.

UK Company

It is rare for a purchase through a UK company to make sense for a holiday home or single investment property. This is despite the fact that the ability to pay for the property with the company's money without drawing it out of the company and paying UK tax on the dividend is attractive. Once again you need expert advice from someone familiar with the law of both countries.

Offshore (Tax Haven) Company

This has the added disincentive that, in Spain, France and Portugal, the governments have passed laws to combat such ownership. For example, in Spain and France you will have to pay a special tax of three per cent of the value of the property every year. This is to compensate the government for all the inheritance and transfer taxes that they will not receive when the owners of these companies sell them or die. This tax treatment has more or less killed off ownership via such companies, yet they still have a limited role to play. These rules do not yet exist in Italy but anyone thinking of buying in this way should, in the light of harmonization of taxes in Europe, bear them in mind.

If the person who controls the offshore company is tax resident in the UK, keep in mind that he may be treated as a director or shadow director of the company. He may thus be liable to UK income tax on the 'benefit in kind' he gets if the company allows him to use the property in Italy. If the property would rent out for €1,500 (£1,000) per week, then this can amount to a lot of benefit – for most people, taxed at 40 per cent.

This does not mean that this type of ownership is never a good idea. A 93-year-old buying a £10,000,000 property, or someone who wishes to be discreet about the ownership of the property, might think the cost is a small price to pay for the avoidance of inheritance tax or privacy respectively.

The Use of Trusts

As a vehicle for owning a property, trusts are of little direct use. Italian law does not fully recognize trusts and so the trustees who are named on the title as the owners of the property would be treated as 'private individual' owners, having to pay all of the income, wealth and inheritance taxes applicable in their case. In a few cases this could still give some benefit, but there are probably better ways of getting the same result.

This does not mean that trusts have no place for the owner of property in Italy. A trust could still, for example, own the property via a limited company if this fitted the 'owner's' overall tax and inheritance planning objectives. Again, careful specialist advice is essential.

Which is Right for You?

The choice is of fundamental importance. If you get it wrong, you will pay massively more tax than you need to, both during your lifetime and on your death. The tax consequences arise not only in Italy, but also in your own country.

For each buyer of a home in Italy one of the options set out above will suit perfectly. Another might just about make sense. The rest would be an expensive waste of money.

The trouble is, it is not obvious which is the right choice! You need in every case to take advice. If your case is simple so will be the advice. If it is complex, the time and money spent will be repaid many times over.

Choosing a Lawyer

The Notary Public (*Notaio*)

The notary is a special type of lawyer. He is in part a public official, but he is also in business, making his living from the fees charged for his services. Notaries also exist in England, but they are seldom used in day-to-day transactions as they are in Italy.

Under Italian law only a legalized private deed of sale (*scrittura privata autenticata*) or a public deed approved and witnessed by a notary (*atto pubblico*) can be registered at the land registry (*ufficio dei pubblici registri immobiliari*).

Although it is possible to transfer legal ownership of property such as a house or apartment by a private agreement not falling into these categories, and although that agreement will be fully binding on the people who made it, it will not be binding on third parties. Third parties – including people who want to make a claim against the property and banks wanting to lend money on the strength of the property – are entitled to rely upon the details of ownership recorded at the land registry. So if you are not registered as the owner of the property, you are at risk.

The notary also carries out certain checks on properties sold and has some duties as tax enforcer and validator of documents to be presented for registration. For example, he will normally check that the property has been declared for tax purposes, that it complies with or is exempt from planning rules, that it is free of mortgages, and so forth.

The notary's basic fee is fixed by law. If he or she undertakes extra work or the documentation is unduly long, the charge will increase. He or she will also charge you 15 per cent for 'general expenses'.

The notary is, in theory, appointed by the buyer but, in many cases – particularly with new property – the seller will stipulate the notary to be used. This is a practical time- and cost-saving measure: the notary will have already drafted the documents gathering together all the bits of land bought by the seller and then split off the various individual plots to be sold, so it makes sense for him to deal with all the resultant sales. Otherwise all of the powers of attorney, etc., would need to be produced before lots of different notaries, potentially all over the country.

The notary is strictly neutral. He is more a referee than someone fighting on your behalf. He is, in the usual case, someone who checks the papers to make sure that they comply with the strict rules as to content and so will be accepted by the land registry for registration.

Many Italian notaries, particularly in rural areas, do not speak English – or, at least, do not speak it well enough to give advice on complex issues. Very few will know anything about English law and so will be unable to tell you about the tax and other consequences in the UK of your plans to buy a house in Italy. In any case, the buyer will seldom meet the notary before the signing ceremony and so there is little scope for seeking detailed advice. It is, anyway, rare for notaries to offer any comprehensive advice, least of all in writing, to the buyer.

Most Italian people buying a home in Italy will not use the services of a lawyer (as opposed to the *notaio*) unless there is something unusual or contentious about the transaction. But for the English buyer the notary is no substitute for also using the services of a specialist UK lawyer familiar with Italian law and international property transactions. This is the clear advice of every guidebook, the Italian and British governments and the Federation of Overseas Property Developers, Agents and Consultants (FOPDAC). It is therefore baffling why so many people buying a property in Italy do not take this necessary step.

The Price

This can be freely agreed between the parties. Depending on the economic climate, there may be ample or very little room for negotiating a reduction in the asking price. There is, however, probably rather more than the estate agent suggests. Italians haggle when it comes to the price of property – or almost anything else for that matter!

How Much Should Be Declared in the Deed of Sale?

For many years there was a tradition in Italy (and in other Latin countries) of under-declaring the price actually paid for a property when signing the deed of sale (*rogito*). This was because the taxes and notaries' fees due were calculated on the basis of the price declared. A lower price means less property transfer taxes for the buyer and less capital gains tax for the seller.

The days of major under-declarations have now largely gone. In rural areas you can still sometimes come under pressure to under-declare to a significant extent, but it is now rare. In many areas the seller will still suggest some more modest form of under-declaration. Under-declaration is illegal and foolish. There are severe penalties. Nonetheless you may find that you have little choice but to under-declare. The seller will often refuse to sell unless you do. Fortunately, there is a semi-legitimate 'grey area' for manoeuvre over declared price, rather like doing 40mph in a 30mph limit.

Where Must the Money Be Paid?

The price, together with the taxes and fees payable, is usually paid by the buyer to the seller in front of the notary. This is the best and safest way. You can, in fact, agree to pay in whatever way and wherever you please. So, for example, in the case of a British seller and a British buyer the payment could be made in sterling by bank transfer. This can produce some complications, particularly in a rural area where the notary has no experience of such transactions.

Try to avoid arrangements, usually as part of an under-declaration, where part of the money is handed over in cash in brown-paper parcels. Apart from it being illegal, it is dangerous at a practical level. Buyers have lost the bundle – or have been robbed – on the way to the notary's office. Sometimes there is even a suspicion that the seller, who knew where you were going to be and when, could be involved!

General Enquiries and Special Enquiries

Certain enquiries are made routinely in the course of the purchase of a property. These include, in appropriate cases, a check on the planning situation of the property. This enquiry will reveal the position of the property itself but it will not, at least directly, tell you about its neighbours and it will not reveal general plans for the area.

If you want to know whether the authorities are going to put a prison in the village or run a new road through your back garden (both, presumably, bad things) or build a motorway access point or railway station a couple of kilometres away (both, presumably, good things) you will need to ask. There are various organizations you can approach but, just as in England, there is no single point of contact for such enquiries.

If you are concerned about what might happen in the area, then you will need to discuss the position with your lawyers at an early stage. There may be a considerable amount of work (and therefore cost) involved in making full enquiries, the results of which can never be guaranteed.

Normal enquiries also include a check that the seller is the registered owner of the property and that it is sold (if this has been agreed) free of mortgages or other charges.

If the person who sells to you goes bust within two years of the sale, his creditors may be able to take possession of the property. There is some protection for the person who bought in good faith, but it can still be sensible to make some enquiries about the seller or to obtain a guarantee.

In order to advise you what special enquiries might be appropriate, your lawyer will need to be told your proposals for the property. Do you intend to rent it out? If so, is it on a commercial basis? Do you intend to use it for business purposes? Do you want to extend or modify the exterior of the property? Do you intend to make interior structural alterations? Agree in advance the additional enquiries you would like to make and be sure to get an estimate of the cost of those enquiries.

The Community of Owners (*Condominio*)

This is a device familiar in continental Europe but most unusual in England. The basic idea is that, when a number of people own land or buildings in such a way that they have exclusive use of part of the property, but shared use of the rest, then a *condominio* is created. Houses on their own plots with no shared facilities will not be members of a *condominio*.

In a *condominio* the buyer of a house or an apartment owns his own house or apartment outright – as the English would say, 'freehold' – and shares the use of the remaining areas as part of a community of owners. It is not only the shared pool that is jointly owned but (in an apartment) the lift shafts, corridors, roof, foundations, entrance areas, parking zones, etc.

The members of the *condominio* are each responsible for their own home. They collectively agree the works needed on the common areas and a budget for those works. They then become responsible for paying their share of those common expenses, as stipulated in their title.

The community is managed by an elected committee and appoints a president and secretary – both of whom are residents in the community. Day-to-day management is usually delegated to an administrator, who need not be a resident in the community. There is often also a resident caretaker.

The charges of the *condominio* are divided in the proportions stipulated in the deed creating the *condominio*. You will pay the same *condominio* fees whether you use the place all year round or only for two weeks' holiday. Of course your other bills (water, electricity, etc.) will vary with usage.

The *condominio* should provide not only for routine work but, through its fees, set aside money for periodic major repairs. If it does not – or if the amount set aside is inadequate – the general meeting can authorize a supplemental levy to raise the sums needed.

The rules set by the *condominio* are intended to improve the quality of life of residents. They could, for example, deal with concerns about noise (no radios by the pool), prohibit the use of the pool after 10pm, ban the hanging of washing on balconies, etc. More importantly, they could ban pets or any commercial activity in the building. These *regolamenti di condominio* are important documents. Every buyer of a property in a *condominio* should insist on a copy of the rules. If you do not speak Italian, you should have them translated or, at least, summarized in English.

Be careful when buying a property in a *condominio*. Disputes are common and the legal framework governing the *condominio* is somewhat lacking compared to other Latin countries.

If you do buy a home in a jointly owned building, consider attending meetings. The building administrator (*amministratore*) will announce when and where the assembly (*assemblea*) is held. Depending on how the meetings (*riunione di condominio*) are scheduled, you will be called to sit in on hours of negotiations and discussions every few months. These get togethers, though administrative in nature, help you get to know your neighbours. More importantly, they allow you some control, or at least knowledge, of your yearly home-owners' expenses (*spese condominiale*), which can shift drastically if it is decided to install a new electric gate or modern elevator. Ask if any major works are being planned, such as exterior restoration and painting, when buying a property.

'Vacant Possession'

In Italy there is a tendency to sell the property stripped bare. If you want the sale to include light fittings, fireplaces, etc., you must say so.

The Surveyor (*Geometra*)

Especially when buying in rural areas, you will almost certainly need the services of a *geometra*. This will not be to carry out a structural survey but to establish the planning status of the property and its boundaries. He may also be needed to help subdivide a larger plot of land of which you are buying a part. His fees will typically vary from about £600 to £1,200 depending on the complexity of what he needs to do.

Often the *geometra* will be linked to the selling agent or know the owner. In a small rural community there will be few surveyors and few agents, so this is not surprising. You then have the choice between using the local *geometra* – with the possibility that he might not be entirely independent – or appointing someone from further afield. This has two drawbacks. Travelling time adds to the cost of the work, and he will not have the intimate local contacts upon which life in Italy depends. Generally it is better to use the local person unless there are strong contra-indications.

Sometimes the *geometra*'s work will be done before signing the initial contract or *compromesso* (*see* below), sometimes afterwards.

Initial Contracts

In Italy most sales start with a preliminary contract. The type of contract will depend upon whether you are buying a finished or an unfinished property. The signing of any of these documents has far-reaching legal consequences, which are sometimes different from the consequences of signing a similar document in the UK. Whichever type of contract you are asked to sign, always seek legal advice before doing so.

Generally the preliminary contract is prepared by the estate agent – who is professionally qualified in Italy – or by the developer. Estate agents' contracts are often based on a pre-printed document in a standard format.

Some contracts coming from estate agents are legally muddled and not properly thought through. They can blur or mix different types of contractual obligation, often referring to mutually exclusive concepts in the same document – for example, referring to it as a contract of sale as well as an option contract.

Sometimes the contracts are extremely one-sided, giving their client – the seller – all the rights and taking away all the rights of the buyer.

It is very important that these contracts are not just accepted as final. In many cases they will need to be modified, in some cases extensively.

If You Are Buying a Finished Property

You will be invited to sign one or more of three different documents. Each has different features. Each has different legal consequences. And each is appropriate in certain circumstances and inappropriate in others.

Offer to Buy

The offer to buy is, technically speaking, not a contract at all. It is a formal written offer from the potential buyer to the potential seller. It will state that you wish to buy the stated property for a stated price and that you will complete the transaction within a stated period. The offer will normally be accompanied by the payment of a deposit to the estate agent or seller. The deposit is not fixed but will usually range from two to five per cent of the price offered. In return for this deposit the property should be taken off the market. The offer must be in writing.

This document can bind you. Unless you stipulate that it is not binding, it is not a mere enquiry as to whether or not the seller might be interested in selling. If he says that he accepts the offer then you (and he) become legally bound to proceed with the transaction.

Generally we do not like written offers. We prefer the idea of making a verbal enquiry as to whether or not the seller would accept a certain price and, once he says yes, for a binding bilateral contract of sale (*compromesso*) to be signed. Often, however, the local practice is to make formal offers. It is then a case of 'when in Rome, do as the Romans do'.

Just make sure that the offer is very clear and that it specifies that it is not binding. If it is a binding offer make sure that it stipulates any key conditions to which it is subject, such as 'this offer is only binding if I am offered a mortgage from X for at least €50,000 at an interest rate no higher than X per cent' or 'This offer is subject to a satisfactory survey'.

Reservation/Option Contract

This is relatively rare but can be useful. It is a written document in which the seller agrees to take a stated property off the market for a fixed period and sell it at a stated price to a stated person at any time within a stated period.

The seller will usually require that any person taking up his offer pays him a deposit. Once he has received this deposit, the seller must reserve the property for you until the end of the period specified in the contract.

This is similar to an English option contract. If you want to go ahead and buy the property you can, but you are not obliged to do so. If you do not go ahead, you lose your deposit.

The contract could contain special 'get-out clauses' stipulating the circumstances in which the buyer will be entitled to the refund of his deposit if he decides not to go ahead. The drafting of these clauses is of vital importance. See your lawyer.

If you do want to go ahead you can exercise the option at any point up to the end of the agreed period. If the seller refuses to go ahead, the buyer is entitled to claim compensation.

Full Preliminary Contract (Compromesso)

The *compromesso* is, in most parts of Italy, the most common type of document. It is also known as the *contratto preliminare di vendita*.

It is an agreement that commits both parties. The seller must sell a stated property at a stated price to a stated person on the terms set out in the contract. The buyer must buy.

Other types of preliminary contract – binding only either the buyer (*promesso d'acquisto*) or the seller (*promesso di vendita*) are sometimes seen and have different legal consequences from the *compromesso*. Because they are relatively rare, they are not considered further here.

The *compromesso* is the most far-reaching of the three documents covered in this section and so it is particularly important that you are satisfied it contains all of the terms necessary to protect your position. Always take legal advice. Remember that, under Italian law, by signing and completing this contract you become, in some senses, the owner of the property, though you will need to sign a deed of sale (*rogito*) and register your ownership to be safe as far as third parties are concerned.

The contract will contain a variety of 'routine' clauses.

- **The names of the seller and buyer should both be stated fully.**

- **The property should be described fully, both in an everyday sense and by reference to its land registry details.**

- **If the property is part of a condominium the common parts (pool, etc.) should be described.**

- **A date for the signing of the deed of sale (*rogito*) will be fixed or the contract will permit either party to require the signing of the *rogito* at any point by giving notice to the other.**

- **A statement will be made as to when possession will take place – normally, on the date of signing the title.**

- **The price is fixed.**

- **A receipt for any deposit is given.**

- **The property should be sold with vacant possession.**

- **The property should be sold free of any charges, debts or burdens and all bills should be paid up to date before signing the *rogito*.**

- It will provide for who is to pay the costs of the purchase.
- It may confirm the details of any agent involved and who is to pay his commission.
- It will set out what is to happen if one or both of the parties break the contract.
- It will establish the law to cover the contract and the address of the parties for legal purposes.

It will probably also contain some 'conditional clauses' (*clausoli resolutivi*). These are clauses that say, in effect, if X is not true or does not happen, then the deal is off and you get your deposit money back.

Examples might be as follows.

- The seller has good title (you might not have been able to get confirmation of this before signing the *compromesso*, especially if you were under pressure to sign quickly or lose the property).
- The seller has planning permission.
- You will be successful in an application for planning permission – for example, to build a pool.
- There are no pre-emption rights or they will not be exercised.
- The property is to be surveyed (or inspected for mortgage purposes) and the sale is conditional upon a satisfactory outcome to that inspection.
- The seller is required to fix various things or complete some work on the property.
- You are applying for a mortgage and the sale is conditional upon that mortgage being offered.
- The sale is conditional upon the sale of your exising property within a certain time.

These all need careful drafting if there are not to be any 'loopholes'. If the buyer or seller drops out of the contract or otherwise breaks it, various arrangements may be made.

A deposit is paid at the time of signing the contract. Normally a special type of deposit is payable by the buyer. If he fails to complete, he will lose the deposit. If the seller fails to satisfy the conditions imposed upon him, and to complete, he will have to return double the deposit paid.

Alternatively the contract may provide for a deposit to be paid as a simple part of the price of the property. The contract can provide for all or part of this deposit – and any other sums paid up to the relevant moment – to be lost if the buyer does not proceed. It is important to understand the difference.

The amount of this deposit varies from place to place and seller to seller. It is sometimes the 'standard' 10 per cent we are used to in the UK but often it is 20, 30 or even 33 per cent. The larger deposit is a mixed blessing. Obviously it puts more strain on your cashflow and puts you at greater exposure if anything goes wrong and you have to recover it from the seller. Getting money back is never as simple as paying it over, however strong your legal position! On the other hand, if you have paid 30 per cent, this acts as a very real barrier to the seller's pulling out of the transaction – or entering into a transaction where there are conditions he is not going to be able to meet. This is because if he can't go ahead he will usually be required to give you back double that amount – 60 per cent of the price of the property.

If, as is often the case, you are to pay all or a part of the estate agent's fees on top of the price of the property, you will often be expected to pay these at the time when the *compromesso* is signed. This will typically be three per cent of the price of the property.

If the parties fail to comply with their obligations there is the ultimate remedy of seeking a court order. As in any country, this is very much a last resort as it is costly, time-consuming and (as in any country) there is no guarantee of the outcome of a court case. If a court order is made in your favour this order can be registered at the land registry.

If You Are Buying an Unfinished Property

Reservation Contract

Often in these cases there is a preliminary contract. This is the reservation contract (*see* above). This allows you to reserve a plot when you see it and allows you time to sign one of the other types of contract when you have made the necessary enquiries.

Full Preliminary Contract

There are three likely types of contract in this case.

• **Contract for immediate sale of the land**: You sign a contract agreeing to sign title deed in respect of the land – and anything the seller has so far built on it – now. This involves paying for the land and work so far undertaken in full at this stage.

At the same time you enter into a contract to build your house on the land. This will normally be an *appalto*. The contract contains detailed provisions as to what will happen, for example, if any changes are needed to the works agreed or costs rise and as to arrangements for inspection and handover of the property.

As the building continues, it automatically becomes the property of the buyer. The buyer, of course, has the obligation to pay the agreed price, usually by instalments dependent upon the progress of the building work.

This has the great advantage of securing the money you pay to the builder. If the builder goes bust you own the land and everything built on it. It only really works for property built on its own plot rather than, say, apartments. It can be tax- and cost-inefficient.

• **Contract 'on plan'**: You agree to buy a property once it has been built and agree to make payments in stages as the construction progresses. Sometimes the payments are dependent upon the progress of the building works. On other occasions they are due on set dates. The latter are now the more common, though less attractive to the buyer.

Once the property has been built, you will sign the deed of sale and pay the balance of the price. It is only then that you become the owner of the property and register your title. Until then, if the builder goes bust you are simply one of many creditors.

The contract can provide for an independent guarantee to secure completion of the construction in the event, for example, that the seller went bust. Remember that big companies and honourable men go bust. Rolls-Royce. Barings Bank, Enron.

Where possible, it is much better to have separate contracts for the purchase of the land and subsequent building work.

• **Contract to buy once the property has been built**: You agree to buy a plot of land and building. You agree to pay once it has been built. Simple! You take title and pay the money at the same time. This is really the same as buying a resale property. This type of contract is little used.

Other Documentation

Has the property got planning permission/a building licence? You should be given a full specification for the property, a copy of the community rules and constitution if the property shares common facilities.

Pay particular attention to the specification. It is not unknown for the show flat to have marble floors and high-quality wooden kitchens but for the specification to show concrete tiles and MDF.

Checklist – Signing a Contract

Property in the Course of Construction	Existing Property
Are you clear about what you are buying?	
Are there any 'extras' included in the sale?	
Have you taken legal advice about who should be the owner of the property?	
Have you taken legal advice about inheritance issues?	
Are you clear about boundaries?	
Are you clear about access?	
Have you seen the seller's title?	
Have you seen an up-to-date land registry extract?	
	Are you sure you can change the property as you want?
	Are you sure you can use the property for what you want?
	Is the property connected to water, electricity, gas, etc.?

Property in the Course of Construction	Existing Property
	Have you had a survey done?

Have you made all necessary checks OR arranged for them to be made?

Have you included 'get-out clauses' for all important checks not yet made?

Is your mortgage finance arranged?

Is the seller clearly described?

If the seller is not signing in person, have you seen a power of attorney/mandate to authorize the sale?

Are you fully described?

Is the property fully described? Identification? Land registry details?

Is the price correct?

Are there any possible circumstances in which it can be increased or extras described fully?

Property in the Course of Construction	Existing Property
Are the stage payments fully described?	Does contract say when possession will be given?
Are arrangments for stage payments satisfactory?	Is there a receipt for the deposit paid?
Is the date for completion of the work agreed?	In what capacity is the deposit paid?
Does the property have planning	Does the property have a habitation licence/permission/licence to build?

Is the date for signing the *rogito* agreed?

Does the contract provide for the sale to be free of charges and debts?

Does the contract provide for vacant possession?

Which notary is to act?

Is the estate agent's commission dealt with?

What happens if there is a breach of contract?

Are there any financial guarantees of satisfactory completion?

Are all the necessary special 'get-out' clauses included?

Steps between Signing the Contract and Signing the Deed of Sale (*Rogito*)

Searches

If you were pressured into signing a preliminary contract (*compromesso*) without doing searches or seeing proof of title, do it now. The sooner you find a problem, the sooner you can fix it or take protective action.

Registration of the *Compromesso*?

It is possible to register the written preliminary contract, so protecting your rights against third parties. This can sometimes be a good idea, particularly if there is going to be a long period from the signing of the *compromesso* to the signing of the *rogito*. It does, however, increase the costs of the purchase.

Power of Attorney

Completion dates on Italian property are notoriously fluid and so you could plan to be there but suffer a last-minute delay to the signing that makes it impossible.

The solution to this problem is the power of attorney. This document authorizes the person appointed (the attorney) to do whatever the document authorizes on behalf of the person granting the power (the grantor). Please note that being appointed under a power of attorney is nothing to do with being a lawyer. Anyone can be appointed – though you need to choose the person with care as you are giving them power to do things on your behalf.

The most sensible type of power to use will be the Italian style of power that is appropriate to the situation. The power will be signed in front of a notary, either in the UK or Italy. If it is signed in front of a UK notary it has to be ratified by, of all people, the Foreign and Commonwealth Office for use overseas. This sounds very grand but is actually quick and simple.

The type of Italian power of attorney that you will need depends on what you want to use it for. Your specialist English lawyer can discuss your requirements with you and prepare the necessary document. Alternatively you can deal directly with the Italian notary who will ultimately need the power.

Even if you have granted a power of attorney, if you get the opportunity to be present at the time of the signing, you don't have to use the power of attorney.

Tax Identification Number

You will need to obtain your *codice fiscale* before you sign the deed of sale. If you do not yet have one (*see* **Red Tape**, p.118), this is a simple process (usually) that will be initiated by your lawyer or the estate agent.

Getting Money to Italy

If you are paying for your property from the UK, there are several ways of getting the money to Italy.

Electronic Transfer

The most practical is to have you money sent electronically by SWIFT transfer from a UK bank directly to the recipient's bank in Italy. This costs about £10–£35, depending on your bank. It is safer to allow two or three days for the money to arrive in a rural bank, despite everyone's protestations that it will be there the same day.

IBANK numbers (unique account numbers incorporating a code for the identity of the bank and branch involved as well as the account number of the individual customer) should be quoted, if possible, on all international currency transfers.

You can send the money from your own bank, via your lawyers or via a specialist currency dealer. For the sums you are likely to be sending you should receive an exchange rate much better than the 'tourist rate' you see in the press.

There is no such thing as a fixed exchange rate in these transactions. The bank's official interbank rate changes by the second and the job of the bank's currency dealers is to make a profit by selling to you at the lowest rate they can get away with!

Thus, if you do a lot of business with a bank and they know you are on the ball, you are likely to be offered a better rate than a one-off customer. For this reason it is often better to send it via your specialist UK lawyers, who will be dealing with large numbers of such transactions. This also has the advantage that their bank, which deals with international payments all the time, is less likely to make a mistake causing delay to the payment than your bank, for which such a payment might be a rarity.

You or your lawyers might use a specialist currency dealer to make the transfer of funds instead of a main UK bank. Such dealers often give a better exchange rate than an ordinary bank. But do make sure that the dealer you are using is reputable. Your money is paid to them, not to the major bank, so could be at risk if the dealer is not bonded or otherwise protected.

However you make the payment, ensure that you understand whether or not you or the recipient is going to pick up the receiving bank's charges. If you need a clear amount in Italy you will have to make allowances for these, either by sending a bit extra or by asking your UK bank to pay all the charges.

Make sure you have got the details of the recipient bank, its customer's name, the account codes and the recipient's reference precisely right. Any error and the payment is likely to come back to you as undeliverable – and may involve you in bearing the cost of it being converted back into sterling.

The bank in Italy will make a charge – which can be substantial – for receiving your money into your account.

Bankers' Drafts

You can arrange for your UK bank to issue you with a banker's draft (bank certified cheque), which you can take to Italy and pay into your bank account. Make sure that the bank knows that the draft is to be used overseas and so issues you with an international draft.

Generally this is not a good way to transfer the money. It can take a considerable time – sometimes weeks – for the funds deposited to be made available for your use. The recipient bank's charges can be surprisingly high. The exchange rate offered against a sterling draft may be uncompetitive as you are by then a captive customer.

Cash

It is not recommended that you pay in cash. You will need to declare the money on departure from the UK and on arrival in Italy. Even then, if you declare £200,000 or so, they will think you are a terrorist or drugs dealer! That suspicion can have far-reaching consequences in terms of listings in police 'dodgy people' files and even surveillance.

To add insult to injury, the exchange rate you will be offered for cash (whether you take sterling and convert there or buy the euros here) is usually very uncompetitive and the notary may well refuse to accept the money in his account. Don't do it.

Exchange Control and Other Restrictions on Moving Money

For EU nationals there is no longer any exchange control when taking money to or from Italy. There are some statistical records kept showing the flow of funds and the purposes of the transfers.

When you sell your property in Italy you will be able to bring the money back to the UK if you wish to do so.

Fixing the Completion Date

The date stated in the contract for signing the *rogito* could, most charitably, be described as flexible or aspirational. Often it will move, if only by a day or so. For this reason, if you are buying in advance of moving to Italy, it is not sensible to book your travel to Italy until you are almost sure that matters will proceed on a certain day.

Checklist – Steps Before Completion

Property in the Course of Construction	Existing Property
Prepare power of attorney	
Check what documents must be produced on signing the *rogito*	
Confirm all outstanding issues have been complied with	
Confirm all other important enquiries are clear	
Confirm arrangements (date, time, place) for completion with your lender if you have a mortgage	
Confirm arrangements (date, time, place) for completion with notary	
Send necessary funds to Italy	
Receive rules of community	
Insurance cover arranged?	
Sign off work or list defects	Proof of payment of community fees
	Proof of payment of other bills

The Deed of Sale (*Rogito*)

To be registered at the land registry – and so protect your ownership of your property from claims by third parties – your purchase must be either by way of a legalized private document (*scrittura privata autenticata*) or public title deed (*atto pubblico*). The deed of sale signed is called the *rogito*.

The vast majority of overseas buyers buy by way of an *atto pubblico* signed in front of a notary (*notaio*). This must be signed in front of an Italian notary either by the parties in person or someone holding power of attorney for them. Generally it is at the moment of signing that the title to the property is transferred into your name.

At the same time as the *rogito* is signed, the balance of the price is paid to the seller, usually by way of an Italian banker's draft handed over in front of the notary. If you are taking out an Italian mortgage it is also at this time that the paperwork in relation to the mortgage will be completed, again by the notary. Also at this time the various taxes and stamp duties and the notary's fees are paid.

The *rogito* will contain a variety of 'standard' clauses, largely replicating those in the contract. It will contain a statement of the price and a statement that the notary has advised you of your fiscal obligations arising out of the sale.

Formalities

Certain procedures are followed at the signing of the *rogito*. The parties are identified by their passports or identity cards. This will normally be done, initially, by the notary's clerk and then also by the notary. The notary's clerk may also go through the content of the *rogito* with the parties. This tends to be very superficial and often the person concerned will have limited or no English.

The parties will then be ushered into the presence of the notary. In addition to the buyer and seller, it would be possible for the group to comprise also the notary's clerk, your lawyer, a translator, a representative of your mortgage lender, the estate agent and any sub-agent appointed by the estate agent. Most of these people are there to receive money! Needless to say, if they all turn up, it can get a little loud and confusing!

If you do not speak Italian, an **interpreter** should be present when you sign the *rogito*. The attitude of notaries when it comes to assessing when an interpreter is necessary varies enormously. No written translation is provided as a matter of course. If an interpreter is required, you will generally have to pay for it.

After the *Rogito* Has Been Signed

The taxes must be paid. Once the taxes are paid, your title and any mortgage should be presented for registration at the land registry. This should be done as quickly as possible. He who registers first gets priority.

After several months the land registry will issue a certificate to the effect that the title has been registered.

The Cost of Buying a Property in Italy

There are fees and taxes payable by a buyer when acquiring a property in Italy. They are sometimes known as completion expenses or completion or closing costs. They are impossible to predict with total accuracy at the outset of a transaction. This is because there are several variable factors that will not become clear until later. We can, however, give a general guide.

These costs are calculated on the basis of the price that you declared as the price paid for the property in the *rogito*. The size of these expenses, coupled with the Italian dislike for paying tax, has led to the habit of accidentally under-declaring the price in the *rogito*. These days are now largely over and we can only suggest that the full price of the property is declared. *See* 'How Much Should Be Declared in the Deed of Sale', p.146.

Notary's Fees

These are fixed by law, so are not negotiable. They will depend on the type of property being bought and its price. As a general guide, allow one per cent. If you have asked the notary to do any additional work over and above the transfer of title to the property or for any advice there will, of course, be additional charges.

Taxes

VAT *(Imposta sul Valore Aggiunta – IVA)*

This applies only to properties bought from a company or business. It is 10 per cent of the declared purchase price of the property unless the property is classified as a 'luxury dwelling', in which case the rate is 20 per cent. The meaning of luxury dwelling is defined. This VAT is sometimes, but not always, included in the price of the property quoted to you.

Stamp Duty

This is charged instead of VAT on properties bought from private individuals. The rate is usually seven per cent. Some historic properties bear a reduced rate of three per cent.

Real Estate Tax *(Imposta Ipotecaria e Catastale)*

If bought from an individual, it is three per cent of the value of the property. If bought from a company it is a small sum usually not exceeding 0.5 per cent.

Local Tax

This is based on the official tax value of the property (*valore catastale*) – not at all the same as the market value. It varies from 0.4 to 0.8 per cent of that value depending on the type of property bought.

Mortgage Costs (If Applicable)

If you are taking out a mortgage, there will be additional costs. These costs typically amount to three to four per cent of the amount borrowed.

Estate Agent's Charges (If Payable by the Buyer)

If an estate agent has sold the property, his fees are often split between the buyer and seller. If this is so, then you are likely to pay three per cent of the true price paid. This can be varied by agreement. These fees will be subject to IVA.

Miscellaneous Other Charges

Architect's fees, surveyor's fees, UK legal fees (typically one per cent), first connection to water, electricity, etc. – most of these will be subject to Italian IVA at varying rates, but your UK lawyer's fees will be outside the scope of UK VAT.

Overall Costs of Acquisition

In the case of a house bought without a mortgage, this is likely to amount to about 15 per cent of the price of the declared price of the property.

Restoration and Remodelling

Rome's ancient downtown skyline is one of the best preserved in Europe, if not the world, thanks to stringent planning permits that don't allow modern constructions over a certain height, of a particular colour, and so on. Too bad that the rules don't apply to the outskirts of the city, where illegal constructions are simply a blight. In some regions and areas planning regulations are applied stringently but in others not. When they are ignored the results can be dire and can be seen by all.

However, if you buy a property and have plans for carrying out building work on it, don't do so without finding out what the local regulations are first and if the area you are in allows you to make the changes you propose. Do this through the municipality (*comune*). Your estate agent will know if your land has planning permission (*permessi comunali*), but always double check. Estate agents eager to sell a property may not be the best source of such information.

Checklist

When visiting properties you are considering buying, have a checklist of things to look out for and enquire about. Many of these are the same as for renting, but several points are more specific when you are buying. These are some factors to keep in mind.

• **Heating** – Is it *autonomo* or *centralizzato*? If *autonomo*, find out when the system was installed and if the boiler system (*caldaia*) is the same that is used to heat your shower water. Some systems heat the water as it goes through, giving you plenty of warm water for long showers or baths. However, if you have a small *caldaia*, the water is heated as it is consumed, so you literally use up the hot water and then have to wait for it to reheat before you can use it again.

• **Mortgages**: are there any outstanding mortgages from previous owners that could roll over to you?

• **Property tax**: has it all been paid?

• **Rubbish tax**: one of the most menacing of fees, it always catches up with the home owner.

• **Renovations and licences**: have all refurbishments or alterations been properly authorized? If not, you could have a fine levied for unlicensed work carried out before your purchase. This includes electrical wiring.

• **Water**: are the average bills high, medium or low? Is the area part of the state-subsidy scheme that would lower your bills? Are there shortages in your area?

Making the Move

As you pack your boxes, close up your house in Britain and prepare to make the move to Italy, make sure you have considered the following.

- Is your paperwork in order, including visas and stay permits if required?

- Is your passport valid throughout your intended stay in Italy? Keep photo-copies of your passport at home and with you, as they are often required when compiling official documentation and will be invaluable in getting a quick replacement should your passport go missing at any time.

- Pets should be accompanied by a Certificate of Good Health supplied by your local vet and translated into Italian (although officials are familiar with English-language ones and rarely put up a fuss). Your pet should also have had a rabies vaccination at least one month prior to departure (but no longer than one year prior). However, *see* pp.162–3 for details of the legal requirements should you wish to take you pet back to the UK.

- If you bring a computer from England, make sure it has the correct plug adapters. You can sign up with an internet service provider once you get to Italy (*see* pp.186–7) but, if you choose to stay with your current provider, check that you won't incur the painfully high surcharge often associated with connecting from abroad.

- If you intended to bring large amounts of money – for the restoration of your new house, for example – you should consider opening a *conto estero* with an Italian bank branch office at home. A *conto estero* allows you to keep your savings in sterling and euros.

- If you are moving permanently, notify your credit card companies and mailing lists of your change of address.

- Also contact the post office, to forward your mail to your new address.

- If you have regular debts to pay in England, such as a mortgage, arrange to prepay them or request that payments be made automatically on your behalf by your bank.

- Make sure you have access to your British tax forms before they are due.

- Terminate or suspend your utility contracts back home.

- Set up a British account with an overseas courier service if you plan on doing a lot of shipping. It will cost you less than an Italian account and is easier to set up.

- Bring books or sheets of British postage stamps with you. You will need them if you have to send self-addressed stamped envelopes to the UK.

- Make a list of any medical conditions from which you suffer, such as diabetes or allergies. Have this translated into Italian.

- Check that your insurance company covers you overseas and, if you will be away for some time, arrange a last round of dentist and medical appointments before your departure.

- Take ample supplies of prescription medicine – from painkillers to the Pill – that you will not be able to fill in Italy before you have signed on with an Italian doctor. Or arrange with your UK doctor for repeat prescriptions and for someone to fill them and send them to you while you are away.

- If you are particularly attached to any beauty or other products you can't find in Italy, stock up before leaving.

- Bring plug adapters and power surge protectors that fit your appliances. Don't bring a television set as it won't work in Italy.

- Stock up on English-language software since it is difficult to find in Italy, and bring your English computer keyboard since Italian ones have all the letters in the wrong places. You'll discover the meaning of cyber torture.

Removal Companies

As a British or other European Union citizen you will be able to take your possessions with you to Italy without paying taxes or customs duties. All foreigners should have certain documents in order before they can move their household goods to Italy, such as a *codice fiscale* and a valid *permesso di soggiorno*. Non-EU citizens may also be asked for a *nulla osta* (no obstacle document) if they intend to import electronic goods like a stereo.

You will also be required to produce a full inventory. You should give the removal company a photocopy of your passport, your *codice fiscale*, your *permesso di soggiorno* and the inventory. If you are a non-EU resident, give them the original *nulla osta*. If you can produce all of the above, the mover will get your goods through customs with no import duty.

If you cannot produce the above documentation, some moving companies can negotiate the payment of a bond to clear customs. Make sure you appoint a removal company that is an accredited customs clearing agent. All items you import to Italy must be for personal, not commercial, use. That means you should not plan on selling them once in Italy.

For a list of removal firms, consult the English *Yellow Pages* (**www.intoitaly.it**). This excellent phone book also has detailed listings for Rome, Florence, Genoa, Catania, Palermo, Bologna, Milan and Naples.

The alternative to a removal company is to move your goods yourself. You could pack everything into a truck or van and, with the Schengen Convention in place, you wouldn't have to produce any documentation whatsoever at the Italian border. If you are making a light move, you might be able to squeeze your belongings in suitcases for air travel and bring a bit over with each trip.

Home Security and Insurance

Anything can happen. If we live by that creed, then insurance is not a bad idea. Most Italians opt out of it, though apartments have communal coverage for damage that is caused by building defects (water leaks from main pipes, fire caused by faulty wiring in the central system, and so on). And if someone from above or below you is responsible, then you're set – if they have insurance. Consider, however, that household insurance (*assicurazione sulla casa*) can be taken out to cover both the building – your home (*edificio*) – and its contents (*contenuto*). A specific policy for theft and fire (*incendio e furto*) is common in Italy and insuring a holiday home is more expensive because of the higher risk of burglary during extended absences of more than three weeks at a time.

In case of burglary or forced entry, file a report (*denuncia*) with the police within 24hrs. This is necessary for an insurance claim. A foreign policy can be taken out and is valid in Italy, but may be more expensive. Always check with the company before putting the final signature on the dotted line. Also, ask for an information number to call if you need to make a claim. The obvious benefit of having a UK insurer is having information in English. But many Italian insurance companies have translation services and English-speaking employees.

Premiums are calculated on the property's size and age. The sum is usually unlimited. If the area is a high-risk zone, either for natural disaster or standard city dangers like theft, the premium will be higher. Those living in burglary risk zones will be required to increase security by installing particular types of locks on doors, adding window locks and even installing an alarm system.

- **Make sure that the level of cover is adequate. Just as in the UK, if you under-insure the building and the worst happens, the company will not pay you out for the full extent of your loss.**

- **If you are using the property as holiday accommodation (or spend long periods away from home) you must specify a policy which is a holiday policy. If you do not, you are likely to find that one of the conditions of the policy is that cover will lapse if the property is empty for 30 or 60 days. Premiums will be higher for holiday homes because the risk is higher.**

- **If you intend to let your property, you must notify the insurance company and comply with any of its requirements with regard to the lettings.**

- **If you need to make a claim, make it quickly. There are usually time limits for doing so. If the claim involves a theft or break-in you will usually have to report the matter to the police. This should normally be done immediately after discovery of the incident and in any case within 24 hours. The claim should be notified to the insurance company without delay. Check the maximum period allowed in your policy, which could be as little as 48 hours. As with all-important documents in Italy, the claim should be notified by recorded delivery post. Make the claim by registered post.**

There are some UK-based insurance companies who offer cover in respect of properties in Italy. The main advantages in dealing with a UK company are that the documentation is likely to be in English and that if you have to make a claim it will be processed in English. There are some Italian companies that also have the facility for dealing with claims in English. This should not be under-estimated as an advantage. Unless your Italian is fluent you would otherwise have to employ somebody to deal with the claim on your behalf or to translate what you have said into Italian – something that is never entirely satisfactory.

Taxation

All tax systems are complicated. The Italian system is no exception. It is helpful to have some sort of understanding about the way in which the system works and the taxes that you might face. Be warned: getting even a basic understanding will make your head hurt. You also need to be particularly careful about words and concepts that seem familiar to you but have a fundamentally different meaning in Italy. Of course, the rules change every year.

The contents of the following pages are only a general introduction to the subject. Books (and lengthy ones at that) have been written about the subject of Italian taxation. This general introduction does little more than scratch the surface of an immensely complex subject. It is intended to enable you to have a sensible discussion with your professional advisers and, perhaps, help you work out the questions that you need to be asking them. It is *not* intended as a substitute for proper professional advice.

Your situation when you have a foot in two countries – and, in particular, when you are moving permanently from one country to another – involves the consideration of the tax systems in both countries with a view to minimizing your tax obligations in both. It is not just a question of paying the lowest amount of tax in, say, Italy. The best choice in Italy could be very damaging to your position in the UK, and vice versa. The task of the international adviser and his client is to find a path of compromise that allows you to enjoy the major advantages available in both countries without incurring any of the worst drawbacks. In other words, there is an issue of compromise.

What should guide you when making a decision as to which course to pursue? Each individual will have a different set of priorities. Some are keen to screw the last ha'penny of advantage out of their situation. Others recognize that they will have to pay some tax but simply wish to moderate their tax bill. For many, the main concern is a simple structure that they understand and can continue to manage without further assistance in the years ahead. Just as different clients have different requirements, so different advisers have differing views as to the function of the adviser when dealing with a client's tax affairs. One of your first tasks when speaking to your financial adviser should be to discuss your basic philosophy concerning the payment of tax and management of your affairs, to make sure that you are both operating with the same objective and that you are comfortable with his or her approach to solving your problem.

Are You Resident or Non-resident for Tax Purposes?

The biggest single factor in determining how you will be treated by the tax authorities in any country is whether or not you are resident in that country for tax purposes. This concept of tax residence causes a great deal of confusion.

Tax residence can have different meanings in different countries. In Italy tax residence is known as *domicilio fiscale*.

Let us first look at what it does not mean. It is nothing to do with whether you have registered as resident in a country or obtained a residency permit or residency card (though a person who has a card will usually be tax resident). Nor does it have anything to do with whether or not you simply have a home (residence) in that country – although a person who is tax resident will normally have a home there. Nor is it much to do with your intentions.

Tax residence is a question of fact. The law lays down certain tests that will be used to decide whether you are tax resident or not. If you fall into the categories stipulated in the tests then you will be considered tax resident whether you want to be or not and whether it was your intention to be tax resident or not.

It is your responsibility to make your tax declarations each year. The decision as to whether or not you fall into the category of resident is, in the first instance, made by the tax office. If you disagree with the decision you can appeal through the courts.

Because people normally change their tax residence when they move from one country to another, the basis upon which decisions are made tends to be regulated by international law and is pretty, but not totally, consistent from country to country.

The Rules that Determine Residence

You will have to consider two different questions concerning tax residence. The first is if you will be treated as tax resident in the UK and the second is if you will be treated as tax resident in Italy.

UK

It is outside the scope of this book to go into any details about UK taxation but some basic points will have to be dealt with for the explanation of Italian taxation to make any sense.

In the UK there are two tests that will help determine where you pay tax. These assess your domicile and your residence.

Domicile

Your domicile is the place that is your real home. It is the place where you have your roots. For most people it is the place where they were born. You can change your domicile but it is often not easy to do so. Changes in domicile can have far-reaching tax consequences and can be a useful tax reduction tool.

Residence

Residence falls into two categories. Under English law there is a test of simple residence – actually living here other than on a purely temporary basis – and of ordinary residence.

A person will generally be treated as **resident** in the UK if he spends 183 or more days per year in the UK. A visitor will also be treated as resident if he comes to the UK regularly and spends significant time here. If he spends, on average over a period of four or more years, more than three months here he will be treated as tax resident.

A person can continue to be **ordinarily resident** in the UK even after he has stopped actually being resident here. A person is ordinarily resident in the UK if his presence is a little more settled. The residence is an important part of his life. It will normally have gone on for some time.

The most important thing to understand is that, once you have been ordinarily resident in the UK, the simple fact of going overseas will not automatically bring that residence to an end. If you leave this country in order to take up permanent residence elsewhere then, by concession, the Inland Revenue will treat you as ceasing to be resident on the day following your departure. However, they will not treat you as ceasing to be ordinarily resident if, after leaving, you spend an average of 91 or more days per year in this country over any four-year period. In other words, they don't want you to escape too easily!

Until 1993 you were also classified as ordinarily resident in the UK if you had accommodation available for your use in the UK even though you may have spent 364 days of the year living abroad. This very unfair rule was cancelled but many people still worry about it. It is not necessary to do so provided you limit your visits to the UK to less than the 91 days referred to above.

Italy

Tax residence in Italy – *domicilio fiscale* – is tested by a number of rules, the main ones of which are as follows:

• If your main home is in Italy you will be classified as resident there however much – or little – time you spend there. If you have been classified as a resident in your *comune* – which gives you various tax advantages – you will be classified as resident for all tax purposes.

• If you spend more than 183 days in Italy in any tax year, you are tax resident in Italy. This time can be in one block or in bits and pieces through the year. The tax year runs from 1 January to 31 December.

- If your centre of economic interests is in Italy, you are tax resident in Italy. Your centre of economic interests is where you have your main investments or business or other sources of income and, usually, where you spend much of your money.

- If you work in Italy, except where that work is ancillary to work elsewhere, you will be tax resident in Italy.

- If you have an Italian residency card you will be *usually* be tax resident in Italy.

- If your family is resident in Italy you will be *assumed* to be resident in Italy unless you show the contrary. If you satisfy the taxman that you are not resident in Italy then you will pay tax on your income and assets as a non-resident but your husband/wife will pay taxes on their income and assets as a resident.

Tax Residence in More than One Country

Remember that you can be tax resident in more than one country under the respective rules of those countries. For example, you might spend 230 days of the year in Italy and 135 days in the UK. In this case you could end up, under the rules of each country, being responsible for paying the same tax in two or more countries. This would be unfair so many countries have signed reciprocal 'Double Taxation Treaties'. The UK and Italy have such a treaty. It contains 'tie-breakers' and other provisions to decide, where there is the possibility of being required to pay tax twice, in which country any particular category of tax should be paid. *See* 'Double Taxation Treaties', p.176.

Decisions You Must Make

The most basic decision that you will have to make when planning your tax affairs is whether or not to cease to be resident in the UK, whether or not to cease to be ordinarily resident in this country and whether or not to change your domicile to another country.

The second consideration is when in the tax year to make these changes. That decision has many consequences.

For many ordinary people getting these decisions wrong can cost them tens of thousands of pounds in totally unnecessary taxation and a great deal of irritation and inconvenience. It is vital that you seek proper professional advice before making these decisions. You will need advice from specialist lawyers, accountants or financial advisers, all of whom should be able to help you.

Taxes Payable in the UK

The significance of these residence rules is that you will continue to be liable for some British taxes for as long as you are either ordinarily resident or domiciled in UK. Put far too simply, even once you have left the UK to live in Italy:

- you will continue to have to pay tax in the UK on any capital gains you make anywhere in the world for as long as you are ordinarily resident and domiciled in United Kingdom

- you will continue to be liable to British inheritance tax on all of your assets located anywhere in the world for as long as you remain domiciled here – this will be subject to double taxation relief – and other more complex rules apply in certain circumstances

- you will always pay UK income tax (Schedule A) on income arising from land and buildings in the UK – wherever your domicile, residence or ordinary residence

- you will pay UK income tax (Schedule D) on the following basis:

    - income from 'self-employed' trade or profession carried out in the UK (Cases I & II) – normally taxed in the UK in all cases if income arises in the UK

    - income from interest, annuities or other annual payments from the UK (Case III) – normally taxed in the UK if income arises in the UK and you are ordinarily resident in the UK

    - income from investments and businesses outside the UK (Cases IV & V) – normally only taxed in the UK if you are UK domiciled and resident or ordinarily resident in the UK

    - income from government pensions (fire, police, army, civil servant, etc.) in all cases

    - sundry profits not otherwise taxable (Case VI) arising out of land or building in the UK are always taxed in the UK

- you will pay income tax on any income earned from salaried employment in the UK (Schedule E) only in respect of any earnings from duties performed in the UK unless you are resident and ordinarily resident in the UK – in which case you will usually pay tax in the UK on your worldwide earnings

If you are only buying a holiday home and will remain primarily resident in the UK, your tax position in the UK will not change very much. You will have to declare any income you make from your Italian property as part of your UK tax declaration. The calculation of tax due on that income will be made in accordance with UK rules, which will result in a different taxable sum than is used by the Italian authorities. The UK taxman will give you full credit for the taxes already paid in Italy.

On the disposal of the property you should disclose the profit made to the UK taxman. He will again give full credit for Italian tax paid. Similarly, on your death the assets in Italy must be disclosed on the UK probate tax declaration but, once again, you will be given full credit for sums paid in Italy.

Paying Tax in Italy

Under Italian law it is your responsibility to fill in a tax return in each year when you have any taxable income unless that income is:

- **taxed in full at source**
- **outside the scope of Italian tax**

The tax office (*ufficio delle imposte*) provides a lot of help and advice over the internet. It is, not surprisingly, almost all in Italian.

It is probably simplest to arrange for an **accountant** (*commercialista*) to complete and file your various tax returns as these are complicated and in Italian. There are many different deadlines for payment of the various taxes.

Local Italian Taxes

Both residents and non-residents pay these taxes. The taxes payable fall into various categories.

ICI (*Imposta Comunale sugli Immobili*)

The ICI is paid if you own a residential property and use it yourself (or have it available for your use). It is paid by the person who occupied the property on 1 January in any year. It is not usually apportioned if they later move.

The tax is raised and spent by the town hall (*municipio*) of the area where you live. It is calculated on the basis of the notional rental value (*valore catastale*) of your property. You can appeal against the valuation decision, but the sums involved are usually so small it is not worthwhile.

The amount you will be charged will be the rental value multiplied by the tax rate fixed in your locality. This will vary between 0.4 per cent and 0.8 per cent depending mainly on the category into which your house falls – as shown in your deed of sale (*rogito*).

The sum claimed must be paid in two instalments by the specified dates, one by 30 June (90 per cent of the sum) and the other between 1 and 20 December (the remaining 10 per cent). Those who fail to pay on time can be fined up to 200 per cent of the amount due.

These taxes are generally low, perhaps £100 for a country cottage or £300 for an apartment in an average area. For uninhabitable structures and properties, *ICI* is reduced by 50 per cent.

Refuse Tax (*Tassa Rifiuti*)

Rubbish collection charges are, in some areas, raised separately.

Other Local Taxes

Town halls can also raise taxes for other projects and to cover shortfalls. You will also pay car tax (*bollo auto*), scooter tax (*bollo moto*) and a variety of other asset-focused taxes – including TV tax, *see* p.188.

Other Taxes Payable in Italy – Non-residents

In general a person who is non-resident for tax purposes has few contacts with the Italian tax system and they are fairly painless.

Income Tax (*Imposta sul Reddito delle Persone Fisiche – IRPEF*)

As a non-resident you will generally only pay tax on the following.

- **Income generated from land and buildings located in Italy. If you own a building in Italy and rent it out, the Italian government collects the first wedge of tax from you.**
- **Income from Italian securities and capital invested in Italy.**
- **Income from business activities in Italy.**
- **Earned income if you are employed or self-employed in Italy.**

Income tax is calculated on these amounts at rates varying from 18.1% to 45.1%. Note that if you are renting out your property you will usually have the normal deductions or allowances to set against your income.

You must file the tax return (available from the tax office's website). This must generally be filed by 30 June for the period ending 31 December of the previous year. Tax on your income for the year 1 January 2004 to 31 December 2004 is declared and paid in May/June 2005.

Corporation Tax

A company will pay tax on the profits it makes from activities in Italy but not its activities elsewhere.

Taxes on Wealth

There is no Italian wealth tax.

Taxes on Capital Gains

- **On the sale of real estate (*imposta comunale sull'incremento di immobili – INVIM*):** Unless you bought your house before 1993 *and* you sell it before 2003 there is no capital gains tax on the sale of real estate.

- **Stocks and Shares:** The gain (the difference between the sale price and the purchase price adjusted to take account of inflation since the date of purchase) will usually be taxed at 12.5 per cent. You can offset any losses.

- **Other Gains:** You will pay tax on the capital gain you make on the sale of any other capital asset, less various exempt items. The gain is taxed as if it were income for the year in question. Payment of the tax on the gain can usually be spread over five years.

Taxes on Death (*Imposta sulle Successioni e Donazioni – ISD*)

This was abolished in October 2001. There is a strong feeling that this is a political gimmick and that it will be reinstated. It is therefore worth looking at the rules prevailing before October 2001; *see* p.175.

Stamp Duty

Many documents need an official stamp (*marca da bollo*), *see* p.111. These are normally about €10. They are bought from the tobacconist.

Other Taxes Payable in Italy – Residents

The Italian tax system is very complex. What follows can only be a very brief summary of the position. The detail is immensely complicated and is made worse because it is so different from what you are used to.

Income Tax (*Imposta sul Reddito delle Persone Fisiche – IRPEF*)

As a permanent resident in Italy you will generally pay tax on your worldwide income – including benefits in kind – from all sources. There are one or two sources of income exempt from tax, the most significant of which are certain social security and invalidity benefits.

Types of Income Tax

Income is divided, as in the UK, into various categories. Each category of income is subject to different rules and allowances. Remember that Italy is (taken overall, not just in relation to income tax) a high-tax society. There are, however, quite legitimate tax-saving devices that you can use to reduce your liabilities. These issues are best addressed *before* you move to Italy as there are then many more possibilities open to you.

See also **Working in Italy**.

Income from Employment (Including Unemployment Benefits)

The income is your total income including all benefits in kind.

Certain items are excluded when calculating income. These include:

- **various personal allowances**
- **certain mortgage allowances**
- **any payments made to the Italian social security scheme**, *see* p.211
- **certain medical insurance payments**
- **limited pension fund contributions**
- **certain expenses related to your work**

There is a type of PAYE in operation whereby your likely tax liability is collected in 12 equal instalments with a final annual adjustment either way. A contributions to the health care system (SSN), which in Italy is separate from social security benefits (*previdenza sociale*), is included in this tax.

Income from Self-employment

See **Working in Italy**. There are various different ways in which tax is calculated for the self-employed. You may be:

- **a *collaboratore*, in which case you are treated more or less as an employee**

- a *lavoratore occasionale* (casual worker) where you are paid your fee less a standard 20 per cent deduction

- a *libero professionista* (consultant or professional) where you must register for VAT and where your clients will make a 20 per cent retention for withholding tax and you submit accounts claiming a credit for that tax already paid

Business Income

This includes income as an entrepreneur where you operate in some form of structure such as a partnership. *See* **Working in Italy**, p.256.

Income from Land and Buildings

This includes rental income. The usual deductions for management, repairs and depreciation are allowed. The resulting sum is taxed as normal income. If you let out your property you will need an accountant. You will then probably find that, after all allowances, little tax is payable! There is also a tax on a notional income based on the mere fact that you own real estate. This is based on the *valore catastale* of your property.

Dividends and Interest Payments

Subject to various allowances, these are taxed as normal income.

Sundry Other Income

Deductions from Taxable Income

From your gross income you can deduct:

- any compulsory payments made to the Italian social security scheme

- payments made by way of financial provision for a separated or divorced spouse or children

Tax Rates

Tax payable is calculated in tranches. That is, you calculate the tax payable on each complete slice and then the tax at the highest applicable rate on any excess. Taxes are paid partly to the national government and partly to the regional government.

Tax Credits

Various tax credits are available. These are deducted from the tax otherwise payable as calculated above.

The rules are complex. They include credits for:

- various personal allowances

- certain mortgage allowances in respect of your primary residence

- limited pension fund contributions

- limited life insurance premiums

- certain expenses related to your work
- certain medical and funeral expenses
- certain university tuition fees
- tax paid abroad (or part of it) on income also taxable in Italy

The personal allowances are complicated and include the following.

- **For you: an allowance that varies depending on your taxable income and whether you are employed or self-employed. This will vary between €50 and €1,000.**

- **For your dependent spouse – i.e. a spouse earning less than about €3,000 per year: an allowance that varies, depending on your joint income, between about €400 and €600.**

- **For each of your dependent children under 18: about €105. Double if you are a single parent.**

If you are a pensioner with no other income there are additional allowances.

If you are married and have income of less than about £2,000 per year you can file a joint return. The allowances are then split between you.

See your adviser.

Payment of Tax Due

If you are not exempt from submitting a tax return, you must complete your tax form.

If you are self-employed you must file the *dichiarazione dei redditi* (tax return) otherwise known as the *modulo unico*. This was formerly known as form 740. This must be filed by 31 July for the period ending 31 December of the previous year. Tax on your income for the year 1 January 2004 to 31 December 2004 is declared and paid 2005. Late submission incurs a substantial penalty.

Most other people, including the employed – if they have to file a tax return at all – will use form 730, which is a lot simpler.

You must make an advance payment of tax equal to 100 per cent of the tax calculated for the year or 98 per cent of the tax paid the previous year, whichever is the lower. Of this payment, 40 per cent is payable by 31 May with the balance being payable by 30 November.

Business Tax (*Imposta Regionale sulle Attivita Produttive – IRAP*)

Levied on all types of business activity, this is a tax based on the profit of the business *before allowing for labour costs*. It is charged at a rate fixed by each region – normally four per cent. It pays for health care for you and your employees.

Taxes on Wealth

There is no Italian wealth tax.

Taxes on Capital Gains

• **On the sale of real estate (***imposta comunale sull'incremento di immobili –*** INVIM):** Unless you bought your house before 1993 *and* you sell it before 2003 there is no capital gains tax on the sale of real estate.

• **Stocks and shares:** The gain (the difference between the sale price and the purchase price adjusted to take account of inflation since the date of purchase) will usually be taxed at 12.5 per cent.

If the gain is from the sale of a company quoted on the stock exchange and you sell more than two per cent of the capital *or* the company is not quoted on the stock exchange and you sell more than 20 per cent of the capital the rate is 27 per cent.

You can offset any losses.

• **Other Gains:** You will pay tax on the capital gain you make on the sale of any other capital asset, less various exempt items.

The gain is taxed as if it were income for the year in question. Payment of the tax on the gain can usually be spread over five years.

Taxes on Death (*Imposta sulle Successioni e Donazioni – ISD*)

This was abolished in October 2001. There is a strong feeling that this is a political gimmick and that it will be reinstated. It is therefore worth looking at the rules prevailing before October 2001. If you were domiciled in Italy then inheritance tax was paid in Italy on the value of any assets that you owned anywhere in the world at the date of your death.

The tax was an inheritance tax rather than, as in the UK, an estate tax. That is, the tax was calculated by reference to each individual's inheritance rather than on the basis of the estate as a whole. Thus two people each inheriting part of the estate would each have paid their own tax. Even if they each inherited the same amount, the tax they would have paid on the sum received would have been different, depending on their personal circumstances.

The overall value of the part of the estate you inherited was calculated in accordance with guidelines laid down by the tax authorities. Assets were generally valued as at the date of the death. The value was declared by the person who inherited but was subject to challenge by the tax authorities. Any debts (including mortgage or overdraft) were deducted from the asset values.

Some gifts – mainly to the State and various charitable organizations – were partly tax exempt. The tax rates on the taxable amount of any gift to you depended on your relationship to the deceased and the amount you inherited.

The tax was calculated in slices. The basic tax was paid in every case. If there was more than one beneficiary it was split between them pro rata to the value of their inheritance. Also, additional tax may have been payable. The rate depended on your relationship to the deceased. No additional tax was payable if you are the spouse, child or parent of the deceased.

- Group A – brothers and sisters and direct relatives.
- Group B – relatives closer than the 4th degree.
- Group C – other more distant relatives and unrelated persons – including common law wives and gay partners.

For example, a gift to a stranger (who is the sole beneficiary) of €70,000 used to bear tax at three different rates:

- first €5,000 – tax free
- next €45,000 – 6%
- balance to €70,000 – 8%

VAT

The normal VAT rate is 20 per cent. Lower rates apply to particular types of supply.

Stamp Duty

Many documents need an official stamp (*marca da bollo*). These are normally about €10. They are bought from the tobacconist.

New Residents

New residents will be liable to tax on their worldwide income and gains from the date they arrive in Italy. Until that day they will only have to pay Italian tax on their income if it is derived from assets in Italy.

The most important thing to understand about taking up residence in Italy (and abandoning UK tax residence) is that it gives you superb opportunities for tax planning and, in particular, for restructuring your affairs to minimize what can otherwise be penal rates of taxation in Italy. To do this you need good advice at an early stage – preferably several months before you intend to move.

Double Taxation Treaty

The detailed effect of double taxation treaties depends on the two countries involved. Whilst treaties may be similar in concept they can differ in detail. Only the effect of the Italy/UK treaty is considered here.

The main points of relevance to residents are these.

- **Any income from letting property in the UK will normally be outside the scope of Italian taxation and, instead, will be taxed in the UK.**
- **Pensions received from the UK – except for government pensions – will be taxed in Italy but not in the UK.**
- **Government pensions will continue to be taxed in the UK but are not taxed in Italy, nor do they count when assessing the level of your income or when calculating the rate of tax payable on your income.**
- **You will normally not be required to pay UK capital gains tax on gains made after you settle in Italy except in relation to real estate in the UK.**

- If you are taxed on a gift made outside Italy then the tax paid will usually be offset against the gift tax due in Italy.

- If you pay tax on an inheritance outside Italy, the same will apply.

Double tax treaties are detailed and need to be read in the light of your personal circumstances, so it is suggested that you get professional help.

Tax Planning Generally

Do it and do it as soon as possible. Every day you delay will make it more difficult to get the results you are looking for.

There are many possibilities for tax planning for someone moving to Italy. Here are some points worth considering.

- Time your departure from the UK to get the best out of the UK tax system.

- Think, in particular, about when to make any capital gain if you are selling your business or other assets in the UK.

- Arrange your affairs so that there is a gap between leaving the UK (for tax purposes) and becoming resident in Italy. That gap can be used to make all sorts of beneficial changes to the structure of your finances.

- Think about trusts. They can be very effective tax-planning vehicles.

- Think about giving away some of your assets. You will not have to pay wealth tax on the value given away and the recipients will generally not have to pay either gift or inheritance tax on the gift.

Investments

Most of us don't like making investment decisions. They make our heads hurt. They make us face up to unpleasant things – like taxes and death. We don't really understand what we are doing, what the options are or what is best. We don't know who we should trust to give us advice. We know we ought to do something, but it will wait until next week – or maybe the week after. Until then our present arrangements will have to do.

If you are moving to live overseas you must review your investments. Your current arrangements are likely to be financially disastrous – and may even be illegal.

What Are You Worth?

Most of us are, in financial terms, worth more than we think. When we come to move abroad and have to think about these things it can come as a shock.

Take a piece of paper and list your actual and potential assets. Think of your current assets. These may include your main home and its contents, holiday home and its contents, car, boat, bank accounts, other cash-type investments, bonds, stocks and shares, PEPs, Tessas, ISAs, SIPS, the value of your business and the value of your share options. Also think of future assets – value of share options, personal or company pension (likely lump sum), potential inheritances or other accretions, value of endowment mortgages on maturity, and so forth.

This will give you an idea as to the amount you are worth now and, just as importantly, what you are likely to be worth in the future. Your investment plans should take into account both figures.

Who Should Look After Your Investments?

You may already have an investment adviser. You may be very happy with the service you have received. But they are unlikely to be able to help you once you have gone to live in Italy. They will almost certainly not have the knowledge to do so. They will know about neither the Italian investment that might be of interest to you nor, probably, of many of the 'offshore' products that might be of interest to someone no longer resident in the UK. Even if they have some knowledge of these things, they are likely to be thousands of miles from where you will be living.

Nor is it a simple question of selecting a new local (Italian) adviser once you have moved. They will usually know little about the UK aspects of your case or about the UK tax and inheritance rules that could still have some importance for you.

Choosing an investment adviser competent to deal with you once you are in Italy is not easy. By all means seek guidance from your existing adviser. Ask for guidance from others who have already made the move. Do some research. Meet the potential candidates. Are you comfortable with them? Do they share your approach to life? Do they have the necessary experience? Is their performance record good? How are they regulated? What security/bonding/ guarantees can they offer you? How will they be paid for their work – fees or commission? If commission, what will that formula mean they are making from you in 'real money' rather than percentages?

Above all, be careful. There are lots of very dubious 'financial advisers' oper-ating in the popular tourist areas of Italy. Some are totally incompetent. Some are crooks, seeking simply to separate you from your money.

Fortunately there are also some excellent and highly professional advisers with good track records. Make sure you choose one of these.

Where Should You Invest?

For British people the big issue is whether they should keep their sterling investments. Most British people will have investments that are largely sterling based. Even if they are, for example, a Far Eastern fund they will probably be denominated in sterling and they will pay out dividends, etc. in sterling.

You will be spending euros. As the value of the euro fluctuates against sterling, the value of your investments will go up and down. That, of itself, isn't too important because the value won't crystallize unless you sell. What does matter is that the revenue you generate from those investments (rent, interest, dividends, etc.) will fluctuate in value.

This is unacceptable, particularly as you will inevitably have to accept this problem in so far as your pension is concerned. In general terms investments paying out in euros are preferable if you live in a euro country.

Trusts

Trusts are an important weapon in the hands of the person going to live in Italy. Trusts offer the following potential benefits.

- **Allowing you to put part of your assets in the hands of trustees so that they no longer belong to you for wealth tax or inheritance tax purposes.**

- **Allowing you to receive only the income you need (rather than all the income generated by those assets) so keeping the extra income out of sight for income tax purposes.**

- **Allowing a very flexible vehicle for investment purposes.**

So how do these little wonders work? After leaving the UK (and before moving to Italy) you reorganize your affairs by giving a large part of your assets to 'trustees'. These are normally a professional trust company located in a low-tax regime. The choice of a reliable trustee is critical.

Those trustees hold the asset not for their own benefit but 'in trust' for whatever purposes you established when you made the gift. It could, for example, be to benefit a local hospital or, more likely, school or it could be to benefit you and your family. If the trust is set up properly in the light of the requirements of Italian law then those assets will no longer be treated as yours for tax purposes.

On your death the assets are not yours to leave to your children (or whoever) and so do not (subject to any local anti-avoidance legislation) carry inheritance tax. Similarly, the income from those assets is not your income. If some of it is given to you it may be taxed as your income, but the income that is not given to you will not be taxed in Italy and, because the trust will be located in a nil-/low-tax regime, it will not be taxed elsewhere either.

The detail of the arrangements is vitally important. They must be set up precisely to comply with Italian tax law. If you do not do this. they will not work as intended.

Trustees can manage your investments in (virtually) whatever way you stipulate when you set up the trust. You can give the trustees full discretion to do as they please or you can specify precisely how your money is to be used. There are particular types of trusts and special types of investments that trusts can make that can be especially beneficial in Italy.

Trusts can be beneficial even to Italian resident people of modest means – say £350,000. It is certainly worth investing a little money to see if they can be of use to you, as the tax savings can run to many thousands of pounds. If you are thinking of trusts as an investment vehicle and tax-planning measure you must take advice early – months before you are thinking of moving to Italy. Otherwise it will be too late.

Keeping Track of Your Investments

Whatever you decide to do about investments – put them in a trust, appoint investment managers to manage them in your own name or manage them yourself – you should always keep an up-to-date list of your assets and investments and tell your family where to find it. Make a file. By all means have a computer file but print off a good old-fashioned paper copy. Keep it in an obvious place known to your family. Keep it with your will and the deeds to your house. Also keep in it either the originals of bank account books, share certificates, etc., or a note of where they are to be found.

As a lawyer it is very frustrating – and expensive for the client – when, after the parents' death, the children come in with a suitcase full of correspondence and old cheque books. It all has to be gone through and all those old banks contacted lest there should be £1,000,000 lurking in a forgotten account. There never is, and it wastes a lot of time and money.

Home Utilities

Understanding bills and billing can be as challenging as deciphering the Red Sea Scrolls, though much is being done to simplify the process as major utilities undergo privatization.

Payment

There are three main ways to pay your utilities, and unfortunately none of them involves sending off a cheque. Instead, a good amount of footwork may be required. Bills usually come every two months or quarterly depending on the service. Utilities are paid in cash or by bank transfer. No other financial instruments are accepted.

- **Pay at the utility company**: This is highly inconvenient because it usually means trekking across town at dawn to wait in a queue with everybody else.

• **Pay at the post office**: This is the way most Italians pay their bills. Bring your remittance slip from the utility company and the amount due in cash and wait in line at one of the *sportelli* (service windows) to make your payment. Based on the *conto corrente* number on your slip, the post office knows where to send your money. Keep your receipt handy as proof of payment. The post office is not only where you pay household bills, you can pay taxes and even magazine subscriptions there. However, you cannot pay more than four bills at a time. If you have more than that, pay the first batch and head back to the end of the queue for a second round. Most post offices also accept payment by *bancomat*, or a cash debit card (not a credit card).

• **Pay through your bank**: The easiest way to handle utility bills, especially if you do not live in Italy year-round, is to have your Italian bank pay them for you via automatic *bonifico bancario* or wire transfer. You pay a few euros in fees each time a bill is processed, but you save having to go to the post office every few months. The bank will keep track of payments on your statement and the utility company will also send you a receipt for payment. Make sure to keep enough money in your account, as utility companies are very quick to pull the plug on services if a payment request is refused due to lack of funds. They will first send you a warning letter, but if you are not in the country to read it you won't be warned.

• **Internet**: You cannot yet pay your bills on the internet, although this will probably change soon. However, you can keep track of your expenditure and account online. You can check your electricity usage on **www.enel.it**, by clicking on *controlla e paga*. The website for water (and also sometimes electricity, *see* below) **www.aceaspa**. It is not as user-friendly, but you can send your meter readings to them electronically, and there is a list of helpful phone numbers under *telefoni utili*. The website **www.italgas.it** (or the more direct **www.italgasclienti.it**) also lets you check usage and bills online. Many foreigners set up automatic payment through their bank and check that it has gone through from abroad via the internet. You will need to sign on to all the above web pages with a user ID and password, and will need account information found on your bill and your *codice fiscale* number to set this up.

If you need to dispute a bill, don't count on an easy ride. The best thing to do is never get to this point by regularly and religiously checking your meter and comparing notes with what you are billed by the utility company.

Electricity

The 1998 deregulation of Italy's largest electric utility, **Ente Nazionale per l'Energia (Enel)**, has effectively failed to reduce electricity costs. **Acea Spa** is Italy's second-largest electricity distribution company (and water supplier) after Enel made a push to simplify the billing process and give the crusty old industry

Calling Acea

Dial **t** 800 130330 and you will hear:

'Siete in linea con Acea Spa servizio clienti.

Per contratti, disdette, aumento o diminuzione di potenza, e variazioni di recapito, digitate sulla vostra tastiera 1.

Per informazione sul bollette, digitate 2.

Per inviare la lettura del misuratore, avere informazioni sulle fatture emesse o comunicare il pagamento delle fatture insolute, digitate 3.'

'You are connected to Acea Spa customer service.

For contracts, cancellations, voltage increase or decrease and change of address, press 1 on your phone.

For billing information, press 2.

To register usage, or get information on past or outstanding bills, press 3.'

An operator will come on after some wait, if a real person is needed. Asking for an English-speaking operator may be futile, but worth a try.

a sleeker appearance with automated billing, online services and a 24-hour 800 (freephone) number. Enel, too, has modernized its operations. Depending on where you are living, the electricity bill that arrives will be from Enel (**t** 800 114499, **www.enel.it**) or Acea (**t** 800 130330, **www.aceaspa.it**).

Meters are read randomly. You are recommended to read your own meter and dial the toll free number of your provider to give them the reading. This easy process guarantees that you will be billed for what you consume, instead of an average, which is never accurate. If your consumption is higher than the amount you have paid for, you must pay the difference or, what is more likely, if the average you pay is higher than the amount you have used, and you are due a refund, you will have to check whether or not your subsequent bill is credited. Easier said than done.

Water

Three-quarters of Italy is lapped by water, and there is plenty of water in the land itself, which has numerous lakes, rivers, streams and glaciers. Italy is a land of mariners and sea-lovers, enthusiastic drinkers of mineral waters, and wielders of *l'arte d'acqua* expressed through millions of decorative fountains throughout the peninsula.

Despite the obsessive presence of bottled water, Italians swear that their drinking water is among the purest on earth. And they are right. The mass consumption of *acqua minerale* is a matter of taste and habit, not a sign that tap (*rubinetto*) water is non-drinkable.

Prices, once you start paying your bills, can be a choker, however. The 2003 OECD *Economic Survey of Italy* notes that in some areas water prices are cheap by international standards, but the level of service is low. In fact water prices vary greatly, depending on where you are, what kind of home set-up you have (private house, apartment) and what your level of use is. Each municipality (*comune*) sets usage rules, and water is supplied by Azienda Communale Energia e Ambiente (**Acea**) – the same company that provides electricity. *See* 'Electricity', above.

Private homes will probably have a meter (*contatore*) installed at the owner's expense. This goes especially for northern Italy. Users pre-reserve the amount of water that they estimate to consume throughout the year (measured in cubic metres). If consumption exceeds that amount, there will be another and higher rate for the extra they have used. A separate contract for different usage (*uso vario*) must be taken out for irrigation or swimming pools.

By the same measure, apartment complexes (*condomínii*) have communal water meters, so the cost you pay is divided among the home owners (*condómini*) in the building. If your home is just for holiday use, that could be an extra expense to consider.

For rural inhabitants, several cost-saving options are available. One is to have your garden and/or pool water supplied by tankers (*autobotte*). Many country homes have a water basin (*cisterna*) that collects water during the rainy seasons to be used during the dry months. If your property already has a well (*pozzo*), have it checked for bacteria levels. If the local health department certifies it (don't trust anyone but the health department here) as drinkable (*potabile*), then you have an extra resource. If not, test it for salt levels or any other antagonistic garden substances, and if the authorities give you the green light, your plants and flowers will be all the happier for it.

Gas

Considerably less expensive than electricity, gas is supplied by the company **Italgas** (**t** 800 900 700, **www.italgaspiu.it**). There are several uses for locally produced methane, which is one of Italy's few natural resources.

Heating (*riscaldamento*) can be either *autonomo* or *centrale/condominiale*. *Autonomo* means you have control over your heating and can turn it off and on

Air-conditioning

Air-conditioning is considered a luxury item in Italy and is consequently expensive to install and operate (this will be reflected in your electricity bills). However, once you have spent a sleepless night in Milan at the end of July (you can't open windows to cool down otherwise vicious mosquitoes will turn you into a bloody pulp) you'll run to the nearest electrical appliance shop. It is highly recommended that you install air-conditioning, especially if you are buying a home for retirement or expect to have elderly visitors.

at will since you have your own boiler (*caldaia*). Many apartment buildings, instead, have *riscaldamento centrale* or *condominiale*, which means that your body temperature is in the hands of your building administrator. In northern towns, where the cold weather is harsher and lasts longer than in the south, they take their heating seriously. But in the central-south, where homes are built to stand the heat and stay cool, having your heating controlled by an apartment administrator can lead to some shivery winters. Having a spare heater (*stufetta*) on hand is never a bad idea.

With *autonomo* heating, keep your *caldaia* maintenance in mind. Plan yearly check-ups by the producer of your boiler, or the store where it was purchased. The *caldaia* also heats your water.

Most cookers run on gas, and have a direct line that feeds into the appliance, with a knob that cuts the supply. If leaving your residence, even for a short time, it is wise to turn off the gas. Some older homes and remote, country residences have tanked gas (*bombole/bomboloni*) in cylinders, which are refillable and changed when they run out. Weapon-looking, metal bottles are delivered to your doorstep or you can stock up yourself if you have storage space.

In case of suspicious gas odours, immediately call the Italgas **t** 800 number, or the fire department emergency **t** 115 and explain that you may have a leak (*una perdita di gas*).

Telephone

There's no greater dinosaur than **Telecom Italia**. Years of state monopoly management are hard to shake off and, despite burgeoning competition, all lines (or most) lead to Telecom (**t** 187, **www.telecomitalia.it**). At least for now.

Some competitors are now able to take over the entire billing process, therefore eliminating the need to deal with Telecom. **Wind**, through its internet service **Libero** (**t** 155, **www.wind.it** or **www.libero.it**), is one company that offers ADSL lines, internet packages and special phone rates. **Vodafone Omnitel** is another option (**t** 190, **www.vodafone.it**).

In some parts of Italy, fibre optic cables are being laid, though at a slow rate. The company that can wire your home and eventually save you from Telecom, **Fastweb** (**www.fastweb.it**), can either pull in a fibre optic wire to your home or adapt your existing Telecom line to become ADSL. Fastweb is controlled by **eBiscom** (**www.ebiscom.it**).

Exorbitant telephone costs can be kept at bay without changing over from Telecom by using low-cost alternative services. You'll have to dial a number first, and then will be billed separately, and receive a Telecom bill. One of these alternatives is the Canadian company **Ultranet** (**t** (416) 588 7054, **www.ultranet-telecom.com**). Once your service is activated, the line is accessed by dialing **t** 1077, or your phone can be adapted so it automatically uses the service. Wind has the same type of service (**t** 155, **www.wind.it**) and their dialling number is **t**

1055. Tobacconists and newsagents sell calling cards that are cheap and well worth the effort it takes to scratch them.

Remember, if you have Telecom, bills are not itemized (*dettagliata*) unless you request them to be.

Mobile Phones

It took the 1990 World Cup to launch the first national cellphone services in Italy, and it has been like a growing madness from there on out. Back then, some 400,000 fans clutched the first mobile technology available, their Tacs-system cell phones, to keep up with the latest scores during Mondiale matches.

Now there are more than 36 million mobile phones in operation in the country. *Il telefonino* is so much the rage that it is debatably vying for first place with *la mamma* in Italians' hearts.

The Tacs dinosaurs have now been replaced by GMS technology, with 2.5 technology and GPRS rolling in steadily. Text or SMS (Short Message Service) sending verges on the manic with over 35 million SMS messages being sent per day. Ringers jingle everything from Dixie to Moby, and electronic games can be downloaded from the internet or by phoning numerous telephone services. Aside from just making life easier in a country that has a functional public phone service deficit, anyone who is someone has a mobile.

Telecom Italia Mobile or TIM (**www.tim.it**) is the leading wireless telecommunications carrier in Italy, with 24 million subscribers, placing it just ahead of the second Italian mobile phone company **Vodafone-Omnitel Italia**

No Cells Allowed

Mobile (*cellulare*) owners are not only increasing in Italy, they are also getting younger. A recent study showed that 56 per cent of Italian children aged 10 years and under own a mobile. Adolescents with *telefonini* shoot up to 93.8 per cent.

Etiquette rules that have been popping up in the form of signs and announcements in restaurants, cinemas and churches for years have now been extended to schools. Not just any school, but elementary schools. Last year an exasperated teacher in Livorno sent a letter to parents requesting children to refrain from bringing their *telefonini* into class. In the end, however, the teacher had to reach a compromise. Her 7-year-old students now chuck their phones into a basket upon entering the classroom in the morning and pick them up during recess and lunch breaks if need be. Worried parents, it seemed, felt that kids should have phones in 'case of emergencies'.

The same study on *bambino*-owned mobiles revealed that the average monthly expenditure of those aged 10 and under was €47. At 52 cents per minute a call, there sure are some emergency-prone kids toddling around.

(**www.vodafoneomnitel.it**). **Wind** (**www.wind.it**) screeches in at third, but is holding its ground, despite its small stake in the abundant Italian market.

Mobile telephones, including the handset, can be purchased and activated at one of the millions of telecommunications shops throughout Italy. You will be able to spot them by the spread of mobile phones gleaming on display, and the numerous stickers and signs of the various mobile companies plastered to their shop windows. To get signed up, show a document and your *codice fiscale* (*see* **Red Tape**, 'The *Codice Fiscale* and *Partita IVA*', p.111). Some shops now let you sign up without a *codice* as the result of a recent regulatory adaptation. However, you will only be allowed to have limited credit on your phone, and must sign up with your *codice* to recharge later on.

If you take out a contract (*contratto*) you will be billed bi-monthly. The charge can be paid at any local post office, or through your bank. There are now direct debit services to your bank or credit card. If you choose a rechargeable (*ricarica-bile*) option, then you can load money on to your phone in several ways – by buying a scratch-off card at news stands or tobacconists, with your ATM card at a bank machine, or by phone with a credit card, if your card company has an active service.

Your UK phone and number will work in Italy, but the cost will knock the breath out of you. A new SIM card can be purchased and used in your present handset without a problem, or keep your UK number and phone on the answering machine mode, and return calls with your Italian mobile for a lower fee. When your Italian mobile is out of credit, you can still receive calls from anywhere in the world, despite not being able to make any.

Internet, Faxes, Post and Television

The Internet

After a slow take-off, the internet is finally catching on. Broadband is helping reduce the internet aversion that many Italians seem to have. As is usually the case, teens and pre-teens have bravely forged ahead, showing the more mature generation that getting tech is not as hard as it may seem.

Though there are plenty of free **internet service providers** (ISPs) in Italy, dialling up is not free. Local calls in Italy cost. But to start with, if you want to get an Italian ISP, there are choices galore. If you are choosing the free route, unless you don't mind changing e-mail addresses often, stick with the bigger providers. The sector is in upheaval and many free ISPs are now charging (like Libero.it, which ironically means 'free'). Also, you can't get away without a *codice fiscale*, one of the few requirements for opening an ISP account. It's also best to have the actual *codice fiscale* card in front of you as you complete the procedure. Your ISP will check your *codice fiscale* information online before giving you an

Free or Low-cost Italian Portals and ISPs

Portals come and go. For an up-to-date look at what is out there, run a search engine check, or go to **www.freedomlist.com**. However, this is a list of servers that was current on publication of this book.

www.aruba.itaruba.it
www.clubnautilus.net
www.clubnet.tin.it
www.freefast.it
www.freepass.it
www.freepop.it
www.i-2000net.it
www.ics-vdc.it
www.infinito.it
www.interfree.it
www.inwind.it
www.jumpy.it
www.kataweb.it
www.libero.it
www.lombardiacom.it
www.monrif.net
www.net4free.it
www.netscream.net
www.nopay.it
www.openaccess.it
www.quipo.it
www.supereva.it
www.tiscalinet.it
www.worldonline.it

account. For example, if you go by the name of 'John Smith' but your *codice fiscale* card reads 'John N. Smith', your request will be denied until you add 'N'.

Some packages, like Telecom Italia's Alice, keep costs low by including ADSL hookup, a flat monthly rate that includes the ADSL line, unlimited navigating hours and an e-mail address. This is preferable to a regular line, and even to an ISDN, as it is cost-effective and much speedier for internet browsing. In some parts of Italy, fibre optic cables have been laid. A company that can either pull in a fibre optic wire to your home or adapt your existing line is **Fastweb** (**www.fastweb.it**), controlled by **eBiscom** (**www.ebiscom.it**).

If you want to keep your UK ISP, check if there are local access numbers in Italy, otherwise you will be paying a fortune to dial up. Some companies can forward your mail from your UK ISP to your new Italian one for a brief period. Or some ISPs can be accessed through the server's website.

Faxes

With an ISDN or ADSL line you can receive faxes while making calls or surfing the web. Otherwise, with an analogue line, remember that slower band rates will run up extra charges in a hurry.

Television

Rai is the state broadcaster and is divided into three main channels – Raiuno, Raidue and Raitre (*see* **Italy Today**, p.67). Italy's three leading private television stations were founded by Silvio Berlusconi, who is now prime minister, and are part of the Mediaset empire. Those six channels make up the core of the Italian national media landscape.

Satellite TV has taken off and there are thousands of shops that will come into your home, rent you a decoder, and get you set up. Be warned, if you have an English credit card, shops will generally not accept it for billing, as an Italian bank-issued card is preferred. Sky is now the exclusive satellite provider and can be reached at **t** 199 100 400 or **www.skytv.it**. Sky Italia is the outcome of a deal completed in April 2003 when News Corp took over the Telepiu platform. Its birth came from the fusion of Telepiu with Stream, in which News Corp had an 80 per cent stake. If you are a Sky user in the UK, you are not authorized to use your UK card in Italy. That doesn't mean that it doesn't happen.

Trash Tax or Television Tax?

In 2001 it was recorded that several towns in southern Italy were almost completely without television. A small hamlet with fewer than 1,000 inhabitants in the region of Calabria had only one television set, owned by the bar on the main strip. These figures, based on state television tax payments, show that either there is a resistance to paying TV tax or that in some areas there aren't many viewers. Many would assume the former assumption is correct.

Technically, the yearly subscription fee (*pagamento canone*) to Rai, for state television is mandatory, and is based on the number of sets per house. It runs at approximately €100 a year and is paid at the post office by filling out the voucher with pre-printed information for *canone* Rai.

Post

Before the Poste Italiana was privatized to become Poste Italiane, Spa., in 1998, it was one of the most frightening of Italian institutions, the land of never-ending queues, crabby personnel and inefficiency. Prospects for the 1998 turnaround were dismal: losses that year totalled $1.3 billion, service was appalling and throughout the monolithic organization there was not a single computer – every transaction was done by hand. All may not be solved now, but a numbered queuing system, air-conditioned branches and financial services run through BancaPosta (generating 45 per cent of Poste Italiane's revenues) have helped pull the institution out of the Middle Ages.

However, there can still be long delays, and not every one of the country's thousands of branches is up to speed. To avoid wasting days at the post office, buy stamps in bulk (€0.41 regular post, €0.62 priority post, both valid in Italy, EU and the world) from the post office or tobacconist. Put letters into the red post boxes outside, and arrange for your bills to be paid through your bank or use your ATM card when possible.

Those two major events are usually carried out through the post office. Or, find a branch in a quiet neighbourhood near you, or somewhere that is easy to reach. Busier areas have more crowded post offices. For information on costs, branches and services, visit the website at **www.poste.it**.

Money and Banking

La banca, Italians will remind you, was invented in Italy. The first cheque was issued through an institute in Prato, and the Florentine Medici family banks had branches as far away as Paris. Italian banks have been making charges for loans since Lombard Lorenzo di Antonio Ridolfi won a case in 1403, which made charging interest legal. As far back as the 14th century, the Republic of Genoa was organizing currency exchange, loans and transfers.

Though some of the present-day procedures – such as issuing a statement (*estratto conto*) only every three months under Italian law, monthly only on request – may be different from what you are used to, essentially Italian banks operate in the same way as most other European banks do. In the 1990s there was a massive privatization of state-owned banks, which led to concentration in the industry and contributed to stock market growth. About two-thirds of the overall market capitalization increase, which grew from 18 to 65 per cent of the GDP (PIL) between 1989 and 1999, was thanks to new listings of privatized companies, many of them banks.

Depending on your needs and how long you plan to stay there are various banking options. Consider opening an account if you're staying in Italy for a significant period of time.

Foreigners opening a bank account are sometimes asked for a residence certificate (*certificato di residenza*), though a *codice fiscale* and your passport or identity card are generally enough. Most banks offer a *conto estero* for non-residents, which means that a *codice fiscale* and a passport are sufficient. The benefits of a *conto estero* are that you can bank in sterling and exchange money as you need it. The account lets you write cheques (*assegni*) in *divisa diversa*, in other words in either euros or sterling. On *conti esteri*, for every transfer of more

Quick Banking Tips

• Get used to writing the date in Italian. The 7th November 2003 is 7/11/03. Remember to cross the '7' so that it is not confused with a '1'.

• Remember that, in Italy, a comma replaces a full stop and vice versa. We write €2,500.00. An Italian would write €2.500,00.

• When you write a cheque, put your location before the date, as in 'Roma, 7/11/03'.

• If, for any reason, you have to express prices in lire (for example, when dealing with the elderly), the easiest thing to do is take off three zeros and divide by two to get the euro amount. (The exact exchange is €1 = 1,936 lire).

than €12,500 you will then be asked to fill out a declaration (*dichiarazione*), explaining why you are making or receiving the transfer. Your bank will file this paperwork with the Ufficio Italiano Cambi (UIC), a government regulatory body. This is to discourage money laundering and to monitor funds that could be destined for illegal purposes.

With fiscal residency (*residenza fiscale*), which indicates that you are earning your wages in Italy (even if in pounds from your UK headquarters), you can open one of several types of accounts. The *conto corrente* is a basic bank account. You can open a savings account with a *libretto di conto* (passbook savings account) or a current account with a *libretto di assegni* (cheque book). A joint account (*conto corrente a firme congiunte*) is an account for two people where both signatures are necessary for transactions. As an alternative, the *conto corrente cointestato*, also for two people, allows either party to carry out transactions without the signature of the other. The terms of a simple *conto corrente*, as far as interest and options, will be explained by your bank.

With a *conto corrente* you can ask for a debit or ATM card (*bancomat*), which allows you to withdraw up to €500 per day, and most stores will accept it. You can also request a CartaSi card that has a debit and credit card function. Many shops are reluctant to take credit cards, and the *bancomat* is more widely accepted. Some shops do not accept foreign credit cards for operations like setting up satellite television accounts or paying bills. *Pazienza* ... the idea of what Visa means is slowly catching on. Until then, pay with your Italian card (*carta*), cheque (*assegno*) or, even better, cash (*contanti*). There is no set rule about what kind of shop accepts what kind of payment, so have several forms available and ask what they accept before paying.

Italian banks with offices (*filiali*) in the UK, like Banca Commerciale Italiana, Banca di Roma or Banca San Paolo Imi, are often more user-friendly. The UK branch may be able to liaise with the branch of your choice in Italy, nudging along transfers and other dealings if need be.

Shopping

In Italian there is *lo shopping*, which is shopping for pleasure, usually clothes but sometimes stereos, CDs, make-up and other self-pampering sundries. And then there is *la spesa* for groceries and household goods – the staples.

La Spesa

Until recently *la spesa* was an exercise in shop-hopping. The butcher, green-grocer, dairy store, bakery and household goods shop were all individual entities. In most towns, they still are, but the entry of the *supermercato* means that there are now all-in-one markets, and even the super-supermarket known as a *hypermart* has arrived and is here to stay. And they are packed, especially at weekends, when it seems to be a family activity to stroll through the wide aisles and marvel over the onslaught of non-Italian labels.

The closest thing to a *supermercato* (GS and SMA are two major chains) is the *alimentari*. As a small shop with a bit of everything from legs of *prosciutto* to washing-up liquid, the selection is limited and prices are usually a bit higher than for the same goods in individual stores. The *alimentari* certainly can't offer the discount that supermarkets can, but they retain all the charm that their more impersonal big brother lacks. Neighbourhood *alimentari* may be down-market but they could be a culinary smorgasbord. Since they are private or family-owned, there is a great variety.

Though supermarkets are obviously not going to go away, there are still plenty of small shops for everyday needs. Often this is because it is simply easier to shop near home than to struggle with traffic and parking difficulties, but it can also be attributed to the Italian's love of the finer gastronomic traditions. Quality beats quantity any day, and you'll see shoppers cooing over the first artichokes of the season as they would over a newborn child. One Irish woman recalls the first time she went to buy tomatoes at the fruit and vegetable shop, and was berated for selecting a sauce tomato when what she had asked for was one for a salad.

When you are in a food shop, you are usually expected to order first, pay at the *cassa* and then pick up your order. This is so that the person who handles your food is not also touching your money. Remember to get a *scontrino*, or fiscal receipt, because it is just as illegal for you not to request it as it is for the shopkeeper not to give it. The *scontrino* is the only means by which tax authorities can keep tabs on store earnings, but shopkeepers are hit with such high taxes that it's no wonder so many 'forget' to give receipts. If you turn a blind eye when this happens, it is customary to receive a *sconticino*, or 'little discount' on your purchase.

Shopping in Monteverde

Window on one block in the Roman neighbourhood of Monteverde:

Every morning, at 7-ish, Raffaele shouts out '*A Maaa-rioooo!!!!!*' That cry, from the barber to the leather shop, reverberates through the courtyards (*cortile*) of the surrounding apartment buildings – most roosters couldn't do better. At that point, horns are already beeping on the street; shutters are swinging open; and heavy, roll-up blinds are rattling upwards as locks are being snapped open. Shopping for the day has commenced in Monteverde, as it has throughout Rome and all of Italy.

Finding your way through the shopping maze means understanding where to go for what, and how to ask for it. The shops you will find in most of Italy are:

• *Caseificio*: Dairy shops sell cheeses, creams, milk and other dairy products.

• *Enoteca*: Wine shops in Italy sometimes have tasting corners, and some, like Il Goccetto in Rome, are cosy hangouts with cheeses and cold cuts to nibble on while choosing a few take-away bottles.

• *Forno* or *fornaio*: An Italian bakery can be mind-boggling with choices and local bread varieties. *La rosetta*, a hollow roll that resembles a rose because of its markings on top, is mostly found in Rome. Throughout Tuscany bread is unsalted and sold in kilo loaves.

Emilia-Romagna is known for its flat bread, the *piadina*, that is made fresh and sold either plain or stuffed like a sandwich at the numerous *piadineria* kiosks along the roadside.

• *Fruttivendolo* or *frutta e verdura*: The produce shop generally sells cheap local wines and herbs, or *sapori*, for flavouring. Wild greens in season, or *la misticanza*, which come from the surrounding countryside, are sold in bulk in shops and at roadside stands.

• *Macelleria*: In Italy the butcher sells everything from beef steaks (*bistecche*) to quail (*quaglia*) and rabbit (*coniglio*) to horse meat (*carni equine*); where horse of the non-galloping kind is still popular in northern Italy, there are specific equine butchers called *macelleria equine*.

• *Pasticceria*: Pasticcerie sell cakes, desserts, mignons and sweets, as well as the spumante to accompany them in case you are buying for a celebration.

• *Pescheria*: Fresh fish and seafood shops – if they say *surgelati* or *congelati* then the products are frozen.

• *Salumeria* or *norcineria*: Delicatessens sell salamis, hams and other seasoned meats. Norcineria is the word used in the region of Lazio, and sometimes in Umbria.

• *Vini e olii*: Though these are a dying breed, literally the wine and oil shop sells local wines by the litre and oils. Bring your own bottle to be filled.

Mercati

Shopping at open-air or closed-in markets with stands and vendors provides an economical way of picking up meals and gives a snapshot of the neighbourhood. In large cities, every few blocks there is a small pocket that turns into a bustling outdoor shopping venue every morning, excluding Sundays. Smaller towns usually have one central market that is easy to find by tailing the older women pushing bicycles early in the morning. Historic markets, like the fish and flower market at the Campo de' Fiori in Rome, or the Vucciría in Palermo, have been supplying the masses for centuries.

Measurements are counted in *etti* (100 grams is one *etto*) for smaller portions, like cheeses and cold cuts, and larger portions can go up to half a kilo or a kilo, *un mezzo chilo* or *chilo*, when ordering meats and produce.

Lo Shopping

Perhaps the biggest impediment to shopping is getting around the opening hours – generally 9–1.30 and 3.30–7.30 Mon–Sat. When most people take their lunch breaks, so do the shops, making it very inconvenient to pop out and pick up a few things midday. For anyone suffering from claustrophobia, Saturday shopping will take sedation since the crowds that couldn't shop during the week, do it all on their one day off when stores are open. To throw in a twist, shops have a weekly closing day (*giorno di riposo*). For example, hairdressers throughout most of the country are closed on Mondays. Often closing days vary with each store. Opening times (*orario*) should be posted outside all shops.

Mega markets with discounted prices are appearing throughout Italy, but *i sconti* are best used for products like toilet rolls and cleaning liquid that you can buy in larger quantities and stock up on, without needing the highest quality on the market. On the periphery of most large cities there will be at least one *megamart* of some kind. There are branches of IKEA, but they are not always easy to get to and they have an amusement-park atmosphere, with large families on outings blocking aisles and socializing. It's best to get familiar with the neighbourhood shops (*negozi*) and department stores (*grandi magazzini*) in town. The biggest chains are Upim, Coin and Standa. Most *grandi magazzini* also have supermarkets attached to them.

General Shops and Services

• *Calzolaio*: Shoe repair shop; in Italy, there are some of the finest cobblers who can turn around a worn out pair of shoes for next to nothing.

• *Cartoleria*: Stationery stores have wrapping paper, best-selling books and other paper-related items.

- **Farmacia**: The chemists in Italy can fill prescriptions and dish out over-the-counter medication. They also have homeopathic (*omeopatia*) and herbal remedies. Some even have an in-house herbal doctor who will mix tisane and make herbal extracts on request.

- **Ferramenta**: Hardware stores often have knick-knacks and key-cutting services. A specialized locksmith store that only deals with locks (*cereture*) is called a *fabbro*.

- **Gioelleria** or **orafo**: Jewellers or goldsmiths; *gioellerie* **are jewellery shops with manufactured goods, whereas** *orofi* are artisan craftsmen who can make on order, or sell individual pieces.

- **Libreria**: Bookstore; Feltrini is one of Italy's largest bookstore chains.

- **Mangimi** or **Alimenti per animali**: Specialized pet-food stores have taken off in Italy over the last several years. Though the mega-chains that exist in other countries aren't around, there are plenty of shops selling well-known brands like Iams, Purina and Eukanuba, Nutro and others.

- **Pelletteria**: Leather goods from bags, to shoes, and jackets; some *pelletteria* also have a workshop attached and can repair leather items.

- **Profumeria**: Perfumeries carry soaps, cosmetics, skincare products and everything one might expect, including perfume.

- **Sarto**: Seamstresses and tailors are commonly used in Italy. Most clothing stores have one on call, as do dry cleaners and laundrettes.

- **Tabacchi**: Tobacconists are the only other place where you can buy stamps (*francobolli*) apart from the post office. They are heralds of the state, selling monopoly items like cigarettes and salt, as well as lottery and bus tickets, tax stamps and prepaid calling cards.

- **Tintoria** or **lavasecco**: Laundrettes or dry-cleaners; sometimes the two are not combined in the same shop, though it is more likely that a *lavasecco* will be able to wash and press than a *tintoria* will have dry-cleaning services.

- **Tipografia**: Printer; usually small establishments, they can print out business cards, bind books and carry out other services that printers perform, though at a high price.

Clothing Shops

Some of the specialist names for clothes shops (*abigliamento*) are the:

- **Abigliamento sportive**: sports shop; Cisalfa is a large Italian chain.
- **Accessori**: accessories shop.
- **Camiceria**: shirt store, usually for men.
- **Scarperia**: shoe shop.

Walking into a shop can be a pleasant experience, but it can sometimes be stressful. Shopkeepers (*commesse*) are intrusive and don't believe in the live-and-let-browse philosophy. They also are keen to convince you to buy, whether the item in question is appropriate or not. Chains like Benetton or Max Mara are more accustomed to hands-off treatment. Remember that you are the client, not the victim.

Flea markets are the antithesis of the *negozio*. Smiles and banter go hand in hand with coercion, but in an amusing market manner. Sundays are the days when cities sell their best second-hand goods and antiques. The market in Porta Portese, Rome, has a complete mix of goods for sale. Buy a 1940s dress or a 1920s chair, or the latest model of digital camera – more than likely 'lost' by some poor tourist the week before. In Turin there is Balôn, and Gran Balôn the second Sunday of every month held in the neighbourhood of Porta Palazzo. Furniture aficionados flock to the Milan antique market on the Navigli, and Arezzo's antique bonanza is held on the last weekend of the month on the Piazza Grande.

Life in Cafés, Bars and Culinary Notes

Cafés and Bars

Despite the sing-along Chianti-flask reputation Italians have been stuck with, Italy does not have a drinking tradition of the sort that prevails in the UK. Nor are there any long and meaningful discussions over a cup of coffee. In fact, it takes all of four seconds to drink an Italian espresso. Even the tallest of Italian coffee drinks, cappuccino and *caffè latte*, aren't sipped lazily at outdoor tables. They are only to be consumed at breakfast time. If you order one after noon, be prepared to explain that you woke up late and are just having breakfast, or face sidelong looks from the bar man (*barrista*).

Establishments called *il bar* (indicated by a sign outside saying '*bar*') have many functions. Pop in for a quick breakfast of *cornetti* and cappuccino. In the afternoon, most bars transform into an *aperitivo* joint, with light drinks like Campari-soda (in Rome) or a *prosecco spritz* (in Venice) and snacks (*stuzzichini*) – mostly crisps and peanuts – on the bar. In most towns the clientele in bars is predominantly male with the occasional woman or girl beetling in for a pint of milk or pack of cigarettes, and scuttling out again as soon as possible. There are a few tables nonchalantly placed in the small amount of space available, and perhaps one or two outside on the pavement. Clients stand around the counter to talk and drink, or spend hours abusing video poker machines for under-the-table cash. This is the average bar ... the one on every corner.

Some upper-end bars have more elaborate layouts. Moving beyond *il bar* is *il café*. These are the idyllic spots where tables are filled by loungers in main squares, such as Navona in Rome and San Marco in Venice, sipping expensive cappuccino or *prosecco aperitivo*. Someone with a bottle of wine or pint of beer on the table is most certainly a tourist. But these cafés are great nesting points to sit back and watch the city streets in full glory.

Theme pubs have blossomed over the last decade, and nearly every town has a Fiddler's Bow or O'Grady's. Though they are mostly filled with teeny boppers, they are often the best place to catch a Champions League or other European match on TV, and can be a casual change from the 'only-one-glass' Italian café.

Restaurants

It may come as a shock, but there is no one Italian food – there are hundreds of them. And every region is fiercely proud and protective of their notable dishes and specialities. Neapolitans outside Naples have been known to get teary-eyed while remembering their coffee as made in Napoli. One type of *prosciutto crudo*, sold only in its home town of Parma, gets 'exported' by Emiliani living away from home. And the creamy mozzarella-like cheese from Puglia called *burrata* has such a short shelf-life that most aficionados order it specially and wait at their cheese shop anxiously on its arrival day to keep anyone else from getting it first. In other words, it's not just pizza and pasta. It is as much chickpea fritters (*panelle*), as it is fondue (*fonduta*), made in Italy's Alpine region. It is as much the Romagnolo *squaquerone* cheese as it is cave-aged sheep cheese (*pecorino di fossa*), and the widely exported parmesan (*parmigiano*).

For adventurous eaters, fathoming the complexities of local Italian cuisines can take a lifetime. The best way to taste regional specialities is by travelling, as most towns stick to their own kind of cooking. Big cities have more variety, as a result of internal immigration within the country, than smaller towns or countryside restaurants. For many years southerners have moved north to seek employment in the more industrialized part of the country, therefore Sicilians in Turin, Calabrians in Milan and Neapolitans in Rome often opened restaurants in their adopted towns. In most Italian *Pagine Gialle* these restaurants are categorized as regional restaurants (*ristoranti regionali*) and can be as foreign an experience for an Italian as for a non-Italian.

Going out to eat is not reserved exclusively for special occasions. *Trattorie* or *osterie* are unembellished establishments that serve home-cooked meals and have a more casual atmosphere than *ristoranti*. Children eat there too and most parents do not feel that inhibiting the little ones would be healthy for children's development. Therefore the *bambini* may be crawling under your table or singing loudly at their own. If you are a parent, this warm and welcoming environment can be a pleasant experience and a world apart from the more forbidding atmosphere of pubs and restaurants in the UK, which are so often unsympathetic to children. For the single diner, or couples *senza bambini*, this may be somewhat unnerving. Restaurants (*ristoranti*) above a certain price range almost never have children romping through them, as the more expensive establishments are chosen for special evenings out. If you have an aversion to dining in a lively atmosphere, consider the extra investment for a peaceful meal.

With Italian foods being enshrouded by a near mystical reverence there isn't room for much else. When Italian teenagers were polled recently, 28.4 per cent had never tried any form of ethnic cooking and 22 per cent said that they did not want to try non-Italian cuisine. Another 15 per cent admitted that they had tasted it, but didn't like it and would never do it again. Apart from an abundance of Chinese diners, there aren't many non-Italian choices except in big cities. While in Italy, eat *all'Italiana*.

Transport

Whereas big cities are well connected throughout Italy with the speedy and inexpensive Eurostar (not to be confused with the more recent London–Paris train), getting to smaller towns can feel like a trip back one hundred years in time. Regional trains puttering through idyllic countryside at a snail's pace can be charming if there is no hurry to get from point A to point B, and there is no heavy luggage in tow. But if you have deadlines or appointments on the other end, the frustration can provoke acid indigestion or worse.

However, there is always a way to get to where you want to go, since even the smallest village in Italy is somehow connected by the vast web of trains, coaches, ferries and flights. If you are well informed about what is available you can combine your forms of transport (*mezzi*) creatively and drastically reduce travel time. For example, to get to the town of Citta di Castello in Umbria from Rome, there are several train and coach combinations. For someone living near the bus station Tiburtina, the trip just takes one four-hour bus ride. But if Tiburtina is on the other side of town, Roman traffic can mean that getting to the station takes another 1½hrs. At that point, the train to Florence and a bus or train from there could save as much as an hour. Getting there by car takes a little more than 2½hrs, depending on traffic.

Never underestimate the traffic factor. Italians prefer to travel by car, and do so when work schedules permit. That means that traffic-snarls at rush hour and streams of weekend out-of-towners are sure to be found leaving on Friday and returning on Sunday from major cities. Leave an hour earlier to avoid it.

Getting from Town to Town

Rail

Though prices may be increasing soon, in 2004 Italian railway (*Ferrovie dello Stato*) is one of Europe's most affordable, so much so that the company's strategy director has recently appealed to the government to abolish the state-imposed price caps on the organization. Those cosy caps that make rail users happier have also frozen company profits at only €4.70 per passenger kilometre compared with the European average of €7.70. And those low prices offer a lot of travel possibilities.

The basic train network in Italy was designed before the Second World War and has developed since. There is only one super-fast line, the Florence–Rome train, which takes 1hr 35mins from Santa Maria Novella station to Termini, both in the town centre. Plans for extending the line to Naples by the end of 2004 are in progress, and a high-speed line from Rome to Milan and Verona is planned for 2008. *Ferrovie dello Stato* (FS) is state-owned and controls the majority of rail travel throughout the country. Efficient as these lines are, there are a few that offer poor service. The train from the French border at Ventimiglia to Genoa is painfully slow, as are the trains that cross into Sicily by ferry.

There are different types of train, offering varying degrees of comfort and speed:

• **Eurostar (ES)**, which has taken the place of the Pendolino (CiS), makes all other Italian *treni* pale in comparison. The second class is almost as comfortable as first, there is a dining car, air-conditioning and plenty of leg room. Reservations are compulsory and a surcharge (*supplemento rapido*) for the fast service is added to the ticket price.

• **Eurocity (EC)** trains connect the major Italian cities to each other and with centres such as Paris, Vienna, Hamburg and Barcelona. They do not stop in small towns ,and they require a supplement.

• **Intercity (IC)** trains link the major Italian centres; to avoid standing in crowded corridors, reservations are advised. A supplement is generally added to the price of the ticket.

• **Diretto (DIR), Espresso (EXP) and Interregionale (IR)** trains stop in the towns that the other trains speed through. They should be taken in combination with faster trains if time is important.

Don't bother to try phoning **t** 892021 (landline only, no mobile calls) because it is always busy or never answered. It's better to visit the useful websites **www. fs-on-line.com** or **www.trenitalia.it**. Many travel agents issue train tickets, though that may be changing as a result of negotiations over commission. To buy online you will need a credit card and a *codice fiscale*, and must register first. Most stations have automated ticket vending machines with instructions in English, Spanish, French and German. If paying with a bank card or credit card, make sure that the machine is *abbiliata carta e bancomat*. Otherwise, go prepared with cash (*contanti*) in smaller notes in good condition to avoid not getting a refund or having the machine spit out more worn bills. Before hopping on the train, don't forget to validate (*timbrare*) your ticket at the yellow machines mounted at the head of each line or at an automatic distributor.

Coach

Coaches cover areas that the trains do not reach. Some routes have better services than others, mostly depending on the destination. Each region has its own operator or operators and coach terminals are generally near train stations or metro stops in larger towns. Tickets should be purchased in advance from the ticket office at the terminal, from tobacconists, or directly on the coach if there are no other options. Travelling by coach is a useful alternative when there is a train strike.

The Bus Station website, **www.busstation.net/main/busita.htm**, helpfully lists routes according to region, area and Servizi di Trasporto con Autobus (SITA). SITA is the national authority that all local operators fall under and has a useful site, **www.sita-on-line.it**.

Sea

Ferries (*traghetti*) and hydrofoils (*aliscafi*) not only connect mainland Italy to surrounding islands, they are sometimes used to go from port city to port city. The *aliscafo* from Sorrento to Naples takes less time than the cliff-hanging journey around the Amalfi Coast. When divided into four, taking a vehicle on a ferry from Genoa to Naples is a more cost-effective (if more time-consuming) way of travelling for four people than going by road, which involves the cost of highway tolls and petrol. In Venice, water buses navigate the miles and miles of canals that are the city's main thoroughfares.

But mostly sea travel is used to reach one of Italy's numerous islands. Millions of travellers take one of the major ferry lines to get to Sardinia, Sicily, Croatia on the other side of the Adriatic and other smaller destinations like the Aeolian isles, where the tiniest port in the world has to be accessed by rowing boat. Tirrenia (**www.gruppotirrenia.it**), Grimaldi (**www.grimaldi.it**) and Moby Lines (**www.moby.lines.it**) leave from major ports such as Ancona, Brindisi, Genoa, Naples and Palermo. Corsica Ferries–Sardinia Ferries (**www.corsicaferries.com**) travel from the port of Civitavecchia north of Rome and Livorno and add services from the port at Fiumicino near Rome during summer months.

A general website, **www.fun.informare.it**, has detailed information, as does SNAV (**www.snav.it**). Buy tickets online at **www.traghettionline.net**.

Car Hire

As a great alternative to getting around if your destinations are in the countryside, or if you have more than one place to see, car rental can actually reduce the hassle of keeping up with time tables and fixed schedules. Do not, however, rent a car if the only spot you are going to be in is a major city when you will be fine using public transport and cabs. A car is more of a problem than it is worth when it comes to parking and getting through traffic.

Booking through the internet is easier than ever. There are inexpensive options through **www.cheaprents.com**. All major companies, such as Hertz (**www.hertz.com**) and Avis (**www.avis.com**) serve Italy, and Maggiore (**www.maggiore.it**) and Europcar (**www.europcar.com**) both have bargain deals, especially at weekends. As in any country, you will need a credit card. It's advisable to take out insurance, especially in larger cities where the merest possibility of there being a scratch or dent on the car could result in your credit card being deducted with a vengeance. Hiring for three weeks or more could also be a thrifty move.

Before taking off, go to the Italian Highway (Società Autostrade) website at **www.autostrade.it** or listen to the state radio station with national traffic and weather at 103.3 FM.

For information about owning a car in Italy, *see* pp.201–205.

Getting About in the City

Bus and Tram

Buses are as susceptible to jammed roads during the rush hour as cars. Trams run a bit faster, since many have preferential lanes (*corsia preferenziale*). Apart from hours of heavy traffic (*traffico intenso*) in Milan, Genoa, Rome, Palermo and other major cities, buses and trams are relatively efficient.

Honour and fear is the ticketing creed. Tickets (*biglietti*) cost no more than €1 for 75mins of travel on any number of buses and trams (though only one train ride is allowed) and must be validated once on board. Random checks result in fines if a passenger is caught without a stamped ticket. Buy them at tobacconists, news stands or from automatic dispensers (shaped like green shacks) at central hubs.

The Subway

In Fellini's 1972 autobiographical film *Roma*, workers digging to build a metro line break into a perfectly preserved ancient hall with frescoes as bright as the day they were painted. Within seconds of being corrupted by fresh oxygen, the vibrant colours begin to fade and then disappear. No one knows how much of ancient Rome was discovered and destroyed over the centuries by construction. The fact is that Rome has only three subway lines, largely as a result of the ruins buried directly under the city surface. In 1999, when the St Peter's tunnel was being built, the home of Nerone's mother, Agrippina, was uncovered as it had stood preserved underground until workmen stumbled across it.

Milan, on the other hand, has a metro network that competes with Europe's finest. Venice doesn't need one, nor could they build one without creating a system of chunnels. The subway in Naples works well, as does the overground metro line known as the Vesuviano. Tickets work much like bus tickets, but controllers stand by the rotating gates to ensure passengers' honesty. Monthly passes can be purchased for a discounted price, and include bus and train transport as well as the underground. There are ticket windows at the entrance to the metro, and automatic machines that can be fussy, so be prepared with a selection of coins.

Mopeds and Bicycles

Real adventurers will find it impossible to not mount a moped. You'll see them waiting in herds at traffic lights, then zooming away into the distance, free of the chains of traffic. They cut off your lane, park in tight spots, zip over the pavement like Evel Knievel. If you have any sense of adventure, or wish to avoid big city traffic snarls, try one. It isn't as difficult nor as dangerous as it seems. The Vespa (wasp) is an icon of Italian two-wheelers, and one you'll see around often.

You don't need a special licence to drive a 50cc moped, recognizable by its smaller licence plate with five characters (numbers and letters); anyone over the age of 14 can ride them.

There is even a boxed-in version of the 50cc that looks like a tiny car, but instead is technically (and for all legal purposes) a 50cc moped; the open-back version, called the Ape (bee) is often used in the countryside and rural areas. You must be at least 16 to drive a 125cc moped, and acquire an 'a' licence (*patente a*). Anything over 150cc is considered a motorcycle. Only those aged 18 and over can ride them and a *patente a* is required.

Cars

For those living in a big city, the best reason for having a car is to get out of town. In the city, parking is difficult, the town centres are more often than not restricted, and paying high fines becomes a fact of life.

If you plan to drive in Italy it is safest and easiest to do so with a car that is adapted to right-hand driving. If you are non-resident, purchasing a car in Italy is illegal, even if you are an EU citizen. Once EU laws are hammered out this will change. But to avoid the unnecessary grief of buying a car and not being able to register and drive it, check with the Italian Automobile Club or ACI (**www.aci.it**) before paying unscrupulous salesmen. Many car dealers (*concessionari*) will sell you an automobile despite the law.

For non-EU nationals, make sure you go to the town hall (*comune*) and request an *atto sostitutivo* (declaring you aren't an EU citizen). You can then purchase a car in Italy without paying the 20 per cent tax, and obtain an '*EE*' licence plate (*targa escursionisti esteri*). They are valid for one year and are only renewable once. After two years, you must return the plates or pay 20 per cent tax and remove the vehicle from the country.

For EU citizens, the car must be **registered** (*immatricolata*) at the Ufficio di Motorizzazione (Department of Motor Vehicles) and tax paid. You may also be protected from car theft once you have an Italian licence plate as roving thieves particularly look for foreign vehicles assuming they belong to tourists and are full of goodies.

Insuring a car is easy and essential. Police run random checks and driving without insurance is a crime. There are two kinds of car insurance. The *bonus-malus* means that you pay a premium based on your accident record; for the *assicurazione con franchigia fissa ed assoluta* you pay a premium, but are covered in all circumstances. The best way to find an insurer is to go by word of mouth, asking friends and neighbours who they use. There are also policies that can be purchased online, at significant savings. The largest insurance companies in Italy are Sai and Assisitalia.

To **buy or sell a used car**, the ownership transfer (*passaggio di proprietario*) must be completed and the registration papers (*libretto di circolazione*) put in your name. In the meantime, you will be given a temporary substitute called the *foglio sostitutivo*. An annual tax (*bollo*) has to be paid at the ACI and is priced according to the engine size of the vehicle you own.

You will have to decide what to do about your **driving licence**. Until recently, Italian law demanded that all foreigners living in Italy convert their licences into Italian ones. There was a certain amount of paperwork involved (mostly official translations) but it did not involve taking an Italian driving test. Following the latest European Union directive on the mutual recognition of driving licences this is no longer required for EU nationals. That means you are allowed to drive in Italy on a valid British licence.

To obtain an Italian driver's licence, you must register for both the written test and the practical one at the nearest office of the ACI, the Automobile Club d'Italia, which also offers driving lessons and 24-hour roadside assistance for members. The test is taken at the Ufficio di Motorizzazione and is based on European standards (including kilometres instead of miles). It can be taken in English but, nonetheless, the test is still hard, including questions on the length

A City on a Plate

In the past, licence plates showed which city the car was from. For example, 'MI' is for Milano and 'CA' for Catania, but, because lawmakers argued that racist acts were being committed against drivers from the south (an increase in 'car-keying' was seen at the height of secessionist sentiments in the 1990s), the names of the cities were removed from licence plates. However, a few years ago, a wave of nostalgia moved lawmakers to reinstate the city codes. As a result, Italian roads are a mish-mash of different plates, some of which don't even resemble Italian ones. There are white plates, black ones, ones with blue EU shading and older ones with orange lettering.

Case Study: Driving Lessons

One afternoon 33-year-old Gareth Roberts got a lesson on Italian bureaucracy the hard way. While driving with friends to the town of Nemi near Rome on the historic Appia Antica the group realized that the wind was picking up. Gareth 'noticed small branches on the road and that traffic had slowed to a crawl. Then a man on a Vespa pulled over, and stared back at me. I was wondering what he was looking at when there was an almighty crash, a flurry of leaves and a sudden loss of daylight. A tree had fallen directly onto the car.'

Once the four had checked for injuries, they wriggled out of the car. Gareth, who moved to Rome from Manchester to work for a satellite television company in 1994, continues with a broad grin, 'We had to wait for the police since we were entitled to compensation from the city for the damage to my car. After 20 minutes, two policewomen arrived, examined the car and gave us a form to complete detailing the damage caused by the tree.' It didn't end there, however. 'Once the paperwork was over, I handed over the photocopies of my insurance documents. In the UK one never carries the originals; even a copy isn't required. And I provided my driving licence. It was then that I was informed I had to pay a fine of 108,000 Italian lire [about €57] for not having the original documents.' Resigned to the fact, he agreed to pay then and there, 'But this wasn't enough,' he recalls. 'I was told to wait for another unit to arrive.' The second police car pulled up with orders. 'We were told to help clear the road first, otherwise we couldn't leave. We protested, invented excuses about urgent appointments but to no avail. So for almost an hour we helped pick up the debris – branches, twigs, sections of the trunk. Needless to say, I never received compensation, either,' he shrugs.

Since then he has decided that it isn't worth the stress of owning a car in Italy. 'I'm just not interested,' he says. 'Parking, traffic are two strikes against, and loving my *motorino* keeps me happy. I just hire when I need to – which is rarely. My last car spent over 2 years in my driveway without being moved.' The beauty of Italy for Gareth is that 'everything is on your doorstep, at least socially. I can walk out of my house and be right in the thick of it. No tube, bus or taxi ride. It's as good as teleport. Or so I would imagine.'

of truck axles and first-aid knowledge. ACI can provide you with a 200-page booklet with sample questions. In addition to passing both the written and practical exams, you must take an eye test, provide photos, and pay an application fee. You will get a *foglio rosa* (learners' permit) first and will have to drive around with a large 'P' (for *principante* or 'beginner') on the back of your car. Once you have obtained the drivers' licence you must keep it valid by paying an expensive *marca da bollo* tax each year. This is a driver's licence tax, and is paid in addition to the car tax.

If you have an **accident**, make sure you get the *numero di targa* (licence plate number), *marca e tipo di macchina* (make and model description of the vehicle), the *numero di patente* (driver's licence number), address, name and phone number of the other driver. If you and the other driver agree on what happened, fill out a *constatazione amichevole-denuncia di sinistro* form, which means the case will be settled between insurance companies. If you and the other driver don't have matching versions of events, you will be requested to submit a letter with your side of the story, and might be asked to furnish witnesses.

If you need roadside assistance, call **t** 116 from any phone, free of charge.

Parking is a serious problem in Italy and, if you can afford it, it makes sense to find a dedicated parking space. Cities like Rome – in which there are 300,000 official parking spaces for the city's 2 million registered cars – are parking no man's land for frustrated drivers. Pay parking spaces are marked by a blue line and any other open space you find is undoubtedly illegal. An army of parking police, *vigili urbani*, regularly make the rounds and hand out tickets. Some spaces are guarded by 'self-nominated parking guardians' who will offer to 'protect' your car while you are away and ask a small donation for their efforts. You're better off paying than discovering what happens if you don't. Also remember that the historic centres of most big cities are closed to cars without special entry permits. You can only qualify to receive such a permit if you can demonstrate that you live within the historic centre and have Italian plates. The authorities will not give a *centro storico* pass to a car with British plates even if the owners can prove that they live in the centre. Many big cities, such as Rome, divide the pass by neighbourhood so that, for example, a driver with a pass for Zone A still can't drive in Zone B, and vice versa.

Pesky **parking tickets** and other fines (*multe*) are almost inescapable. If you have Italian licence plates (*targa*) the police officer merely has to write down the number and the fine will be sent to your residence. Contesting it means long hours of queues and arguments, without the guarantee that it will be revoked. One of the benefits of having a non-Italian licence plate is that, unless you are physically stopped, police are less likely to issue tickets because of the complicated transnational process of following the procedure through.

Many of the horror stories you've heard about driving in Italy are really modern myths. **Motorways**, or *autostrade*, are well maintained, brightly lit and have service stations with snack bars or restaurants and petrol every 25km (15 miles) on average. The majority of *autostrade* have tollbooths at which you pay as you leave with cash, credit cards or a pre-paid 'Viacard' (available at tobacconists). Driving on **smaller roads**, *strada statale* (SS) or *strada nazionale* (N), through regions such as Tuscany or Sicily is one of the biggest pleasures life affords. Last, despite city traffic that will make you suicidal, driving from one city to the next is really quite fast. The network of motorways makes it feasible to visit Florence or Naples from Rome in a day trip (for more information, visit **www.autostrade.it**).

Unfortunately, the Italian art of driving is not a myth. Italians are known for turning and passing without signalling, and an acute and incurable inability to stay within the painted boundaries of the lane. One of the most important rules of the road, however (that is not only respected but revered), is not passing on the right. If you wonder why a blue Alfa is tailgating you and flashing its full beams centimetres from your back bumper, it's because: a) you are a snail, and b) you shouldn't expect HIM to break the law and pass on the right.

Speed limits, like traffic lights, are also open to interpretation. The speed limit on motorways is 130km per hour (80mph) for vehicles over 1100cc and 110km per hour (70mph) for all others. In cities, it is 50km per hour (30mph) and 110km per hour (70mph) outside city limits. Secondary state roads are usually 90km per hour (55mph). The wearing of front **seatbelts** (and back seatbelts too, for children) is mandatory, although Italian drivers too commonly 'forget' them.

Crime and the Police

In Italy there are four divisions of police:

- *Carabinieri* **(military police)**: answer to the Defence Ministry; responsible especially for criminal offences; they are elegantly clad in dark blue uniforms with a magenta strip down the trouser leg

- *Guardia di Finanza* **(finance police)**: also military police, but answer to the Finance Ministry; responsible for criminal financial activities such as drug running or tax evasion; they wear drab grey–green uniforms

- *Polizia di Stato* **(state police)**: a civil force that answers to the Interior Ministry; responsible for criminal activity and anti-state crimes

- *Polizia Municipale* **(municipal police) or** *Vigili Urbani*: traffic cops; each city has its own force

An archaic, and mistaken, notion of pistol-toting *mafiosi* and butt-pinching males plagues Italy. The same sorts of crimes happen here as in most other European countries. The chance that you may be in the wrong place at the wrong time applies – sometimes being the victim of a crime simply can't be avoided. But using common sense and being cautious can help reduce risk.

As a general rule, be informed and aware of the sort of area in which you are living, and what the particular dangers of that area are. Break-ins do happen, especially during summer months when many leave for extended periods and burglars know that their job will be easier. Those living in apartments on the ground floor should take extra precautions by installing protective gratings and heavy-duty locks. Alarm systems are recommended in large cities. Perhaps one of the most effective home surveillance methods, however, is simply a matter of socializing and getting to know your neighbours, letting them know if you will

Gypsy Sightings

In 1999 Rome's mayor at that time, Francesco Rutelli, told journalists at a press conference that it was a well-known fact that 'nearly all Gypsies [sic] are criminals and need to be expelled from the capital city'. At the time of his unsubstantiated comment (he had no official source to refer to when questioned), Rutelli was on a campaign to 'clean up the city' for the Jubilee year, which would attract millions of Catholic pilgrims from around the world.

Roma (Gypsies) are Europe's most discriminated-against ethnic minority. A number of them living in Italy scratch out a meagre existence begging and rummaging through refuse for reusable items. Some of the most basic human rights like schooling for their children, housing, work and access to public areas are denied to them or seriously curtailed.

Many guide books and Italians, wanting to do good, will warn of 'Gypsy thieves and pickpockets', and pointing them out on the street as criminals because of their ethnicity is not considered racial profiling or racist by the average Italian. Roma may steal – as may Italians, redheads or prime ministers. For safety's sake, always be alert whatever the person in front of you looks like. For humanity's sake, be informed about ethnic minorities in the country you live in and remember that scapegoating is a habit that shifts the blame and simplifies a more complex question.

be away for any substantial length of time. Also, if you have a second home that is mostly uninhabited, make provisions to make it look as if someone is living there.

For personal safety, common sense applies. Some areas of town are more unsafe than others and, wherever you live, be sure to know the zones that could be riskier after dark. Although generally Italy is very safe from physical violence, mugging and pickpocketing can be a problem. On crowded buses and other places keep your money in your bag or pocket in front of you. Anything on your back can easily be rifled through or even cut away. A direct gaze at a suspicious character who is too near on a bus, or calling attention by shouting for help ('Aiuto!') is usually enough to ward off petty criminals.

Much has been written about the possible risk from gypsies (see box 'Gypsy Sightings', above). Not only is the finger-pointing racist, it does a great disservice to the average traveller who looks only at one type of person as a potential threat. A sound rule of thumb is to try to keep your distance from strangers, watch for strange behaviour like people fluttering bags or cardboard in front of you, or spilling or falling on you, and be conscious of what goes on around. Don't be consumed by paranoia.

In case of emergency, dial t 113. This is a free call from any phone, and even your mobile phone, if out of credit, will allow this call to go through.

Taking Your Pet

Generally speaking, it is more difficult to get your pet back into the UK than it is to take it to Italy – depending, of course, on what kind of animal companion you have.

If you plan to return to the UK with your pet at any time, check first with the British government office Defra (**www.defra.gov.uk/animalh/quarantine/index.htm**, **t** 0845 933 5577, or outside the UK **t** (020) 7238 6951, minicom/textphone number for deaf and hard of hearing **t** 0845 300 1998, **helpline@defra.gsi.gov.uk**). The helpline is a local call rate number within the UK and available 9–5 on working days.

Cats and dogs need a Pet Passport if you are planning to take them on a round trip adventure. A pet travel scheme, known as PETS, has been established with easy steps to follow ensuring a safe return trip for cats and dogs. To get the passport under the PETS requirements you must see a government-authorized vet no less than 6 months before departure. This has replaced the former six-month quarantine, but must be followed according to schedule, since the passport will not be issued at the last minute. Your vet will then:

- **insert a microchip giving your pet a unique identification**
- **vaccinate the animal against rabies and distemper**
- **arrange for a blood test to confirm there is a satisfactory level of anti-bodies against rabies and to certify that there is no dormant disease; the six-month wait is linked to this test and therefore cannot be rushed through.**

24–48hrs beforeyou return to the UK, a qualified vet must check your pet for ticks and tapeworms. An official certificate must be provided to British authorities when entering the UK. If the test is more than 48hrs old, the pet will not be allowed back in. You must also sign a declaration of residency stating that your pet has not been outside any of the PETS qualifying countries during the previous 6 months.

Note that if you are travelling by car you should check with the countries that you are driving through in case there are specific requirements relating to pets. If you need to stay in a country, go to **www.petfriendlyholidays.com** for pet-friendly hotels along the way. Your vet can also provide a mild sedative to ease the animal's journey. If you are flying or shipping your pet into Rome unaccompanied, try to avoid doing this on a Friday. Italian inspectors do not work at the weekend, which means caged pets could spend their first weekend (*fine settimana*) waiting in an airport hangar.

If you are moving for good, and there is no turning back for your pet, then all you need is an export certificate from the British Ministry of Agriculture and a

Let History Roar

Romans have a special place in their hearts for cats. Two thousand years ago the ferocious feline *Leo leonis* was the Roman empire's preferred method of ripping apart the opposition. In 2002, the city government of SPQR made official big plans for Rome's present-day, whiskery co-citizen's *Feles felis*.

Three of the sites best known for their cat colonies – Trajan's Market, the ruins at Largo Argentina and Rome's Pyramid (the Piramide) – are now featuring interactive programmes with the sites' full-time inhabitants. Roma Felix tours give guided visits in English and Italian with an itinerary that is 'half archaeological, half feline'.

The city's kitties have always basked in special treatment. Archaeological areas packed to the gills with 120,000 cats of all shapes and sizes have been immortalized in calendars, posters and gadgets, which are found at every tourist attraction. Vets regularly give check-ups and vaccinations and, unlike pigeon feeders in Central Park, cat aficionados (*i gattari*) as they are called in Roman dialect, are entitled to modest government subsidies and are considered social servants.

health certificate issued by an approved vet within 15 days of your departure. Only two animals per person per entry are allowed. Once in the country, take your pet to a vet for a general checkup and ask about country-specific illnesses. Vets are listed in the Italian *Pagine Gialle* under 'Veterinaria ambulatori e laboratori', or ask your vet before leaving if she or he can recommend colleagues in the town where you are going.

You need a special certificate to bring exotic animals (tropical birds, snakes, lizards, crocodiles, invertebrates and so on) into the country. Contact the Italian Ministry of Agriculture for information. For assistance once in Italy, contact Società Italiana Veterinari per Animali Esotici or SIVAE (Palazzo Trecchi 26100, Cremona, t 0372 460440, **www.anapsid.org/vets/italy.html**).

Health and Emergencies

Public and Private Health Care

Every resident is allowed health care in Italy through the Servizio Sanitario Nazionale (SSN). There are debates over the quality and competence of facilities, but the infinite charity of the Italian soul has created a public medical system that is truly generous, and that includes foreigners. Sick and injured patients will never be turned away at the emergency room entrance, or asked for insurance by ambulance drivers.

Those entitled to state medical care include workers paying taxes (which include SSN contributions), retired people from EU countries and their dependants. Contributions to the UK National Insurance scheme are taken into account when calculating your entitlements in Italy. Thus, you may be entitled in Italy on the basis of your UK contributions for a few months after your arrival. Ask the DSS for form E106 before you leave. If you are a pensioner you should obtain form E121 from your pensions office before leaving the UK. This is your passport to the benefits enjoyed by Italian pensioners.

Whereas emergency care is immediate and adequate, the occasional visit to the doctor can be more difficult. To use the public health care system before getting a stay permit, you will be covered for the first 90 days in Italy if you fill out an E111 form, available at any UK post office, before departing. Fill in the application form at the back of the leaflet, and the form E111 as well. Hand over the completed forms at the post office where the form will be stamped, signed and returned to you. The E111 is free but you must get it stamped for it to be valid. This gives you the same treatment benefits in other EU countries as you have with the NHS at home. You will probably pay for treatment and then request reimbursement through the DSS on your return to the UK or through filling out the request form and posting it. If you intend to stay in Italy for an extended period, or permanently, it is essential to file a change of address with the International Services, Department of Social Security, before packing up and leaving. For more information, go to **www.doh. gov.uk/traveladvice**, or **t** (020) 7210 4850 (Mon–Fri 9–5), Minicom **t** (020) 7210 5025, **dhmail@doh.gsi.gov.uk** or the Department of Health, Richmond House, 79 Whitehall, London SW1A 2NL.

When applying for a stay permit (*see* **Red Tape**, 'The *Permesso di Soggiorno*', pp.116–18) it is necessary also to sign up with USL/ASL – the state health care system. This is done at the Agenzia Sanitaria Locale (ASL) nearest where you live, with your identity card and *permesso di soggiorno*. Once completed, the ASL/USL office will assign you a general practitioner, or *medico generico*. If you have any illness apart from emergencies you must visit the *medico*, who will also makes house calls (*visite a casa*) for bed-ridden patients. Should you need hospital treatment *il dottore* will write out an official request (*impegnativa*) asking for treatment or tests from the hospital. Once you have an *impegnativa* you can go to any public hospital and the staff will direct you to the appropriate department for your needs. This somewhat drawn-out process does not apply for emergencies, in which case you go straight to *pronto soccorso*.

Many opt for private insurance, or supplement public health care with a more comprehensive policy. State hospitals can undoubtedly be daunting. Remote areas often lack the necessary equipment or personnel and big cities usually have overflowing wards and mile-long waiting lists. Private hospitals, on the other hand, are well equipped and efficient, often with English-speaking staff. But they are expensive. There are a variety of policies available that allow the policyholder to access private health care. Italian insurers include Istituto Nazionale delle Assicurazioni (INS), Sanicard, Filo Diretto, Europa Assistance and Pronto Assistance. The English and Italian *Yellow Pages* directories have lists of insurance companies (look under '*Assicurazioni*' in Italy). In the UK Bupa (**t** 0800 001010, **www.bupa.co.uk**, BUPA House 15–19, Bloomsbury Way, London WC1A 2BA) and COE Connections (**t** (01702) 587003, **f** (01702) 316541, **www.coeconnections.co.uk**, International, 138 Aylesbeare, Shoeburyness, Essex SS3 8AG) are two insurance companies that offer short- and long-term international policies, have provided corporate and private policies for years, and have translators on the staff to process the forms filled out by Italian doctors. If you are working for a UK company, ask about corporate insurance policies.

Medicine, Prescriptions and Pharmacies

If you have prescribed medication that you are bringing into Italy, have a copy of the prescription or a doctor's certificate with you to avoid confiscation or unwanted delays at the border. Pharmacies will often sell lighter medication without a doctor's prescription, which can be handy. However, any kind of more serious medicine requires a doctor's prescription. Some medicines are state subsidized, and can cost considerably less.

Home-administered injections are common in Italy when needed and syringes (*siringhe*) can be sold without a prescription. Suppositories (*supposte*) are also common – if you prefer pills (*pasticche*) be sure to make this clear.

You can identify a pharmacy (*farmacia*) by the green neon sign outside. Though more intimate products such as condoms (*preservativi/profilattici*), pantyliners (*salvaslip/assorbenti esterni*) and tampons (*tamponi/tampax*) can be purchased in supermarkets, most Italians still pick them up at a pharmacy.

Asking for a pregnancy test (*testa di gravidanza*) or treatment for a yeast infection (*candida*) at the pharmacy can be embarrassing, but they can only be purchased there. For a bladder infection (*cistite/infezione della vescica*) the pharmacist will usually sell you the medicine Monuril, which works like a charm. However, technically you need a doctor's prescription to buy it.

Social Services and Welfare Benefits

In an ever more mobile world, much has been done to co-ordinate benefits provided throughout the EU and EEA. There are three ways to claim social security and welfare, and many of them overlap. You can claim under the reciprocal EU and EEA rules, under the rules of the country into which you pay contributions, or according to the rules of the country where you live.

EU and EEA rules

This benefits scheme does not replace national ones to which you may be entitled. It coordinates the different national programmes and determines which country should pay which benefits and where the applicant should apply to receive them. It covers health benefits, accidents at work, occupational maladies, invalidity benefits, old-age pensions, bereavement compensation, death grants, unemployment benefits and family benefits.

The EU rules apply to any EEA nationals (including refugees and stateless persons) residing in an EEA country and to their families. Reciprocal social security agreements that include EEA countries help benefits to be paid abroad. Leaflets for each country covered by a reciprocal agreement with the UK are available at local DSS offices, or from the Pensions and Overseas Benefits Directorate, Tyneview Park, Whitley Road, Benton, Newcastle upon Tyne NE98 1BA, **t** 0191 218 2000, or in Northern Ireland at Overseas Branch, Social Security Agency, Commonwealth House, Castle Street, Belfast BT11 DX.

When asking for information, list the benefits you are getting, give your full name, date of birth and National Insurance (or pensions) number, as well as the purpose of your visit, where you are going, and how long you plan to be away.

Italian Benefits

Your entitlement to claim benefits in Italy will be determined by your social security or Istituto Nazionale di Previdenza Sociale (INPS) contributions in Italy and by NI payments in the UK. (These are separate from the health care (SSN) contributions.) Employees' contributions are deducted at source from their salary and amount to 10%; the employer pays another 35% on top of that. The self-employed must register with INPS and and make their own contributions.

- **Maternity benefits**: To receive Italian maternity allowances, you must have an Italian contract of employment. Maternity leave is 5 months paid and since 2000 law 53 (*legge 53*) has allowed fathers parental leave (*congedo parentale*) for 60–150 days.

- **Health benefits**: These were covered in the health care section, above. To summarize, you can qualify for free health care or, if you are a non-EU resident, you may pay a subscription fee to access the system.

- **Accidents at work, occupational maladies and invalidity and disability benefits**: Unless you have worked in Italy at some time you are not likely to benefit from this kind of pension.

- **Pensions**: Unless you have worked in Italy at some time you are not likely to benefit from an Italian pension, but you will continue to receive your UK pension. Pensions in EU countries are paid on the basis of 'totalization.' This means that if you have lived in various countries, all of your contributions in any EU country will be added together to calculate your pension entitlement. For example, if Italy pays a minimum pension after 20 years' contributions and a full pension after 40 years', if you have paid enough contributions – anywhere in the EU – to qualify, you will get a pension. If you have worked for 5 years out of 40 in Italy and the balance elsewhere, the Italian government will pay 5/40ths of your pension at the rates applicable in Italy. If you had worked for 15 years in the UK, the British government would pay 15/40ths. The retirement age is 65 for a man and 60 for a woman, but you can sometimes retire at 57 after 35 years of paying contributions.

• **Unemployment benefits**: If you lose your job, the Italian unemployment benefit authority must take into account any periods of employment or NI contributions paid in other EU countries when calculating your entitlement to benefits in Italy. You must, however, have paid at least some insurance payments in Italy prior to claiming unemployment benefits in Italy. That means you cannot go to Italy for the purpose of claiming benefit. You should obtain form E301 from the UK benefit authorities before going to Italy. If you travel to Italy to seek employment there are restrictions on your entitlement to benefit, and you must comply with all Italian procedural requirements. You must have been unemployed and available for work in your home country for at least four weeks before going to Italy. You must contact your 'home' unemployment benefit authority and obtain a form E303 before leaving for Italy. You must register for work in Italy within seven days of arrival. You will be entitled to benefit for a maximum of three months. If you cannot find a job during that period you will only be entitled to continuing unemployment benefit in your home country if you return within the three-month period. If you do not, you can lose all entitlement to benefits. You are only entitled to one three-month payment between two periods of employment.

• **Family benefits**: If the members of your family live in the same country as that in which you are insured, then that country pays the benefits. You are entitled to the same benefits as nationals of that state. If your family does not live in the same country as that where you are insured, if you are entitled to benefits under the rules of more than one country, they will receive the highest amount to which they would have been entitled in any of the relevant states. Pensioners normally receive family benefits from the EU member state that pays their pension.

UK Benefits

Many UK benefits are still available when residing outside the country. In the UK there are 'contributory' benefits, those earned by accumulating credit with National Insurance (NI) payments, and 'non-contributory' benefits, which are not dependent on National Insurance contributions. There are four classes of contribution:

• **Class 1: mutual contributions by employers and employees based on income**

- Class 2: flat-rate contributions paid by self-employed

- Class 3: non-obligatory payments made by contributors not making Class One or Class Two payments

- Class 4: compulsory and additional 'profit-related' contributions by the self-employed.

Apart from these categories, benefits are divided into means-tested and non-means-tested ratings based on financial status.

For accidents at work, occupational illness and invalidity benefits you are covered in Italy as you were in the UK, meaning that you will receive the same NI payments without alteration. The only exception is for invalidity benefits: you are unlikely to receive Attendance Allowance, SDA and/or DLA if you live abroad permanently.

A new system of bereavement benefits for men and women was introduced in April 2001 and are payable for those living in Italy. This does not affect women already receiving benefits under the previous scheme, provided they continue to qualify.

Unemployment benefits or Job-seekers' Allowance may be available in EU and EEA countries if:

- you have applied and been accepted for the allowance before you depart to go abroad, giving at least four weeks' notice (this is sometimes waived in special circumstances)

- you have been and continue actively to seek employment in the UK up to the day you depart

- you are going abroad explicitly looking for work

- upon arrival and within 7 days you register with the national equivalent of a job centre in Italy

- you follow the other country's system for claiming benefits

- you actively seek work and follow the other requirements relating to obtaining Job-seeker's Allowance that are necessary in the UK

Maternity allowances and incapacity benefits are covered under the more costly Class 2 NI contributions. Apply in the UK using a CF83 form from the DSS.

Check with the Department for Work and Pensions (**t** (020) 7712 2171, **f** (020) 7712 2386, **tvp-customer-care@dwp.gsi.gov.uk**, **www.dwp.gov.uk**, Department for Work and Pensions Correspondence Unit, Room 540, the Adelphi, 1–11 John Adam Street, London WC2N 6HT) for up-to-date information.

Retirement and Pensions

In the same way that Florida is the haven to which Americans flock after retirement, Italy has for years been a popular venue for savouring the flavours of life *post lavoro*. Temperate climates and palate-pleasing meals are two reasons for this; another is that Italy takes on a whole new charm when experienced at a slower pace. No rushing, no getting to work on time and fighting traffic to do so, just leisurely hours immersed in the rich details of art, architecture, dining and aesthetics that Italy does best.

Italians like retirement, too. In fact, the national system is one of the most generous in Europe, at least concerning age. Reforms may shortly change this, but under Italian law in 2004, people who have worked and paid contributions for 35 years can retire at 57. Italy has been under pressure from the IMF and European Union to reform its pension system, which currently costs around 15 per cent of the country's GDP and is hampering efforts to reduce the budget deficit. In 2004 the welfare minister Roberto Maroni pointed his finger at the system, saying, 'We start off every year with a 36 billion euro pension deficit.' If changes do occur, Italy will only gradually fall in line with European standards by raising the earliest possible retirement age to 60 by 2010 and only later to 65.

None of the flurry over whether there should be reform or not will matter if you have exclusively paid contributions towards your pension plan in the UK. If you are retired and move to another EU or EEA country, you will receive your benefits there. If you move during your working career and stop paying NI contributions your pension will be frozen (with adjustments according to increases in the UK) until retirement age.

The Pension Service (International Pension Centre, Tyneview Park, Newcastle upon Tyne NE98 1BA, **t** (0)191 218 2000, **tvp-customer-care@dwp.gsi.gov.uk**, **www.dwp.gov.uk**) will have details about how to receive your pension abroad and other pertinent facts. Company pensions may or may not be funnelled into foreign bank accounts and you may or may not wish to have sterling exchanged directly into euros. Currency dealers can monitor fluctuation rates, and transfer funds at the optimum moment. Government pensions (army, civil service, police, and so on) will be taxed in the UK. In other cases it can be paid tax free in gross and then be taxed in Italy.

If you have worked for an Italian company and accrued a pension in INPS (the ruling Italian pension fund) you will have to pay tax on it in Italy. You are unlikely to be tapping into the Italian retirement system, unless you have chosen to become a resident or citizen and use the country's infrastructure like an Italian (filing tax returns and so on).

Payments made in Italy to a private pension fund of up to 12% of income are deductible from taxable income.

Inheritance and Making a Will

Italian inheritance tax (*imposta sulle successioni e donazioni*) has, until recently, been one of the most financially punitive in Europe. Because of an accident of history this tax was effectively levied twice upon death. First, the whole estate was taxed in its entirety, and later the heirs had taxes levied on the separate shares of their inheritance. Reforms mostly aligned national law with European legislation, abolishing the punitive double charge and reducing the actual rates of tax levied. Italian inheritance tax is no longer charged on the whole estate, but levied once on the value of the assets transferred to the individual beneficiaries. Effectively this exempts small- and medium-sized estates from Italian inheritance tax, and particularly foreign owners of Italian properties, which under Italian law are usually taxed on the local land registry value (*rendita catastale rivalutata*).

Much of Italian inheritance law is based on the pan-European medieval *maggiorascato*. Today, it imposes what may be called 'forced inheritance' for Italian citizens, a term implying that specific relatives, including those not holding Italian citizenship, are entitled to a fixed proportion of a decedent's estate. In some cases even illegitimate children are considered heirs. If you have family or roots in Italy and have lost track of the family real estate or other assets, you may have the right to claim portions of property.

Death

Several years ago light blue advertising boards popped up in several Italian cities inviting Italians to 'sleep with the stars'. This gentle campaign was a small indication that despite being a culturally strong Catholic country with burial the standard practice when someone dies, cremation is beginning to be more acceptable. This is partially the result of increasingly limited space and the high cost of burial. It also stems from a 1987 law encouraging the development of cremation, thus lifting some of the cultural taboo around it. The number of cremations in Italy each year grew from 3,000 in 1988 to 23,500 in 1998.

When a death occurs, it must be recorded with the town hall (*comune*) within 24hrs, as well as with the British Consulate. The once controversial *imposta sulle successioni e donazioni* (*ISD*) or taxes on death were abolished in October 2001. However, it could be reinstated or a new tax initiated. Check with your lawyer or accountant for details of the current tax requirements.

Funerals are expensive in Italy, as is returning a body home. Your consulate will have information on services and agencies to assist in the process.

Inheritance

If you are a UK citizen, you can decide how you wish to dispose of your possessions and property as you wish. This is a luxury that Italians don't enjoy, as restrictive rules mean that certain groups of people have almost automatic rights to inherit their property.

Making a Will

When drawing up a will in Italy, do so with a lawyer versed in UK and Italian laws. Immoveable property must be disposed of under Italian law, regardless of whether or not you are a resident or living in Italy. Moveable property will be disposed of in accordance with the will you have drawn up, and the rules of the country you drew it up in. There are ways around the moveable–immoveable rule, but they will depend on your resident status and should be discussed with your lawyer.

Living with Children

It is widely known that Italians love children. And no matter where you end up in Italy, there is a common thread that stitches the country together – *la famiglia*. The family unit is placed so high on a pedestal that it is unshakeable. Infants are coddled and unbelievably spoiled and *mamma* is as sacred as the Virgin Mary herself.

For someone not accustomed to receiving unsolicited advice, hanging out with Italian mothers and women friends can be an experience in itself. An abundance of old wives' tales are heralded as providing guidelines for keeping children safe and healthy. Often Italy can seem like a 'don't' society. Children are bundled from head to foot, even in the summer, to avoid catching cold. Anxious mothers echo the well-known fact that swimming, or even touching water (that includes taking a bath) after eating can cause vomiting, and even kill a child. Sitting on a cold floor can provoke irreparable internal damage. And the 'don't' list goes on. There is a national obsession around the many dangers lurking that children must be shielded from.

Having a child in Italy means you never find yourself alone among neighbours, colleagues, friends and others poised and ready to jump in and lend a hand. And it is probably one of the safest societies to raise offspring, with its many watchful eyes and open arms. Numerous offers to help with car pooling, pickups, hand-me-down clothing and babysitting come hand in hand with the well meaning but sometimes overbearing counsel that you are sure to hear.

All of that doesn't help much with the challenges of raising a child away from your own country. No matter how much locals adore the beloved *bambini*, moving home with children is not always easy. Major and minor changes in your established routine with your kids can be a hair-raising experience even in your own country. Try doing it in another language.

Much depends on what setting you're coming from, and the one you are moving to. Someone coming from a small town in the countryside who moves to a major city, like Milan or Rome, will be faced not only with cultural change, but also with the environmental adjustment that comes with the shift from rural to urban surroundings. The difficulties that would arise from a similar move within your own country might be annoying, but in a foreign land they can raise the blood pressure, and drastically lower morale.

There are many things that big Italian cities can boast of, but being pram-friendly is not one of them. In towns like Rome, a walk with the baby is an exercise in dodging dog poo, navigating cars parked on the pavement and adjusting your infant's protective gas mask. In compensation, however, there are miles and miles of green expanse around the city in the form of public parks and villa grounds for a stroll and fresh air. It just takes time getting to them.

If you grew up with a garden and treehouse, and you dream of your children having one, then get down to the nitty-gritty of choosing between city and country without ado. Houses with gardens are rare in cities, and living in suburbs has its own difficulties. The choice between living in the centre of a city and its suburbs arises in the UK as much as in Italy, but it can feel more oppressive to deal with on foreign ground. Before moving, find out as much about the area that you are moving to as possible. Look for parks, and think of parking. Take a walk and look for pram or stroller access, including to the building you are moving into. One woman explained that even though she had asked if there was a lift to her fourth-floor apartment, when she got there, it was barely wide enough for two adults engaged in an embrace. She lost three prams and two strollers to thieves, since she would leave them in the building's entranceway while carting her baby and groceries up and down in the minuscule lift. Taking the time to think through the practical implications of living in the area that you are planning to move to can save a lot of difficulties later.

Kids' Activities

If you believe that children's activities should involve more than trips to amusement parks, then here are some ideas and resources for fun and educational recreation.

Check two general websites for UK citizens travelling with children, **www.travellingwithchildren.co.uk** and **www.allkids.co.uk/parents/holidays.html**; **www.activitiesforkids.com/travel/travel_hints.htm** suggests activities to keep children occupied anywhere, any time.

Going on holiday with children in Italy can be a boring if not miserable experience amid the cruising teenagers and beach-orientated adults. Accommodation reviews on **www.mumsnet.com/revhols/summer** help pinpoint ideal spots for parents with kids on vacation in the country. And for outings that hold special interest for youngsters, **www.travelforkids.com/Funtodo/Italy/italy.htm** is brimming with up-to-date and well-researched information.

Sports and activities like ceramics and drawing are generally organized through your child's school. Ask his or her teacher what will be offered throughout the year and if there is a list to sign that will let the organizers know how to contact you. One possibility is the Scouts (*esploratori*), which are organized through the Catholic church, though you need not be a member to sign your child up. Contact national organizations and associations (trekking, equestrian, and so on) directly to ask about child-specific courses and programmes (*see* listings in 'Recreational Courses', pp.227–9). The Unione Italiana Sport per Tutti (**www.uisp.it**) organizes summer camps throughout Italy. For nature walks see **www.compagniadellanatura.it** and for child outings in a *bambino*-friendly environment see **www.kinderheim.it**, **t** 02 498 2588.

If you want to visit the amusement parks, here is a list of venues around the country. Don't expect Disneyland, but do expect good old-fashioned, non-educational fun. There is a list of theme parks at **www.italytourism.it** or **www.themeparkcity.com/EURO_IT.htm**. Some direct links to amusement parks with descriptions, opening hours, directions and events are:

- Edenlandia, in Naples (**www.edenlandia.it**)
- Mirabilandia, in Ravenna near Bologna (**www.mirabilandia.it**)
- Gardaland, near Verona (**www.gardaland.it**)
- Luneur, in Rome (**www.luneur.it**).

Education and Studying in Italy

The Italian School System

Free education has been guaranteed in Italy since 1946. Italian schools are divided into three main levels for compulsory education: primary, secondary and superior, and they are discussed below. Pre-school or nursery school (*asilo nido*) for children aged 0–3 is sponsored by the local authorities or private institutions. For 3–5-year-olds there are *scuole materne*, which are part of the school system and under the responsibility of the Ministry of Education (Ministero della Pubblica Istruzione) (**t** 06 58491, Viale Trastevere 76/A, 00153 Rome, **www.istruzione.it**), the governing body for all public education.

Public (state) schools are the norm in Italy. The majority of Italians attend state schools. Private schools are usually an alternative for weaker students, not superior institutions of higher quality. In fact, as one Italian put it, 'the public school system is as close to a non-denominational, non-classist system there is – most Italian students in public schools grow up knowing each other, not their parents' social standings.' Students in private Italian schools are usually sent there because they are not academically bright and, by paying, their parents can guarantee them at least passing high school. There may also be social reasons for sending them there. However, the choice of international private education is different for non-Italian parents, and will be covered later.

Random oral testing (*interrogazione*) is the basis for grading, along with written examinations and end-of-year tests. Italian students know that they can be questioned on the subjects they are studying at any moment while in class. This is meant to encourage constant and thorough preparation. At the end of the school year, a student is either passed on to the next grade level (*promosso*) or failed (*bocciato*) and required to make up the subjects that are not up to standard, either in summer school or during the next academic year.

Italian state schooling adheres to the characteristic Italian bureaucratic and hierarchical mania, which can be discomforting for expats. One young mother from Brighton says, 'Italian state schools are mildly condescending towards parents. Teachers have a "we know best" attitude. They discourage any efforts to meet with them unless it's on their terms and at their convenience. They don't let you keep your child's report card unless you photocopy it yourself at your own expense. You're only allowed to keep the original for a week or so, and then you must return it, as it is state property.' A report card is printed on official stationery and signed, countersigned and rubber-stamped by regional inspectors in a typical display of Italian bureaucracy.

In spite of this administrative strictness, though, the day-to-day running of schools can be surprisingly sloppy. Graffiti covers most walls, and the general air of disrepair that one associates with state institutions is ever present. Sometimes demolition debris and trash from the street is allowed to pile up in quiet corners of the building's exterior and playground and is not swept away from one month to the next. Funding for new equipment needed for the children's playground seems to be non-existent, so dangerous, ill-repaired equipment remains in use for years.

The syllabus and methods of examination are decided by the Ministry of Education, in co-operation with the National Education Council. Regionally, the *sovrintendenza scolastica* represents the Ministry and then Italy is broken down into districts (*distretti*) administered by provincial education offices. Day-to-day running of primary schools is done by the *dirigente scolastico*, and the *preside* runs secondary and high schools.

Primary School

Attendance at primary or elementary school is compulsory from age 6. Primary education promotes cultural literacy and encourages pupils to interact socially at an early stage. Some 93 per cent of primary education is provided by state-run schools, but there are also a number of private primary schools, mainly sponsored by religious groups.

Most primary school teachers are women. A 1998 reform increased the requirements for teachers, making a four-year course ending in a degree (*Laurea in Scienze della Formazione Primaria*) compulsory for teachers, as opposed to the previous certificate from special colleges. For the first five consecutive years,

Goodbye Gift

Every region has a special way of seeing children off. For example, on completing a child's final primary school year in the Lazio region where Rome is located, all graduating pupils are presented with a gift from the county – an elegant gift-box containing a very large cotton Italian national flag, a music CD with the Italian national anthem and five other European national anthems, and a 200-page hardback book relating the story of how the national anthem was written, together with a message of encouragement to the recipient as a young citizen of Italy. Such patriotism may sound like old-fashioned national-istic propaganda, and perhaps it is, but it's a lot better than being presented with nothing at all.

students have the same class teacher. Italians argue that it is meant to provide stability, but it is unfortunate if a child is unhappy with the teacher in question.

Grade school teaching is very activity- and culture-rich and includes numerous day trips and class drama workshops. Italian kids are often exhibitionists and performers, but demanding homework is routine and Italian children are expected to take home and complete work and projects from grade one. The breadth of school subjects at primary level in Italy is impressive. Over the last decade, foreign language lessons and computer training for children as young as 6 years old have been introduced. By the age of 11 children have received intensive introductory levels of schooling in all disciplines and many basic prin-ciples of science (biology, chemistry, physics), as well as some algebraic maths, and even political and 20th-century history. Field trips are one of Italy's strong points. In a land saturated with Roman, Etruscan, Greek and other ruins from north to south, kids at a very young age can experience archaeology first hand.

Parents have to buy all their children's notebooks and are often requested to donate paper, glue, staples, chalk and other stationery materials to the school. Children are not given lockers or desks with storage space, so they must carry their entire, often heavy, collection of school books back and forth from home to school in their rucksacks. And beware of the fact that there is often a lack of toilet paper and soap in the children's lavatories.

Secondary or Middle School

After primary school follows four years of secondary school (*scuola media*) for students aged 11 to 15. Compulsory education ends here, with an exam that must be completed successfully before pupils can continue on to high school or a vocational institute.

Scuola media aim to provide a general academic education and directional framework. After three years students may choose to opt out of secondary school by taking the exam for the *diploma licenza media* and transferring to a vocational school. Secondary students who wish to continue with higher education continue on to high school (*liceo*) and complete those studies by taking the dreaded *maturitá* exam. As with primary education, secondary education is free for pupils. For children attending private (or non-state-run) schools, families pay enrolment and tuition fees. A recent reform gives families state subsidies for those who choose private education – a move that hasn't gone down well with the government opposition and general public.

Secondary-school teachers are required to obtain a university degree (*laurea*) in teaching, plus a qualification (*abilitazione all'insegnamento*) by taking a competitive state exam. There are more male teachers in secondary schools than in primary schools, but most secondary-school teachers are still female, some 76 per cent according to government figures.

Upper Secondary School or High Schools

The pressure is on at age 14 to decide whether or not to continue on towards university or concentrate on vocationally orientated studies. There are many options: *liceo scientifico* (scientific secondary school), *liceo classico* (grammar school), *liceo linguistico* (language secondary school), *istituto magistrale* (magisterial school), *facoltà di magistero* (teachers' training college), *istituto tecnico* (technical school), *istituto professionale* (professional school) and the artistic institutions *liceo artistico* (art school), *istituto d'arte* (institute of art), *conservatorio di musica* (conservatory of music), *accademia di danza* (academy of dance) and *accademia nazionale d'arte drammatica* (national academy of dramatic art). The diploma you get at the end of this stage of education leads on to the professions either directly or indirectly by admission to university.

University

The Italian university model is still almost exclusively academic, meaning that the focus is on cognitive knowledge with little attention to work tools, methods or other techniques. Students are ready to enter the university after obtaining a secondary high school diploma (*diploma di maturitá*). For some courses there is an introductory first year before going to university, for example, a student with a diploma from the *liceo artistico* would be able to enrol in the *accademia di belle arti*, but would require supplementary courses to enter another university.

Overcrowding is a major problem for Italian universities. For the more coveted degrees there are often entry exams. Each university has different admissions policies and applications must be made to each one individually. The educational and vocational system in Italy has been without radical changes from 1923 and reforms are inevitable. Though university is free for students, there are enrolment fees (*tasse di iscrizione*) and regional taxes to be paid.

Anyone can apply to get on to a course at an Italian university, though there are specific bureaucratic hoops to jump through for non-Italians (*see* 'Foreign Students at University', below). The world's oldest university from the 11th century is in Bologna, and the University of Oriental Studies in Naples has been rated one of the leading institutions worldwide. The **Ministry for Universities** (Dipartimento per l'Autonomia Universitaria e gli Studenti, Piazzale JF Kennedy 20, 00144 Rome, **t** 06 59911, **www.miur.it**) has more information about applying.

Foreign Students in State Schools

Education in Italian state schools is free for all, including foreigners. Non-residents may enrol a student in elementary, middle or high school. Even if your children are infants when you move to Italy, if you plan to stay in the country, at some point you'll need to find a school for them. There are numerous private schools that provide primary and high school English or bilingual education for expatriate children (*see* 'English and International Schools', below), but you may prefer to raise your kids as semi-Italians and enrol them at an Italian state school; this would be cheaper and will probably encourage them to integrate into the local area more closely.

You must apply directly to the school that you wish your child to attend. Information about local schools can be obtained from the local education office (*provveditorato*) or the town hall (*comune*). If transferring from a school in another country, an authorized translation of the student's qualifications and past scholastic experience is needed and a letter from the former head teacher.

There are more than two sides to the public–private, international–Italian school argument. On the personal side, you should consider everything from your language skills to those of your children. Would you be able to help them with their homework in Italian? Are you familiar with the Italian curriculum? Will you be settling permanently in Italy or moving away at some point? Do you want to participate in teacher–parent meetings and is your Italian sufficient?

From an educational point of view, don't be afraid to pull out all the stops when looking into the educational options for your children. A series of reforms of Italian state schools has been introduced to ensure that the national syllabus is in line with the rest of Europe, but it may take some time for some of the weaker points to be ironed out. However, the Italian educational system has been applauded as well rounded and one that encourages independent thinking, and some of the world's most stunning artists, poets, architects, doctors and engineers have come from the *scuola pubblica italiana*.

Foreign Students at University

Foreign students who wish to register at an Italian university should follow the procedure outlined in the circular issued each year in April by Ministero dell'Università e della Ricerca Scientifica e Tecnologica (MURST). It is available at the site of the Ministry (**www.miur.it**) by clicking on '*Atti ministeriali*', and at the site of the Ministero degli Affari Esteri (**www.esteri.it**). The most recent version of the circular is 'Registration of foreign students at courses in Italian public universities and private universities with the authority to issue legally valid degrees – Academic year 2003/2004' (only available in Italian). The places available for foreign students each year are listed at the sites of the various universities or at the Ministero degli Affari Esteri (MAE) or Ministero dell'Istruzione, dell'Università e della Ricerca (MIUR). For information about scholarships, foreign students should contact the Ministero degli Affari Esteri at Direzione Generale per le Relazioni Culturali, Ufficio IX, 00195 Rome.

EU and non-EU students who live outside Italy should hand in their application, indicating the degree programme and university they wish to attend, to the Italian embassy or consulate in their own country usually between May and June. They should include their secondary school diploma or equivalent, which will be translated into Italian and authenticated with a *dichiarazione di valore*. The Embassy or Consulate will forward the application to the universities chosen, which will contact the students who are eligible to sit for the entrance examination no later than August. Students must also take a test in Italian language and culture, which is generally held in September. Only students who have passed the test in Italian language and culture are eligible to sit the entrance exam to faculties with a limited number of places available. Non-EU students who have a permit to study in Italy must report to the police station (*questura*) in the university town they have applied to within 8 days of their arrival (*see* **Red Tape**, 'The *Permesso di Soggiorno*', pp.116–18).

Students who live in Italy can obtain form 'D' for the authentication *dichiarazione di valore* of their school diploma from the foreign students' office of their chosen university. They should send this with their application form to the Italian embassy in their own country. These students do not have to sit the Italian language and culture test. With the qualifications from their school and a certificate that they have passed the Italian language exam (if required), all foreign students can register for any undergraduate degree programme.

When continuing a university degree, or applying for a researcher's position in an Italian university, your previous qualifications must be recognized. Non-EU residents must apply to the Italian embassy or consulate in the country where the qualifications were obtained by the date established by the Ministero dell'Università e della Ricerca e Tecnologia. The Italian diplomatic bodies will then translate, authenticate and forward the documentation to your chosen university. To have your foreign qualifications recognized and declared valid in Italy, you must submit the following documents:

- **your secondary school certificate**
- **academic qualifications**
- **a list of subjects taken and their respective syllabuses**
- **your thesis (if any)**
- **two photographs**

All university students pay a standard fee. Other fees vary according to the student's economic circumstances and the degree or diploma programme. All foreign students must present their parents' income tax declaration(s) for the year before their registration at the university. The tax form must be translated into Italian and authenticated by the Italian diplomatic authorities in the country in which they were presented.

All students registered for degree or diploma programmes can apply for accommodation. Applications are processed according to school exam results and parental incomes. University students can also use the refectory where the Istituto per il Diritto allo Studio (ISU) serves low-cost meals. Information can be obtained from ISU (ISU, Via Santa Sofia 7/9, Milan, **t** 02 5830 8017 or **t** 02 5832 0507, **http://users.unimi.it/~isu/isu.htm**).

English and International Schools

There are a number of major English-language schools (from kindergarten to upper school level) in Italy. Though most are private and have considerable enrolment fees, some provide financial aid or can direct you to helpful sources. If your region is not included, go to **www.international-schools.com**.

In and Around Rome

Ambrit Rome International School
Via Filippo Tajani 50, 00149 Roma
t 06 559 5305, **f** 06 559 5309
www.ambrit-rome.com
Pre-school, primary, middle

American Overseas School of Rome
Via Cassia 811, 00189 Roma
t 06 334381, **f** 06 3326 2608
www.aosr.org
Pre-kindergarten, elementary, middle, high, boarding

Castelli International School
Via degli Scozzesi 13, 00046 Grottaferrata, Roma
/**f** 06 9431 5779
www.pcg.it/cis
Grades 1 to 8

Castelli Kindergarten
Via dei Laghi 8,600, Logetta di Marino, A9 00047 Marino, Roma
t 06 9366 1311
www.romeschools.org
Ages 3 to 6

Core International School
Via Crati 19, 00199 Roma
t 06 841 1137
Nursery, primary

Greenwood Garden School
Via Vito Sinisi 5, 00189 Roma
t/f 06 3326 6703
donnase@tin.it
Early childhood development centre

Kendale Primary International School
Via Gradoli Tomba di Nerone – Via Cassia Km 10.300, 00189 Roma
t/f 06 366 7608
www.romeschools.org
Ages 3 to 11 years

Marymount International School
Via di Villa Lauchli 180 (Via Cassia Antica Km. 7), 00191 Roma
t 06 362 9101, f 06 3630 1738
www.marymountrome.com
Early childhood to Grade 12

The New School
Via della Camilluccia 669, 00135 Roma
t 06 329 4269, f 06 329 7546
www.newschoolrome.com
Nursery, kindergarten, primary, secondary

Rome International School
Viale Romania, 32, 00197 Roma
t 06 8448 2650 or t 06 8448 2651, f 06 8448 2653
ammiserm@mclink.it
Kindergarten, elementary

St Francis International School
Via Borgia 85, 00168 Roma
t/f 06 3551 1023
www.stfrancisinternationalschool.com
Early childhood, primary, middle

Southlands English School in Rome
Via Teleclide 20 (Via Epaminonda), Casal Palocco 00124 Roma
t 06 505 3932, f 06 5091 7192
www.southlands.it
Nursery, kindergarten, primary

St George's British International School
Via Cassia Km. 16, 00123 Roma
t 06 308 6001, f 06 3089 2490
www.stgeorge.school.it
Ages 3 to 18

St Stephen's School
Via Aventina 3, 00153 Roma
t 06 575 0605, f 06 574 1941
www.ststephens.it
Grades 9 to 12, boarding

Tuscany
American International School of Florence
Via del Carota 23/25, 50012 Bagno a Ripoli (Firenze)
t 055 646 1007, f 055 644226
www.aisfitaly.org
Pre-school, middle, upper

Liguria
American International School of Genoa
Via Quarto 13/C, 16148 Genova
t 010386 528, f 010386 700
Ages 3 to 14

Lombardy
American School of Milan
20090 Noverasco di Opera (Milano)
t 02 530 0001, f 02 5760 6274
www.asmilan.org
Primary, intermediate, middle, high

International School of Milan
Via Caccialepori 22, 20148 Milano
t 02 4870 6030452 or t 02 4009 2180
www.ism-ac.it
Pre-school, elementary, middle, high

Sir James Henderson School of Milan
Via Pisani Dossi 16, 20134 Milano
t 02 264 13310, f 02 264 13515
www.sirjameshenderson.com
Pre-school, lower, upper

Campania

British Forces School
Parco Mazzola 80014, Lago Patria (Napoli)
t 08 1509 1653 or **t** 08 15096555
Bfsnaples@libro.it
Elementary

International School of Naples
Viale della Liberazione 1, 80125 Bagnoli (Napoli)
t 08 1721 2037 or **t** 08 1635 753, **f** 08 157 0248
www.intschoolnaples.it/elementary.htm
Elementary, high

Friuli-Venezia Giulia

International School of Trieste
Via Conconello 16, 34016 Opicina (Trieste)
t 04 0211 452, **f** 04 0213 122
www.geocities.com
Early childhood, elementary, junior high

Veneto

Vicenza International School
Contra San Marcello 9, 36100 Vicenza
t 0444 525080, **f** 0444 525083
www.worldwide.edu/ci/italy/schools/15488.html
Kindergarten, elementary, middle, upper

Piedmont

International School of Turin
Vicolo Tiziano 10, 10024 Moncalieri (Torino)
t 11645 967, **f** 11643 298
www.saa.unito.it
Early childhood, elementary, upper

Recreational Courses

Wielding a chisel like Michelangelo or becoming a literary master like Dante may not be on the cards, but being surrounded by creative energy and with a stimulating backdrop has a way of awakening your inner artist. Taking courses, classes, workshops and even university degrees can be rewarding and another way of enjoying living in the country. A quick search on Google will bring up an infinite number of possibilities, but some ideas to get you started are considered below.

Cooking and Wine-tasting

Go to a party, join colleagues for a drink, mingle at an art exhibition. Wherever it is, in most Italian social situations the discussion inevitably turns towards fine cuisine (*la buona cucina*). Taking a course or going on a cooking holiday means that you'll never be at a loss for small (or big) talk when conversations move in that direction. And what better way to make new friends than giving an invitation to a stellar dinner party?

One of the best known culinary training courses is the series (in English) from Diane Seed, held in the splendid Palazzo Doria Pamphili kitchens in Rome (Via del Plebiscito, 00186 Roma, **t** 06 6797 103, **f** 06 6797 109, **www.italiangourmet. com**), Seed is the quintessential voice on getting to know authentic Italian cuisine. The Città del Gusto (City of Taste) in Rome (Via Enrico Fermi 161, Roma, **t** 06 5511 2211, **f** 5511 2266, **formazione@gamberorosso.it**) offers cooking courses and *sommelier* classes in English throughout 2004. Another option in Rome is to enrol for one of the wine courses and tastings at the International Wine Academy in Piazza di Spagna (Vicolo del Bottino 8, 00187 Roma, **t** 06 699 0878, **f** 06 679 1385); the tastings are always an event.

Some schools combine cooking and language, such as Porta e'Oriente (Via Antonio Primaldo 70, 73028 Otranto, Lecce, **t** 338 456 2722, **f** 0836 804431, **porta.doriente@libero.it**, **www.porta-doriente.com**) in the region of Puglia.

For an extensive list of schools throughout Italy, go to **www.italyemb.org** and look under 'cooking schools'.

Art, Restoration and Fashion

Packed with art and cultural courses (such as restoration, painting and fashion), the World Wide Arts website, h**ttp://wwar.com/categories/Academic/ Countries/Italy** lists what's on throughout the country.

Mosaic Art School (Via Francesco Negri 14, 48100 Ravenna, **t** 349 601 4566, **f** 054 436 1920, **mosaic@sira.it**, **www.sira.it**) gives learn-how instruction and the historical background of an art form widely found throughout Italy. Vecchio Atelier d'Artista (Strada Mandoleto 11, 06071 Castel del Piano (Pg), **t** 075 529 3246, **info@vecchioatelier.it**, **www.vecchioatelier.it**) in Umbria has hands-on restoration courses.

Dance, Acting, Theatre and Choir

Acting courses are a good way to break down any embarrassment and exercise your Italian. Arte del Teatro (Via Urbana 107, Rome, **t** 06 488 5608) is one possibility in Rome. Some language schools, like Scuola Leonardo da Vinci, with branches in Rome, Florence and Siena (**www.scuolaleonardo.com**), teach theatre and cinema courses in Italian so you get an extra benefit. *See also* 'English and International Schools', above.

Water Activities

White-water rafting, snorkelling, scuba and free diving are popular because of Italy's clement temperature much of the year and near proximity to clear water. Keep in mind that Leonardo da Vinci was the first known user of air tanks in Italy in the 15th century, and the tradition continues. For scuba classes check with Scuba Schools International in Italy (Via Bergami 4, 40133 Bologna, **t** 051 383082, **f** 383554, **www.ssi-italy.org**) for courses near you, and in English if available. For free diving check with the international free divers association's local office (Via delle Porta 21, 07026 Olbia (SS), **t** 07 895 3511, **Italy@divingFREE.com**). There is excellent rafting to be had in the verdant region of Umbria – try the rafting centre Fiume Corno in Norcia (**t** 0742 23146 or **t** 348 3511798, **www.raftingumbria.it**) or go to the National Rafting Association (Associazione Italiana Rafting, Via Caiolo Alto, 23100 Caiolo Alto, Sondrio, **t** and **f** 342 354018, **airaf@airaf.it**, **www.airaf.it**).

Listings

To see listings of other activities, dip into local magazines, local publications and look out for postings at bars and universities. The back pages of *Roma C'e*, in Rome, for example, publishes courses in the city, as does the City of Rome homepage under '*Corsi in città*'. Every major city now has a website, as do most small towns, with information on municipally sponsored activities and paid courses.

Sports

Spectator Sports

At first glance it may seem that **football** (*il calcio*) has a monopoly on the Italian taste. As Peterjon Cresswell said in his *Fans' Guide to European Football*, 'The Italian game ... is a weekly celebration of noise and colour, fed by a media hyperbole which would put an American presidential campaign to shame.'

But speed isn't enjoyed only on the pitch. Racy Italians like velocity and it doesn't get more lively than with **Formula One motor racing**. Ferrari is associated with Michael Schumacher, who took his team to the top of world racing after decades of unsuccessful competitions. In the land where herds of moped drivers zip around from age 14 (officially) onwards, it is unsurprising that Italian

motorcycle racing has produced the likes of world champions Valentino Rossi (whose fan-club following travel the globe to watch the teenage heart throb), Max Biaggi and Loris Capirossi.

In 1998 Italy entered the **rugby** Five Nation Tournament, making it six. Though hardly vying for a top ranking, they managed to beat Scotland on their own territory – their one and only victory in numerous tournaments, despite having a team with vicious determination.

Tuscany and Emilia-Romagna, with their rolling hills and less busy roads, are prime training grounds for world-class **cyclists**, like Pantani, winner of Tour de France and Giro d'Italia; the historic cycling couple Coppi e Bartali from the 1940s and 50s; and Binda and Guerra from the 1920s who inspired the song by Italian singer Paolo Conte TKT.

Often **winter sports** like skiing and snowboarding aren't associated with sunny Italia, but don't forget Olympic winning skiers Alberto Tomba, Deborah Compagnoni and Isolde Kostner who dominated the ski competition scene throughout the 1990s, raking in the cups and medals left and right.

Participatory Sports

Spectator sports aside, there are numerous activities to get involved with while in the country, such as dance, gyms, amateur soccer teams, horse riding, trekking and cycling. It may take some research to find where to go initially, as Italians tend to organize sports more through friends and acquaintances than through centres where participants sign up individually. Depending on your interest, try investigating at the local *circolo sportivo*. Every town, and in big cities nearly every neighbourhood, has a *circolo* where you can sign up for various sports that you can enjoy at weekends or after work. Be aware that sometimes it isn't clear what exactly is on offer and they can feel a bit exclusive.

If you are interested in one particular activity, start by looking directly for single-interest clubs or organizations. There is a list of some of the main activities and sports, giving Italian terminology, below.

• *Equitazione, andare a cavallo, cavalcare*: **Horse-riding** is popular in Italy, and there are numerous stables (*maneggi*), which are often small and privately run. Ask what is available at bed and breakfasts (*agriturismi*) in the area you want to ride in. They almost always have a stable they recommend. Or look in local listings for stables, either in weekend guides or in the phone book. You can also go to a store that sells equestrian equipment and ask for contacts.

• *Nuoto* (**swimming**): before signing up (*inscriversi*) to use a public or private pool, you will be asked to give a doctor's certificate attesting to your good health. You can also ask for an exam by the pool's staff doctor. Swimming pools are listed under '*Piscine*' in the Italian *Pagine Gialle* (and check the English *Yellow Pages*, too).

Case Study: Do you Rehg-bee?

When 33-year-old Paul Virgo wanted to find a rugby (pronounced *rehg-bee* in Italian) team to play with in Rome, he wasn't clear where to start: 'I wandered around at the weekend looking for pitches with H-shaped posts.' He ended up playing for AS Villa Pamphili, a C2 level team. However, signing on 'wasn't easy as Italy is a bureaucratic country and every year I have to get letters from the English Rugby Union testifying that I am not a pro,' says Virgo. 'You'd have thought one letter would have been enough ... after all, if I wasn't a pro in 1998 and played all the following season in Italy, why did I have to get the same letter from the English RFU, saying the same thing in 1999 and then every year after that?' But, aside from the red tape, life on the playing field for the English teacher, doubling as a journalist, is just as competitive in Italy as in the UK. Italian players 'play to win' says the now injured scrum-half player. 'Either they do things properly or they don't do them at all. There's no glory in being a noble loser – they play to win.'

After four years in Italy Virgo has discovered that the thing he loves about living there is the same thing that drives him crazy – the people. 'Italians are kind, hospitable, interested in things beyond their borders – much more than many of my compatriots – and gentle. BUT, those people I find kind, charming and gentle in social situations must inevitably be the same people who are rude with members of the public in banks, post office, etc., vote for Berlusconi, and try to mow me down when I'm on a zebra crossing.' However, he doesn't agree with the stereotypes about English people being less touchy-feely than Italians and doesn't mind 'the odd *ciao bello*' called his way by male friends. 'I have English male friends who I'm just as touchy with as my Italian pals,' says Virgo. He agrees that there is a lower instance of 'sweet' talk in the locker room than in social situations. 'In the end,' he notes, 'I guess the rugby team is more macho than your average male.'

• *Palestre* **(gym)**: to keep that *bella presenza* polished and impressive Italians spend a lot of time in the gym. Signing up is easy, though most gyms will not give out membership costs over the phone. Visit a few and ask around to find the one best suited to you. Big chain gyms have yet to catch on, meaning that gyms have a lot of variety in size and character.

• *Sci* **(skiing)**: it's really enough to decide where you want to go. Weekends at smaller resorts and slopes are a harrying experience of skiers pouring in from the surrounding towns for a weekend run. But calm weekdays, if your schedule is flexible, can give you the chance to ski Italy's small and big mountains even in a day trip. Alternatively, white weeks (*settimane bianche*) are packages that can be picked up at travel agents and are all-inclusive deals for trips to the numerous Alps and Dolomite ski resorts.

• *Calcio, Pallone, Calcetto*: **Soccer** and all of its variations (five-player, indoor, and so on) are played everywhere and all the time. For a more organized approach, pop into the recreation centre (*circolo sportive*) to see if a team is being organized. Pitches (*campi di calcetto*) for five-player matches can be rented out with an identity card when there is a free time slot. So if you want to take the initiative, organize with friends or co-workers and go to the local sporting centre (*centro sportive*), with each player chipping in their share of the cost.

• **Ciclismo (cycling)**: country roads throughout Italy, but especially in Tuscany and Emilia Romagna, are filled with groups of cyclists in semi-professional gear peddling away for fun or training. In small towns local bike clubs organize bike outings (*giri*). Local cycle shops generally have lists of *gruppi ciclistici*, as well. If you just want a relaxing pedal, bikes can be rented for a modest daily rate.

• *Roccia, alpinismo* and *speleolo*gia (**rock-climbing, trekking and spelunking**): the Club Alpino Italiano or CAI (**t** 02 2505 7231, **www.cai.it**) has numerous groups and instructors for climbing throughout Italy, as does Associazione Amici del Trekking e della Natura (**t** 02 837 2838, **www.trekkingitalia.com**). To get inside the country, try exploring Italy's network of caves with Centro Nazionale di Speleologia (**t** 075 9170 236) or Societa Speleologica Italianana (**t** 051 209 4547, **f** 051 209 4522, **www.ssi.speleo.it**).

• *Pesca* and *caccia* (**fishing and hunting**): for fresh-water fishing, a licence is required through the Federazione Italiana della Pesca Sportiva (Viale Tiziano 70, Rome 00196, **t** 06 3685 8522). Deep-sea fishing is also very popular and does not require a licence. The hunting season in Italy is from September to February. Get informed about local endangered species and the regulations around hunting before picking up a shotgun and heading out with the Association Face Italia (Via San Antonio 11, I-20122 Milano, **t** 02 5830 4902, **f** 5830 5005, **faceit@libero.it**).

Also, look under '*Associazioni e federazioni sportive*' (Sports associations and federations) in the phone book.

Working in Italy

07

Though everyday life may be easy, and quality of life superb, living in Italy comes at a price. Whether moving to study or start a new life, you'll need an income. Students often like to pick up extra cash with a part-time job and even retirees may want to dabble in their old profession or become skilled at a new one. Most people who move to Italy are simply looking for a way to support their dream of living *la vita Italiana* and making enough money to pay the bills.

Typically, Italy has been the land of the 'dream job'. Artists in all media gravitate towards the poetic vision of Venice, the verdant Chiantishire that makes for an endless stream of Kodak moments or the lemon-blossomed Amalfi coast. Endless prose has flown from expat writers' pens. Incessantly clicking camera lenses seek to capture the soul of the country. *Arte* leads the way to fame and fortune, or at least helps to scratch out an income.

Much has also been reported about Italy being a country plagued by complex labour laws and high unemployment. To complicate matters further, regional disparities between north and south are considerable. There is a resistance to hiring non-Italian employees, and nepotism rules when it comes to taking on staff. But more international companies are moving in and Italian companies are going international, creating the need for foreign employees.

If Italy is where you want to live, you will probably have to tangle with the joys and frustrations of seeking employment and eventually working there. Following basic, common sense rules that apply to any labour market, and paying extra attention to the extra-special Italian characteristics described in this chapter, will set you on the road to your professional life (*la tua vita professionale*) in Italy.

Business Etiquette

There is no underestimating the **bella figura** (roughly translated as 'making good appearance'). In the workplace, it is nearly as important as having a university degree and work experience. The *bella figura* umbrella covers everything from being well groomed and sporting smart attire, to using the correct formal tense when speaking, dishing out compliments and displaying the gift of the gab.

Closely linked with the *bella figura* is the **title** (*titolo*). That little nudge before a last name has the power of commanding respect in Italy like in no other country. When Italians graduate from university (at a national average age of 28), the degree earns them the title of Doctor (*Dottore* or *Dottoressa*). It is the crowning moment in the coming-of-age ceremony. And for any professional trying to get things done, or just simply get someone's attention, tossing in a

Dottore or any other title often serves as a crucial catalyst. Other titles include Engineer (*Ingegnere*) or Accountant (*Ragioniere* or *Commercialista*), a pretty low rung on the scale; Lawyer or Attorney (*Avvocato*), as Fiat's Gianni Agnelli was crowned; or Knight (*Cavaliere*), which is something that is granted, for instance to prime minister Berlusconi who is a *Cavaliere del lavoro*, or received for special services in industry.

When going to a **business meeting**, don't be surprised if it is carried out 'over lunch'. The offers to discuss business over a meal (*colazione*), which can mean lunch or breakfast, but usually lunch, is commonplace. And though wine will certainly be on the table, and it is considered polite to have a sip, the casual atmosphere serves mostly to create an atmosphere of co-operation and trust. In the same way, the after-work cocktail (*aperitivo*) sets the stage for relaxed yet serious conversation at which colleagues are also carefully evaluating each other. There is no underestimating the power of casual meetings that set the foundation for confidential working relationships.

So back to the *famosa bella figura*. Italian **office attire** for men can be a classic-cut suit and tie, or even less formal trousers and shirt, but whatever it is, it will always be freshly pressed, starched and immaculate. Many men take an extra shirt to change into at midday and usually have a freshening-up kit at hand. One Italian politician, when jabbed at by a German spokesman (no, not the Berlusconi–Schwartz debacle!), was heard to comment, 'look at the *figura* he makes', which can be taken to refer to the scene he was making, but was also a double-edged reference to his (tasteless) appearance.

Women are also painstakingly well turned out for the office. They are less likely to wear feminine suits than the latest cut of trousers, and blouses and skirts of varying lengths, with an emphasis on quality brands and designer labels. Skirt lengths can be on the short side, linen trousers are popular in summer and blouses are often very light. As one male colleague said, *la bella femmina Italiana* has an air of self-confidence that can be eye-catching, and a bit daunting.

Greetings at the first meeting (*il primo incontro*) should always be formal; greater informality comes later. *'Buon giorno, dottore/dottoressa'* is the correct way to greet another colleague or boss for the first time. Find out as much as you can about the title of the person you are meeting. *Dottore*, though generally a safe formality, could actually be incorrect and *Ingegnere* or *Avvocato* more appropriate. Using the proper title not only sets a confident tone, it reflects your cultural command of the language. Once on comfortable terms with colleagues, *'Salve'* is a warm but more professional greeting and will be heard more often than *'Ciao'*, the least formal of all salutations.

When taking leave, the most common expression is a heartfelt *'Arrivederci'* or *'Arrivederla'* when face to face, or *'Arrisentirci'* or *'Arrisentirla'* if on the phone. If it is a first meeting, thank people for their time and look directly at them while shaking their hand (*stringendo la mano*, literally squeezing the hand). A dodgy gaze could imply that a person is not recommendable (*poco raccomandabile*).

Il primo incontro will probably be arranged by telephone. If you are initiating the meeting, a bit of patience and cajoling is helpful. Secretaries (*segretarie*) may not always take messages, and if you are meeting a higher-level executive, ask to speak directly to his or her assistant (*assistente*). Name-dropping helps considerably, and don't forget to use titles to catch attention.

Once a professional relationship is formed, there are a series of 'kindnesses' (*gentilezze*) that it is sensible to observe. Small **gifts** are given out on public holidays, when employees such as drivers, doormen and cleaning staff are given tips (*mance*) and high-level management gives small gifts, usually food baskets, to other employees. Journalists are often offered costly and substantial gifts that they may have to turn down gently, citing their publication's code of ethics. At the headquarters of one foreign publication a correspondent reported that from early December their one-room office would be packed to the gills with everything from wine to designer clothing. The line was drawn, however, when an automobile was delivered with an eloquently written card inviting the publication's chief to interview the CEO.

The Labour Market

When seeking work in Italy there are different kinds of **contracts** available. Always ask an accounting consultant (*ragioniere*), certified accountant (*commercialista*) or labour union representative (*sindacalista*) what your options are. Your embassy will have a list of preferred certified accountants and the three major labour unions in Italy are CSIL, CGIL and UIL, all of which have an adviser for foreign workers. But there are differences that you can find out about immediately.

Being employed on a long-term or permanent contract by a company (*assunto*) gives you all the rights and privileges of any Italian employee. This is the most difficult of all classifications to secure. Alternatively you might be offered a consultancy contract (*contratto di consulente*), which gives you fewer rights than Italians have, but means that you will be taxed less and have fewer contractual obligations. These are generally offered for short-term projects or for trial period and are a way that Italian companies use to get round the labour law that makes it nearly impossible to fire an employee (*see* box 'Dying for a Change', opposite). Italian companies are wary of being locked into contracts that could leave them burdened with ineffectual employees, so the *contratto di consulente* is common, as is black-market labour (*lavoro in nero*). See 'Contracts', p.245, for a list of the various contracts available and their main characteristics.

Statistics of high **unemployment** in Italy can be misleading. Though the official rate is 12 per cent, it skyrockets to 50 per cent in some parts of the south, and

Dying for a Change

On 19 March 2002 the economist and advocate of labour reform, Marco Biagi, was pedalling home in Bologna, as he did every evening. Biagi had been advising the government on urgently needed reforms to unshackle the country's rigid labour market. That evening the soft-spoken economist was shot dead outside his home with a bullet in the neck. The Red Brigade (Brigate Rosse) admitted responsibility.

The brutal murder shocked Italians, who believed that the savage decades of political assassinations had long since drawn to a close. With this eruption of violence, Italy's debate over labour market reform dramatically polarized. Prime minister Silvio Berlusconi faces one of his toughest challenges trying to deliver on election promises to make Europe's fourth largest economy more competitive.

Less than a week after Biagi's assassination, at the behest of the country's largest labour union CGIL, more than one million Italians streamed into Rome protesting about the legislation proposing changes to article 18 of the 1970 Workers' Statute. This article effectively protects employees from dismissal. Since 90 per cent of Italian workers are not covered by any kind of unemployment insurance, unions staunchly defend this and other job-protection clauses.

Ironically, Biagi's close friends say the gentle 57-year-old economist was a moderate and opposed the government's radical attack on workers' rights, preferring to build consensus for change. He was against putting changes to article 18 in the draft law without prior discussion with labour union leaders. Unlike the government, he knew it would meet with stiff resistance.

Berlusconi's proposed changes are actually minimal. The new law does not affect some nine million existing labour contracts. It would facilitate lay-offs for three types of workers: those hired by small companies with more than 15 employees, employees of companies in the underground economy that come clean, and part-time workers in the south whose contracts are transformed into full-time contracts. However, media tycoon and former entertainer Berlusconi failed to sell the labour reform, assuming he would find little resistance. Says one industry association spokesperson, 'The real message got lost. Italians felt duped. The crucial point was never clearly communicated.'

A now embattled Berlusconi has vowed to push ahead with labour law reforms, undaunted by terrorists or union opposition. But industry leaders question whether the gain is worth the cost in social conflict, and fear that the growing climate of distrust and recrimination could block other crucial reforms and lessen Italy's image among investors. No question, Italy's labour market needs an overhaul, but 'at what price?' asked one national newspaper. An editorial written the day after Biagi's murder put the question, 'Is Italy truly a country that is dying for a change?'

dips to a mere 4 per cent in parts of the north. A significant number of unregistered employees muddle the unemployment figures as well. Young people in Italy are most affected, with 30 per cent of the under-25 age group unemployed. But often the unemployed (or partially employed) in the south won't seek job opportunities in the north for fear of discrimination, or simply because they don't want to move too far from their *casa*. A northern shipping company short of workers offered a fully covered move, housing allowance for the first year and competitive salaries for Sicilians and Calabresi willing to move near Verona, thinking that in the two regions with the highest unemployment rate the applications would come rolling in. For the 57 places they were offering they had 12 applications, and managed to hire one driver.

For this reason and others, northern companies are seeking immigrant labourers to fill the gap. Although the positions are usually at the bottom of the hierarchy, it is a small sign that there is change coming in a labour market that is renowned for its rigidity and tendency to hire Italians over foreign labourers.

British job-hunters will find that, although in general it is difficult to penetrate the Italian labour market, there are certain positions that Italians prefer be filled by non-Italians. Your chances increase depending on your skills, linguistic ability and place you are seeking employment.

Job Ideas

If being non-Italian initially seems more like a hindrance than a boon when seeking employment, keep in mind that you have some of the same skills that Italians do and some that they do not, precisely because you aren't Italian. You may want to look into some of the possibilities discussed below.

• **Editing, researching or writing for English-language publications**: Individual jobs may come and go, but they are always required in Italy.

• **Translating or interpreting**: Though you need proficiency in Italian for this, sometimes agencies, companies or organizations need a native English speaker to 'clean up' translations that sound awkward or are outright incorrect. One woman got her first translating job by informing the restaurant she was eating in that the menu had many errors. After she had corrected the menu at the restaurant the management referred her to friends who ran another restaurant, then another. She now specializes in menu and brochure translation.

• **TV publicity, film and other media productions**: There are often vacancies for extras, actors, technicians or just someone to fill in the crowd. One website to check is **www.mandy.com**.

• Several **UN organizations** (FAO, IFAD, IPGRI, UNESCO, UNICER, WFP) have their base or offices in Italy and there are other international non-governmental organizations (IOM, OXFAM) here, as well (*see* p.244). They often need staff.

• **Bars and restaurants**: It's worth approaching any bars and restaurants that cater to tourists or an English-speaking clientele in case they are interested in taking on English-speaking staff. Not only are kit Irish pubs multiplying like rabbits throughout Italy, Rome has Planet Hollywood and Hard Rock, and every major city has somewhere that attracts non-Italians; they need staff.

• **Hotels and bed and breakfasts or *agriturismo***: Major hotel chains have a constant need for a multilingual staff. With the burgeoning phenomenon of agriturismi, the demand for English-speaking staff has increased. A list of registered B&Bs in Italy can be found through the internet. Similarly, the extensive Italian coast is peppered with resort towns – Cinque Terre, Milano Marittima, Portofino, Positano, Riccione, Rimini and many more – that need seasonal staff with language skills. Club Med has six resorts in Italy and hires bar staff and childcare workers for periods of no less than 6 months.

• **Catering and party organizers**: This is another growing sector for Italians and the expat community. Most hotels use external catering, and private caterers may provide small dinners to private customers, as well as cater for large events. Party organizers can be in demand for anything from children's birthdays to wedding festivities.

• **Public relations or communications**: English-speaking staff are required in any of the many companies with a press office that need an international public relations voice. This could include foreign companies like Texas Instruments or Buena Vista Home Entertainment, as well as Italian companies that need to deal with the foreign press or international companies, such as Alitalia, Telecom Italia, Benetton, or the fast-growing newcomers like Tiscali or EBiscom. If you are interested in public relations, don't hesitate to phone the *ufficio stampa* or *ufficio relazione internazionale* (listed in the reference guide *Uomini e Communicazione* mentioned below, or reached by calling the switchboard and asking to be transferred) and ask if there are any openings.

• **Working with tourists**: There are jobs travelling with groups on package tours as an assistant (*accompagnatore* or *accompagnatrice*). This is not a guide as such. To become a guide, one must pass a local exam for the city one is in. An accompagnatore stays with the group from their arrival to their departure, helping them with practical arrangements such as hotel check-ins, getting to restaurants, getting to their local guides and liaising with the group and the booking agency.

• **Crafts and souvenir shops**: These are in every major town and city, and cater to non-Italian-speaking customers (imagine that!) who are usually tourists. Florence has leather, Rome religious objects and mini-Colosseums, Venice glass and lace. These shops will look for attendants who can cater to customers, both linguistically and in the service they provide. Try going around to shops or local chambers of commerce for a listing of *negozi* selling the wares that tourists look for.

• **Au pair work**: This is for anyone in their 20s (sometimes younger, but it depends on the agency or family); look for au pair work by tapping into one of several well-known international agencies like English-Italian Au Pair in Italy (Aupairitaly.com, Via Demetrio Martinelli, 11/d – 40133 Bologna, **t** 051 383466, **info@aupairitaly.com**) and Angels International Au Pair Agency (**www.payaway. co.uk/dirchild.htm**), based in northwest London. Be warned that au pair work can often require long hours, sporadic scheduling and sometimes additional duties, like cleaning. Female au pairs are preferred. Always ask for details of the exact responsibilities and hours involved before accepting a position, especially one where the au pair is expected to live with the family. One young woman from Brighton told me that when she arrived at her new employer, the 'children' she was supposed to be taking to the park every day were actually three Labrador retrievers – two medium-sized mutts and something that 'looked more like a well-worn hearth rug'. Perhaps a photo of the children wouldn't be a bad idea.

Excellent sources when beginning your job search are the adverts in local English-language publications such as:

• *Wanted in Rome*: a biweekly publication available on international news-stands in and around Rome with classified ads about apartments, work, services provided and so on, and articles on current events, culture and lifestyle; see also **www.wantedinrome.com**

• *Talk aBOut*: a monthly published in Bologna with listings, reviews and classifieds; see also **www.talkabout.it**

• *Roma C'e*: published every Wednesday and available on newsstands in Rome; most of the publication is in Italian, but there's a large section in the back in English with events (in and around Rome) including music, theatre, nightlife, restaurant reviews, outdoor festivals, sports and more; though there are sometimes job listings, use it more as an English language source for possible venues to look for work.

And these websites might be useful:

• **www.noplacelikerome.com/employment.htm** has job listings, legal in-formation and general tips, as well as numerous links to other sites.

• **www.zoomata.com** has news, tips and listings throughout Italy.

A glance at the English *Yellow Pages* or **www.intoitaly.it** for companies under headings of interest to you could be useful. As English-language publications come and go, check on Google (or any other search engine) for a current list of English publications and websites in Italy.

Editoriale Genesis puts out the annual *Uomini e Communicazione*, a list of companies, their head offices, press offices and other vital stats. Go to their website (**www.primaonline.it**) or phone their publisher in Milan (**t** 02 4819 4401) to order a copy if you aren't around to snap it up off the stand when it comes out. Though not specifically designed for job-seekers, it lists companies by type (fashion, automotive, telecommunications, and so on) and can be an invaluable source of employment ideas.

Don't discount newspapers and magazines. Scour them all, from the *Financial Times* and *The Economist* to *La Repubblica* and *La Stampa*. The dream job may not be advertised, but if you are open-minded and look carefully, you might find the name of an interesting company or type of job that hadn't occurred to you.

Being Employed

Living and working abroad can be an exhilarating experience, but also a humbling one. This is the opportunity to explore the skills you know you have, to remind yourself of those you had forgotten or to develop new ones. If you are looking for employment as a means to stay in the country, then leave no stone unturned. There are countless scams (*fregature*), as in any country, so be wary. But don't pass over offers of trial runs or unpaid periods. Set limits of how much time you are willing to invest in trying out a possible position: the rule that one thing leads to another applies in Italy as everywhere else.

If you are established in a profession and ready to seek a job in Italy, remember that professional licensing and certification requirements can be country-specific. You may have to apply for the Italian equivalent **professional qualification** or even take local exams. Ask for advice from your professional body or union at home for information about practising in Italy, or one of the 40 European documentation centres (**EDC**) in England can assist. The **European Commission Information Centre** (8 Storey's Gate, London SW1P 3AT, t (020) 7973 1992) will give you the address of the closest EDC to you. The UK **National Academic Recognition Information Centre** (NARIC) provides information about the overseas equivalents of professional qualifications and can be contacted at ECTIS 2000 Ltd, Oriel House, Oriel Road, Cheltenham, Glos GL50 1XP, t (01242) 260010, **106736.2043@compuserve.com**, **http://europa.eu.int/comm/relays/edc/index_en.htm**.

Looking for Work

Networking (*networking*; net-voork-ing) is only one step away from the Italian vice of nepotism (*racommandazione*), but don't disregard it. An evening discussion at a party or pub, or a casual encounter, has an amazing way of becoming a conversation about someone who knows someone. Perhaps expats living in Italy have picked up the Italian habits, or they simply know the merits of spreading the word – especially as most have been through it all before.

Cold calling is usually not very successful, and résumés and CVs sent on spec often seem to disappear into thin air.

CURRICULUM VITAE
di Mario Salvatore Rossi

DATI PERSONALI

NOME: Mario Salvatore

COGNOME: Rossi

RESIDENZA: Via Segrate 2, 12121 Bologna

DOMICILIO: Piazza Verdi 32, 00122 Roma

TELEFONO: 06-6888883

E-mail: msro@iol.it

DI NASCITA: 11-01-72

STATO CIVILE: Celibe [*Celibe* is masc., *Nubile* fem.]

PATENTE tipo: RN7890457R Guida B

STUDI

SCUOLA SUPERIORE: Diploma Liceo Scientifico conseguito presso l'Istituto A. Einstein di Teramo nel 1994.

CORSI DI FORMAZIONE: Corso di Formazione in Economia e Diritto dei Mercati Finanziari della durata di 60 ore svoltosi dal 13 settembre al 19 ottobre 2002, presso la sede della Federazione delle Banche di Credito Cooperativo.

UNIVERSITARIA: Laurea in Economia e commercio con indirizzo Economia Aziendale orientamento Manageriale conseguita presso l'Università degli Studi di Urbino in Giugno 2003 con votazione 85/110. Tesi di laurea in Organizzazione Aziendale.

CONOSCENZE

LINGUE: Italiano; madrelingua   Tedesco; scolastico   Inglese; buono

INFORMATICHE: Ottima conoscenza del Sistema Operativo Windows, del pacchetto Office (Word, Excel, PowerPoint), di Internet e della Posta elettronica.

ESPERIENZE

LAVORATIVE: Gestione e Amministrazione del 'Ristorante Buona' (300 posti) in Teramo dal 1993 al 1999. Con responsabilità inerenti alla contabilità generale, al controllo delle sale, ai rapporti con i fornitori e alla creazione di eventi di intrattenimento per la clientele quali concerti, spettacoli teatrali e di cabaret.

CARATTERISTCHE PERSONALI

Sono una persona tenace e intraprendente, ho buone capacità comunicative. Amo la musica (suono l'oboe e il sax) e il teatro (ho frequentato un corso di teatro sperimentale ad Urbino), pratico sport (calcio, palestra, piscina, sci). Cerco di viaggiare all'estero per conoscere persone e culture diverse. Sono una persona dotata di una buona capacità di lavorare in gruppo.

PREFERENZE PER L' IMPIEGO

AREE DI INTERESSE: Organizzazione Aziendale, Marketing, Pianificazione Strategica

Autorizzo il trattamento dei miei dati personali ai sensi della Legge 675/96 sulla Privacy

CURRICULUM VITAE
of Mario Salvatore Rossi

PERSONAL DATA

NAME: Mario Salvatore

SURNAME: Rossi

RESIDENCE: Via Segrate 2, 12121 Bologna [Italians are required by law to have a registered residence, which is sometimes different from their home address]

ADDRESS: Piazza Verdi 32, 00122 Roma

TELEPHONE: 06-6888883

E-mail: msro@iol.it

BIRTHDATE: 11-01-72

CIVIL STATUS: Single

DRIVER'S LICENCE type: RN7890457R B Driver

STUDIES

HIGH SCHOOL: Scientific High School Diploma from *l'Istituto A. Einstein* in Teramo in 1994.

CONTINUING EDUCATION: Economic and financial market course, 60hrs, from 13 September to 19 October 2002, at the headquarters of the Federation of Credit Cooperative Banks.

UNIVERSITY: Degree in economy and commerce with a major in Company Economics and Management, from the Università degli Studi of Urbino, June 2003, with the score 85/110. University thesis on company organization.

OTHER SKILLS

LANGUAGES: Italian: native speaker; German: high-school level; English: good

COMPUTER SKILLS: Excellent knowledge of Windows operating system, of Office programs (Word, Excel, PowerPoint), internet and email.

WORK EXPERIENCE

Management and administration of Restaurant Buono (300 seating) in Teramo from 1993 to 1999. Responsible for general accounting, management of the rooms, relations with producers and events coordinator for concerts, theatre performances and cabaret.

PERSONAL CHARACTERISTICS

I am a determined and enterprising person, with good communication skills. I love music (I play the oboe and sax) and theatre (I attended an experimental theatre course in Urbino). I play sports (soccer, gym, swimming, ski). I travel abroad to know different peoples and cultures. I have good interpersonal skills and like working with other people.

WORK PREFERENCES

AREAS OF EMPLOYMENT: Company organization, marketing, strategy planning

Authorized use of personal data according to the Privacy Law 675/96

Temporary employment agencies in Italy are starting to take off, such as Manpower (Via del Corso 184, 2nd floor, stair C, 00186 Roma, **t** 06 695401, **f** 06 6954 0220, **www.manpower.com**), Adecco (**www.adecco.com**; an international page with relevant links) and Ali Temporaneo (Largo Magna Grecia 24–25, 00183 Roma, **t** 06 7720 3670 or 3848, **f** 06 7720 3323, **info.rm@alispa.it**, **www.alispa.it**), and can be a great way of getting a taste of working in the country.

Employment websites like **www.jobs-in-europe.net/italy.html** have listings from English summer camps to au pair agencies, and classifieds with a variety of opportunities; **www.recruitaly.it** has jobs aimed at recent graduates, as well as established professionals.

The Curriculum Vitae

When answering an advert, or knocking on doors, be sure to have an immaculately prepared résumé, both in Italian and English. Online translation services, most of them free, do a decent job, but have a native Italian-speaker look over it for you as well. Since there are peculiarities about the format of a résumé it is becoming quite common practice to have an Italian-style CV, and an English-

Name that Acronym

UN agencies seem to be acronym-dependent and assume that everyone is familiar with their organizations' abbreviations and acronyms. Even more confusing is that not only do Italians do the same, but they often use the Italian translation, spelled out in an acronym, and then tossed into conversation as a proper noun. Need some deciphering? Here is a list of UN agencies based or with offices in Italy, the Italian translation and how in to say it.

• FAO (Food and Agriculture Organization of the United Nations), in Italian pronounced 'Faow', written FAO, but translated as Organizzazione delle Nazioni Unite per l'Alimentazione e l'Agricoltura.

• IFAD (International Fund for Agricultural Development), translated as Fondo Internazionale per lo Sviluppo Agricolo, sometimes called FISA – pronounced 'Fee-Sah'.

• The UN (United Nations), known in Italy as ONU (Organizzazione Nazioni Uniti), 'Oh-noo'.

• UNHCR (United Nations High Commisioner for Refugees) or ACNUR pronounced 'Ack-noor' (Alto Commissariato delle Nazioni Unite).

• WFP (World Food Programme) or PAM (Programma Alimentari Mondiale).

• WHO (World Health Organization) or OMS (Organizzazione Mondiale della Sanità).

When looking up agencies in the phone book Italians will often use local spelling – for example ACNUR is found under 'A', not 'U' for UNHCR.

Case Study: Rosemary

Take one woman's experience. Rosemary, a UK artist who was raised in Jamaica, had degrees in art and English literature from universities in London and Canada. Although she was already an established painter with numerous exhibitions under her belt when she came to Italy in 1989, she struggled to make ends meet as an artist. Using her knowledge of English, she began editing for the Food and Agriculture Organization (FAO) of the United Nations in Rome, at which point she was asked to write for a local English-language magazine. After she had held some exhibitions in Italy, she began to sell her paintings for a substantial sum, and was also asked to work full-time at the FAO. Her love of horses led her to buy one of the horses she rode regularly and now she runs a small stable specializing in taking differently abled children on invigorating trail rides. 'If I had have belligerently insisted on only painting, and living off my art, I might have had to abandon Italy, my adopted home, for lack of resources,' she reflects.

language version of it also. Italians put information on their résumé that seems unnecessary to an outsider, such as their height, age, weight, hobbies and personal characteristics. The curriculum vitae on pp.242–3 is an example of a résumé in Italian, with an English translation. You may choose to leave out personal data, like age, but will probably be asked to provide it before the interview, if you are called.

Contracts

If you want to work for a UK company in Italy it will be easiest for you if the company has hired you before you move there. The company will have to justify to the Italian labour authorities why you should be employed rather than an Italian. You can apply to work with UK (or other non-Italian) companies once you are in Italy, though being hired locally may mean that you have to return to England before beginning your employment.

Getting hired by an Italian company can be a bit trickier as, again, Italians will have precedence over non-Italians applying for any position, unless the employer can prove that the job can only be done by the non-Italian because he or she has a specialist skill.

Under Italian law an employer must provide an **employment contract** in which the pay is negotiated by the employer and employee, but cannot go below the national minimum wage. There are many kinds of contracts, but the two main ones are characterized by specifications about duration:

> • The *contratto a termine* or *tempo determinato* is fixed-duration contract, which ends after a predetermined period without either party needing to give termination notice officially, unless the employee wishes to terminate

his or her position before the end of the contract. This contract is generally used for seasonal labour (*lavoro stagionale*), replacement for employees on maternity or sick leave (*lavoro interinale*), and other situations that call for temporary, stop-gap staff.

• A *contratto a termine*, if renewed, automatically becomes a *contratto a tempo indeterminato* (open-ended contract), which means you become an employee (*dipendente*); this is what all Italians strive for, since it almost certainly guarantees a job for life.

There are also several types of **apprenticeship contracts**. *Contratto di appredistato* or *tirocinio* is the general term for an apprenticeship contract, though *tirocinio* often refers specifically to a law intern. More specifically, the *contratto di formazione* is for employees aged between 16 and 24 and applies for a training period running from 18 months to a maximum of 4 years. The *contratto di formazione e lavoro* is a non-renewable work-training contract and can have various durations – intermediate- to high-level professionals can obtain one for up to 24 months, whereas a beginner's training position can last a maximum of 12 months. All of these possibilities offer the employer the opportunity to pay a lower salary and provide reduced benefits.

Unpaid Trainees

Positions for trainees are not as common in Italy as elsewhere, though the idea of working (free of charge) in exchange for training has been around for ages. Italian companies are becoming more open to taking on trainees as a way of assessing possible future employees, preparing young people for the job market, or filling a rotating position without designating company funds to it. The position must be strictly unpaid to avoid complicated labour contracts, but working as a trainee is often the best way to find out about a job opening in a company before anyone else. The trainee positions available depend on your area of interest and specialization, and your language level.

There are several areas where positions as trainees are available.

• **The media**: The Foreign Press Club or Stampa Estera has a bureau in Rome (**www.stampa-estera.it**) and Milan (**www.stampaestera.it**). Publications, radio and TV correspondents often work from the Stampa Estera and you can post your résumé on their board. Contact their administrative office (find the telephone number on their web page) for information. The two main media trainee positions are with the Associated Press and Reuters news agencies, though many smaller publications take trainees.

• **The UN and other intergovernmental organizations**: The International Fund for Agricultural Development (IFAD), Oxfam, Unicef and Unesco all offer trainee positions for students of international relations, political science, social science, public relations or economics. Proficiency in Italian is required; apply through the human resources department with your CV or respond directly to an advertisement. The UNHCR and the UN Information Centre also accept trainees. *See also* 'Volunteering', pp.257–50.

• **Law**: Working as a trainee with domestic or foreign-based law firms or legal institutions is an excellent way to build a résumé and gain a unique perspective on legal work abroad. Two organizations offer unpaid legal trainee possibilities in Italy. The International Juridical Organization for Economic and Social Development (IJO) and the International Development Law Institute (IDLI) offer 6–9-month trainee positions, limited to students of law or those interested in the legal field. Another resource for law trainee positions is Global Experiences (**www.globalexperiences.com/internships/internshipsitaly.htm, internships@globalexperiences.com**).

• **Art and restoration**: In a country saturated by the arts, this is one of the most attractive areas to seek a trainee position. Every major city has numerous galleries and museums. The International Centre for the Study of the Preservation and Restoration of Cultural Property (ICCROM), an intergovernmental organization based in Rome, promotes the conservation of all types of heritage and has trainee, volunteer and paid positions. Look at the website **www.iccrom.org** for details. If you have a specific town, interest, museum or gallery in mind, try phoning directly and requesting to speak with their educational or conservation departments.

• **Human rights, refugees and immigration**: Despite the fact that Italy has the lowest number of immigrants of all of European countries, it is seen to be on the front line of immigration and refugees entering Italy from any point of the 6,600km (4,100-mile) coastline. As a result, immigration is a key contemporary Italian social issue (*see* **Italy Today**, pp.73–5). The International Organization for Migration accepts trainees and there are limited possibilities for obtaining a trainee position with Amnesty International, Human Rights Watch, Save the Children, Médecins Sans Frontières and numerous smaller groups like the Italian Committee for Refugees (CIR), Caritas and Sant'Egidio.

Employment Conditions

Unless a contract specifically eliminates or waives certain points, employment conditions (*condizioni di impiego*) are valid and apply to anyone employed in Italy. These are the main features.

• Wages (*lo stipendio*) are based on the type of work. Check the minimum wage in the area that you are working in.

• Pay rises (*scatti di anzianita*) are expected every two years.

• The standard working week is 38hrs, with overtime pay 115–130 per cent of your salary, and 120–175 per cent for night shifts.

• There are 12 national holidays (*le vacanze, feste* or *ferie*) each year (*see* p.279) and the saint's day of your home town on top of that. Employees may take paid holidays of 4–6 weeks per year.

• Bonuses are not obligatory, but employees often receive *la tredicesima*, which is the 13th month, equivalent to an extra month's pay.

• Health insurance (*sanità*) is part of the national health package; it is public and free. Contributions towards the SSN, and to the INPS for other benefits, are paid through PAYE; the employer contributes 35% and the employee 10%.

• Maternity leave (*maternità*) is generous. A mother is given five months total, which she can choose to split up using some before the birth and the rest after.

• Sickness leave or disability (*malatia* or *convalescenza*) is covered for up to 180 days of absence. If extended, then the sick leave becomes disability leave and the sick employee can apply for a pension.

• Basic state pensions (*pensioni*) start at 65 for men and 60 for women. After 15 years of contributions, an employee can receive a partial pension. Full pension rights come after 35 years of employment. Italy is currently debating pension reforms.

• Redundancy policies are influenced by a strongly protective labour law, making it nearly impossible to fire an employee.

• If an employee leaves his or her post, termination indemnity (*trattamento di fine rapporto*) is paid – usually the equivalent of a month's pay per year employed. Less than 10 per cent of Italians have or are eligible for unemployment insurance.

The website (**www.informer.it**) and newsletter of the *Informer* probably provide the clearest explanation of the legalities of working in Italy as a foreigner – refreshingly, in English.

Teaching

So widespread is the teaching profession among English-speaking foreigners in Italy that, even if you aren't a teacher, you'll be pestered with requests to lend a hand with translations, homework and work documents, or even to give a few private lessons. It is assumed that if you speak English, you can (and want) to teach it – even if you are the CEO of an electronics company. If you have already come prepared for teaching, you probably won't be unemployed for long. Whether or not you will increase your savings by teaching is another matter. In larger cities like Rome and Milan the pay is higher, but so is the cost of living. There are also more wannabe teachers like yourself knocking on doors, increasing competition and reducing the number of plum jobs available.

Qualifications

Until not too long ago there was still a 50–50 chance that a non-certified instructor could land a decent English-teaching job in any Italian town. That is becoming less and less true, and if your interest is truly in teaching, a Teacher of English as a Foreign Language (TEFL) certificate boosts your value and gives you an edge in the market. This applies to language-school teachers and private

Case Study: English as Art

Teaching English isn't always what it is cracked up to be – sometimes it is better. At least that is what 31-year-old Chris Benninger from the west of England says. During one of his language courses for international business magnates in London, Benninger got an offer he couldn't refuse. 'I knew that my students were mostly upper management, CEOs and industrial bigshots, but didn't realize that "the Italian" of the group was actually the owner of the leading European health and fitness equipment maker.' So bowled over was he by Benninger's capacity to teach business English, the company owner approached Benninger and offered him a job in his firm in Italy. 'The only catch was that I had to decide in less than a week, when the president was leaving.'

As is the case with most artists, Benninger taught English to make ends meet. His real passion, however, is his contemporary, on-glass art that uses multi-media and has won awards such as the Leighton prize in 2001. 'There was no better place that I could think of to expand my work than in Italy. And I had someone offering me a way to get there, and a job, to boot.' Two weeks later, he was sipping Sangiovese wine and savouring a *piadina*, Emilia-Romagna's scrumptious stuffed bread speciality. 'For an artist, Italy is top. It is one of the few countries where business doesn't come first, and the pleasures of life take precedence.'

However Benninger encountered a few problems. Italy's *gioia di vivere* has its disconcerting aspects. 'People promise a lot, but the follow-through is less than desirable. That goes for personal relationships, and business matters.' When he arrived, he found himself caught in a series of catch-22 situations while trying to get settled in. He couldn't buy a car without a residence permit, couldn't get his *permesso di soggiorno* without a contract, wasn't offered a contract that would allow for residency, no bank would let him open an account until he had a fiscal tax code, but he couldn't get a fiscal tax code without a stay permit. 'It was just a big ball of yarn that took forever to unravel.'

Yet, for all of the tricky manoeuvring, time lost on bureaucracy and empty promises, the artful English instructor says that Italy is the place to live. 'Opportunity courted me, and now we are married,' he reflects, six months down the road, 'and, banal as it may sound, it really is beautiful and the food is truly gorgeous.' Well spoken for a pre-Raphaelite, living well and with an unexpected income to do so.

instructors. However, if you are just testing the waters, some schools will accept you on the basis that you are a native speaker. If you are not well versed in grammar, however, beware. One English teacher warns that 'Italian grammar itself is intricately complex and well taught from grade 1, therefore students tend to cling to grammatical structure and will ask tough questions'. So, either brush up your grammar or stick to conversational English. If you do catch the bug and decide to go for the TEFL certificate, you can do so in Italy.

One of the best-known schools offering preparation is the **International House** in Rome (Viale Manzoni 57, 00185 Rome, **t** 06 7047 6894 or **t** 06 7047 6802, **www.ihromamz.it**). It offers month-long courses also in Rome, Milan and Palermo.

Many schools will help with job placement in Italy, once teachers have completed the TEFL course. For TEFL training in the UK (and elsewhere) there are several options.

- **The hub of all English-teaching information is the Cambridge ESOL** page at **www.cambridge-efl.org.**

- **Europa Pages** has a website (**www.europa-pages.com/uk**) that lists some 1,000 schools throughout the UK and Ireland and puts out the EFL Directory, a guide to learning English in Britain, now in its 8th edition. The directory has information for language travel agents or student advisers and can be purchased on **Amazon.com.**

- **International House:** 106 Piccadilly, London W1J 7NL, **t** (020) 7518 6823 or **t** (020) 7518 6823 6900, **f** (020) 7518 6951, **www.ihlondon.com.**

- **I-to-I** offers TEFL certificate courses throughout the UK, weekend TEFL courses in many cities and online TEFL courses. In England contact I-to-I at **t** 0870 333 2332 or **info@i-to-i.com**; in Ireland at **t** 058 40050, **ireland@i-to-i.com**; or go to **www.weekendtefl.com.**

- **Linguarama:** New Oxford House, 16 Waterloo Street, Birmingham B2 5UG, **t** (0121) 632 5925, **www.linguarama.com.**

Getting Down to Teaching

Teaching at **language schools** provides some security (even if some prefer to hire staff on temporary contracts) and benefits, and they are often the springboard to bigger and better English-teaching opportunities. Most of the top schools are members of the **Italian Association of English Language Schools** (Associazione Italiana Scuole di Lingua Inglese or AISLI) and a list of members can be acquired through the **Cambridge Centre of English**, part of the **British Council** (**www.britishcouncil.it**). The British Council has offices in Rome, Milan, Naples and Bologna and you will also find TEFL course information on their website.

Private international grammar, middle and high schools also employ English teachers. Check with the school you are interested in about the requirements;

generally you will be asked for a general teaching certificate, diploma or degree as well as a specialization in English teaching. Universities with English departments ask for a university degree and generally positions are for assistants (*lettori*), though visiting lecturers are not uncommon.

Private lessons can be lucrative and, once plugged in to the network (*giro*), unexpected opportunities can arise. One well-established English teacher found work through the instructor of a theatre course she was taking in her free time, since she had 'so much of it'! The instructor, who also works in film, had an 'entire cast that needed basic English training', and what began as a two-month job has turned into more work than she can handle in the last three years. University students are now being pumped full of English material and children are starting to learn English from the age of five. Though not as secure as a full-time position in a school, teaching privately can supplement income, and even become a more than sufficient way of earning a living.

Freelancing and Part-time Work

For some, freelancing is the result of years and years of building up contacts and finally shaking off the shackles of a 9–5 position. For others, it is not a choice but a necessity as a way of trying to make a living.

Italy is not the easiest place to work as a freelance. The job market is limited and, since many people have a dream of setting up business in Italy, competition is fierce. Nepotism exists in the non-Italian community as much as among the indigenous population and it cannot be stressed enough how important it is to socialize and network.

Though quite a few freelancers begin operating informally, they are unlikely to be able to sustain this for long. Loopholes abound when it comes to legal requirements. Italians themselves have an aversion to following regulations to the letter, partly because controls are lax. Even the best intentions of operating according to the law are often muddled by ambiguities in the regulations themselves, and the plethora of choice on just how one wants to be classified.

Different rules apply to different freelance or part-time positions. As an EU citizen, the basics you will need are a *codice fiscale*, possibly a *partita IVA* and, if you plan to work part-time in an establishment, possibly a worker's registration card (*libretto di lavoro*), which you can obtain at the town hall (*municipio*).

A *permesso di soggiorno* is not sufficient for you to work – it is merely a permit to stay in the country. To work officially as a freelance you have to register your services or skills with the relevant professional organization. You should also change your *permesso* or request a new one called the *permesso di soggiorno per lavoro autonomo/independente*.

With a *codice fiscale* employers (and you) can operate under a semi-legal umbrella by holding the tax contribution (*ritenuta d'acconto* or *r d'A*) required of all workers for you. To get paid, you will probably be asked to present an invoice (*see* box 'Invoicing', opposite). You can ask your employer to pre-calculate the *ritenuta* for you based on what you will be paid. As the tax will be deducted from your pay, be aware that the price you are asking will be reduced. Therefore, ask your employer to adjust your pay accordingly so that what goes into your pocket will be what you are expecting.

Invoicing

An example of how to make out an invoice for an Italian employer is given below. The name of the person requesting payment goes at the top, with address and tax number (*codice fiscale*). After the biller's details the name and address of the company being billed is given, and their *partita IVA*. Directly below give the date in full and invoice number (also specify which project number it is for you with the company). Before the amount that you are charging the company, explain what the bill is for (rights to an article, in this invoice), then give the invoice amount with the *ritenuta d'acconto* calculated. There is a standard legal phrase to be added below the amount, and you should add the *marca da bollo* for €1.29 (*see* p.111), and an original signature.

Mary Smith
Via Verdi 10
00151 Roma
cod. Fiscale: MSL LLT 68R99 Z308R

Spett.le
The Best Magazine
Via Stampa 1
00193 Roma
P.IVA 12345123456
Ricevuto del 1 Luglio 2003
No. 1

Compenso cessioni diritti
Articolo *Best Magazine*

importo lordo €112,50
R d'A –€16,88
Netto €95,62

Fuori campo IVA ai sensi dell'art. 5 legge 633/72 e sue successive modifiche ed intergrazioni. Ritenuta d'acconto sul 75 per cent dell'importo ai sensi DL 669 del 31/12/96.

Marche da bollo €1,29 sull'originale.
In fede,
Mary Smith
Payment details here

You will have to fill in a tax return annually, and also pay contributions towards the health service (SSN); *see* pp.170–77.

Various connotations apply to the term freelancer, from 'glamorous' to 'obviously struggling', and it is important to treat a freelance career as seriously as any other form of employment. Have catchy business cards made and always keep plenty at hand. Most freelancers who work from home find that keeping a separate area for their working space makes all the difference. Keep up to date with technical and computer matters in the area in which you are working and have a good fax and email service. Try to set a schedule, with regular hours. Get tips from established freelancers and don't forget to network! As a freelancer, it is more important than ever.

Starting Your Own Business

Toto, a much beloved Neapolitan comedian actor known for his never-ending ability to poke fun at Italians and society in a bittersweet way, played out a great parody on Italians' 'creative business skills'. Playing a trickster in the film *Toto Truffatore*, he manages to sell the Trevi fountain to a wealthy American tourist, though it wasn't his to sell.

Despite the legal ambiguities, ever-pernickety regulators, tax burdens, zoning issues and an entire barrage of obstacles, small business is the lifeblood of Italy and more than four million micro-businesses thrive throughout the country today.

Setting up business as a freelance requires patience. Consider exactly what benefits you will get by doing so and ask yourself if it's worth going through the tedious procedures or if you couldn't continue to operate as you are. This is not encouraging illegality but being blatantly realistic. Keep in mind that many of the support structures that help small businesses in some countries, like bank loans and state-offered consultation for new entrepreneurs, are lacking in Italy.

Start in Italy (**www.startinitaly.it**) is an internet portal with information on starting and doing business in Italy, usually for a fee. The Italian embassy (**www. italian-embassy.org.ae/Embassy/business_in_italy.htm**) provides up-to-date information in English.

Using Agencies

Don't consider setting things up on your own as there are many matters that have to be dealt with, there is no comprehensive do-it-yourself guide to help you and you will be faced with papers, forms and much bureaucracy. Agencies, informally called *galoppini*, specialize in obtaining documents and making applications for businesses getting started, and can help get the ball rolling and take care of numerous time-consuming tasks. Various relocation agencies and project managers claim to be able to get you up and running in no time. Much of this is *bravura* – be wary about such claims as even the most expert agency can find tangling with the authorities time-consuming and obstructive. Location is another key element that determines how long it will take to become operational as a freelance. The average time for getting started in Milan varies from the time it takes to become established in Rome or Palermo. Any agency that says otherwise is either inexperienced or giving you false hope.

What *galoppini*, more costly notaries (*notaii*) and relocation agencies are usefully able to do for you is deal with the irritating paperwork by registering your business at the tax registrar's office (*ufficio registro*), registrar of enterprises (*registro delle imprese*) and companies' registrar (*ufficio delle ditte*) located at the chamber of commerce (*camera di commercio*). Your company will also be listed at the local tax office (*intendenza di finanza*) and you will have to obtain a value added tax code (*partita IVA*) to be registered at the VAT office (*ufficio IVA*). Before you sign legal forms, consult with a tax adviser about what implications the kind of business you are opening will have for you. You can find the names of local agencies and notaries in the telephone book looking under *certificati, notaii* and *agenzie*.

Different Types of Business

Sole Proprietor

To operate a business as a sole proprietor (*ditta individuale*) there is no capital requirement; all you need is a *partita IVA* and to be registered with the *camera di commercio*. You are, however, solely responsible for tax obligations and company liability.

Branch Office

A branch office (*sede secondaria*) is an Italian branch of a foreign company operating in Italy and is subject to taxation and corporate law.

Companies

To operate commercially in Italy, a company must have a structure that is recognized by Italian authorities. The Italian equivalents of the UK limited liability company are the *S.r.L.* and *S.p.A.*; both are corporations (*società di capitale*). By forming a corporation you are protected against liabilities, except where the initial investment is concerned. An *S.r.L.* or *società a responsabilità limitata* requires a minimum quota capital of €10,000. The *S.p.A.* is the big sister of the *S.r.L.* and entails minimum initial investment of €100,000 and a sizeable deposit of €30,000 with the Banca d'Italia, which is refunded after the company is registered. You can estimate that the cost of setting up a *S.p.A.* runs to roughly

6 per cent of the initial capital. For example, a €250,000 company will require an investment of approximately €15,000. Once the company memorandum (*atto costitutivo*) and articles of association or statutes (*statuto*) are submitted by a notary to the local tribunal court or local business registry office, the court will ascertain if the legal requirements are in order to enter the company on the register. Then the company must be entered in the chamber of commerce registry and public gazette called *BUSARL*. You will be issued a company number (*numero REA*) and company register (*registro imprese*).

Both the *S.p.A.* and the *S.r.L.* can have a single director or a board and there are no requirements for Italian partners, so they may be fully foreign-owned. There are stringent income tax requirements, and corporate tax (*IRPEG*) and an *IVA* (value added tax code) must be obtained for both.

Partnerships

Setting up a partnership is much less complicated than forming a corporation, and there is no rule about minimum initial investment. A disadvantage is that participants are liable for company debts, so be careful about choosing your partner or partners. There must be a minimum of two partners, but there is no maximum.

There are three possibilities for setting up a partnership:

- *Società in nome collettivo* **(SNC)**: An unlimited partnership is a business entity whose partners have unlimited liability for all the acts and transactions entered into by the partnership. All or any of the partners may be appointed as directors of the partnership. Italian law generally restricts the transfer of a partner's interest in the partnership.

- *Società in accomandita semplice* **(SAS)**: Limited partnership has a combination of limited and unlimited liability. There are two categories of partners: general partners who have unlimited liability, and special partners who are liable only to the extent of their capital contributions to the partnership. Only general partners may be appointed as directors of the partnership.

- *Societá in accomandita per Azioni* **(SAPA)**: A partnership limited by shares has a structure and characteristics similar to those of a limited partnership, except that the capital contribution of the partners is represented by shares; generally, the law relating to limited liability companies will apply.

Taking Over a Business

Another option from starting a business from scratch is to purchase one that already exists. A considerable amount of registering, licensing, paperwork and other start-up related hassles will already have been dealt with. However, be certain that you know the financial state of the company beyond the shadow of a doubt. Get several external, objective evaluations and have your own infrastructure (business plans, lawyer, banking facilities and employees if you don't inherit them from the previous staff) organized before starting operations. It may be possible to keep previously hired employees, in which case consider whether to retain their services or to find new staff.

Taking on Staff

Once you have the proper permits and licences and are up and running you may need to hire employees. There are several options for temporary contracts (*see* 'Contracts', pp.245–6) that give the employer and employee the chance to see if they work well together or else to fill positions for a short time during a hectic period or to cover another employee's absence. When it comes to hiring staff Italian labour laws work vigorously in favour of the employee and once someone is on the staff it is nearly impossible to fire them. Companies can find themselves saddled with a less than desirable worker at a very high cost. In addition to salaries there are additional social security contributions for 13, sometimes 14, paid months per year, up to 6 weeks of paid holidays annually, public holidays, sickness and other unexpected costs. Social security contributions alone add approximately 45 per cent to the wages bill. Italians hope to be hired for life. As one contemporary comedian joked, most job contracts last longer than marriage.

Taxes

Taxes are complicated in any country. If you are opening your own business, filing your taxes or doing anything connected with your businesses tax obligations, never do so without a tax consultant.

Italian taxes fall into two categories – direct and indirect. Value-added tax (*imposta sul valore aggiunto* or *IVA*) is an indirect tax (*imposta indiretta*) and is imposed on virtually all transactions involving goods and services.

Non-residents can obtain an *IVA* refund on goods purchased in the country with the mandatory validation stamp on the invoice plus the purchasing documentation. These must be presented at customs upon departure from Italy (or at the border of final departure from the EU). For an overview and updated information on taxes go to the government site for the *Ministero delle Finanze* at **www.finanze.it**.

Direct taxes (*imposte dirette*) include an income tax on individuals based on income earned (*imposta sul reddito delle persone fisiche*, *IRPEF*), whether in money or in kind, an income tax on corporations (*imposta sul reddito delle persone giuridiche*, *IRPEG*) and the local income tax (*imposta locale sui redditi*, *ILOR*). *See* **Living in Italy**, 'Taxation', pp.165–77 for more details.

Sources of Advice and Help

Chambers of commerce promote the business and trade of their country. In Italy a chamber of commerce (*camera di commercio*) is the place where you must register your business if you open one, but they also serve as information hubs, often having a list for job-seekers. The **British Chamber of Commerce in Italy** (BCCI, at **www.britchamitaly.com**) is a private, non-profit-making entity. It works closely with the British Embassy and the British Consulate General in Milan, but is not government-funded. The BCCI was founded in Genoa in 1904 and has its headquarters in Milan, just 100m (330ft) from the Milan Chamber of Commerce. Branches of the Chamber operate in Campania, Emilia Romagna, Friuli, Lazio, Liguria, Piemonte, Puglia, Tuscany and Veneto, with area secretaries for Bergamo, Brescia, Gorizia, Padua, Pordenone, Taranto, Udine, Venice, Verona and even London.

Loans for starting up a business in Italy are virtually impossible to obtain for two simple reasons: UK banks cannot provide start-up loans for anyone intending to become a resident abroad; Italian banks, on the other hand, are not prone to giving loans to foreigners for start-ups. However, there are **EU incentive programmes** for much of the *Mezzogiorno* – southern Italy – and other pockets throughout the country. Chambers of commerce have information about incentives and there is a government agency, Istituto Assistenza Sviluppo Mezzogiorno (IASM), dealing with these matters based in Rome.

More information on starting up and operating in Italy can be found at Doing Business in Italy: Web Site Translation and Promotion to Italian Search Engines (**www.ddc-on-line.com/TradeServices/BusinessOpportunities.html**), which lists trade services and consulting for small- to medium-sized business starting in the Italian market. Try **www.italbiz.com** for directories, listings, news and consultants.

Volunteering

There is nothing like volunteering as a way of immersing yourself in the best and sometimes most gratifying of Italian work experiences. It is also a way to begin to come into contact with the culture and become more proficient with speaking Italian. Meeting and working with others will help you form a network of friends and contacts for future business or work opportunities. There are many organizations that take volunteers; they vary considerably in their requirements about age, length of service and occasionally application fees. They exist in all sorts of fields such as archaeology, environmental and animal care, social services and human rights, religious organizations, and work or summer camps. If you are interested in working as a volunteer, it is best to check what the options are in the areas in which you are interested before you arrive in Italy as some organizations insist that you must apply through your resident country.

Start by looking through online resources or contacting organizations that take volunteers in Italy. Some of them are listed here:

- **ANPAS** (Associazione Nazionale Pubbliche Assistenze) at **www.anpas.it**, Via Baracca 209, 50127 Firenze, **t** 055 374887, **f** 055 375002.

- **FIVOL** (Fondazione Italiana per il Volontariato) or Italian Foundation for Volunteers with headquarters in Rome, **www.fivol.it**, Via Nazionale 39, 00184 Roma, **t** 06 474811, **f** 06 481 4617.

- **SPES** (Associazione Promozione e Solidaritá) or Association to Promote Solidarity, **www.spes.lazio.it**, Via del Pigneto 12, 00176 Rome, **t** 06 7030 4704, **f** 06 7030 4745.

- **CNCA** (Coordinamento Nazionale Communitá di Accoglienza) or National Coordination of Welcoming Communities at **www.cnca.it** list national opportunities for volunteering.

- **Movimento Volontariato Italiano** (Italian Volunteer Movement) **www.volontariato.it**, Via Degli Adelardi 4, 41100 Modena, **t** 338 268 2995, **f** 059 226133.

The website **www.volunteerabroad.com/Italy.cfm** has extensive listings and requirements for organizations of all kinds.

Archaeology, Art and Architecture

- **Gruppo Archeologici d'Italia** (Archaeologists of Italy Group) is one of the largest Italian archaeological organizations and snaps up volunteers for excavations. Contact them at Via degli Scipioni 30a, 00192 Roma, **t** 06 3973 3786, **www.gruppiarcheologici.org**.

- **Europe Conservation in Italy** (Via Bertini 34, 20154 Milan, **t** 02 331 3344, **f** 02 331 04068) recruits volunteers for excavations mostly from July to September.

- **Archeoclub d'Italia** (Via Sicilia 235, 00100 Roma, **t** 06 488 1821) has archaeological work camps.

Social Services and Human Rights

Someone who is self-sacrificing in Italian can be called a *Croce Rossina*, or in other words a volunteer with the **Red Cross**. The website of the Croce Rossa Italiana (**www.cri.it** or international site **www.crossnet.org**) describes trainee and volunteering possibilities. **Amnesty International** (**www.amnesty.org**) also has offices in Italy.

Volunteers for Peace (1034 Tiffany Rd, Belmont VT, 05730-0202, US, **t** 802 259 2759, **f** 802 259 2922, **www.vfp.org**) offers short-term voluntary service projects in more than 80 countries, and in 2001 had 225 opportunities in Italy. People working on their international workcamps perform a community service while living and interacting in an intercultural environment. There are work projects of all sorts: in construction or renovation of low-income housing or community buildings, historic preservation, archaeology, on environmental projects such as trail building, in environmental education, wildlife surveying, park maintenance, organic farming, social services – working with children, the elderly, physically or mentally handicapped, refugees, minority groups, drug and alcohol recovery, AIDS education – and arts projects or festivals.

These are three organizations you may wish to consider:

• **Casa Diritti Sociali** (CDS) and **Centro Servizi Volontariato** (CESV) are composed of hundreds of small volunteer associations throughout the region of Lazio. Contact Casa Diritti Sociali-Rome, Manfred Bergmann, **manberg@tin.it**, **www.dirittisociali.org** or **www.december18.net**, **t** 34 7473 5067.

• **Caritas** (**www.caritasroma.it** or **www.caritasitalia.it**) is a religious organization but takes on non-religious staff; it is the pinnacle Catholic volunteer organization in Italy, operated by the Vatican, and has trainee positions and volunteer opportunities, as does Communità di Sant'Egidio (Piazza Sant'Egidio 3/a, Roma, **t** 06 5730 0510, **f** 580 0197, **info@santegidio.org**, **www.santegidio.org**).

• **Helpline** is run by the Samaritans, who work to prevent suicide worldwide with 31,000 volunteers in over 40 countries. They run 24-hour hotlines, have face-to-face meetings and deal with much correspondence. Contact them at Via San Giovanni in Laterano 250, 00184 Roma, **t** 06 7045 4444 or **t** 06 7045 4445.

Environmental, Animal Care and Alternative Medicine

There are several organizations in this area; details of some are listed below:

• The **World Wide Fund for Nature** (WWF) (Via Garigliano 57, 00198 Roma, **t** 06 844971, **www.wwf.it**) and **Greenpeace** (1436 U Street, NW, Washington, DC 20009, US, **t** (202) 462 1177, **www.greenpeace.org**) has work in Italy. Amici della Terra or Friends of the Earth (Via di Torre Argentina 18, 00186 Rome, **t** 06 686 8289, **f** 683 08610, **www.amicidellaterra.org**) also has volunteer possibilities.

• The **Earthwatch Institute** (3 Clocktower Place Suite 100 Maynard, MA 01754-0075, US, **t** 800 776 0188, **f** (978) 461 2332, **www.earthwatch.org**) has trainee positions studying the works of doctors like Hippocrates, Dioscorides, and Galen, on the grounds that many modern drugs have their origins in ancient medicinal plants.

• The **Torre Argentina cat sanctuary** shelters anywhere from 250 to 300 abandoned cats permanently, and hosts up to 600 cats at a time, amid the ancient Roman ruins in the city centre. It acceps volunteers for cleaning and taking care of the cats, giving administrative help, and carrying out clerical work such as stuffing envelopes, making photocopies and various other administrative tasks; they also take on tour guides (mostly English-speakers). To work with the modern-day lions of Rome (*see* p.208), go to **www.romancats.de**.

Reference

Italy at a Glance

Capital city: Rome
Official name of country: Repubblica Italiana
Type of government: Parliamentary republic
Head of government: Prime Minister
Area: 301,230 sq km (116,306 sq miles) Note: includes Sardinia and Sicily
Length: 1,223km (760 miles)
Greatest distances north–south: 1,139km (708 miles)
Width east–west: 515km (320 miles)
Geographic highlights: Italy's stunning countryside includes such winter resorts as Cortina d'Ampezzo in the Alps. Europe's three active volcanoes – Etna, Stromboli and Vesuvius – are all located in Italy. Hundreds of miles of coastline are lapped by azure waters and adorned by seaside villages, yacht-filled bays and industrial ports. The moderating influence of the sea and the protection given by the Alpine barrier from the cold north winds join to bless Italy with a temperate climate. Nevertheless, the weather varies considerably according to how far one is from the sea or the mountains. The winter is gelid in the Alps, cold and foggy on the Po Plain and the central Apennines; mild and even warm on the Ligurian coast, the Neapolitan coast and in Sicily
Independent states within the country: The Vatican State and Republic of San Marino.
Languages and dialects: Italian (official), German (parts of Trentino-Alto Adige), French (in Valle d'Aosta region), Slovene (in the Trieste-Gorizia area); numerous other minority dialects are spoken. (*See* **Getting to Know Italy**, 'The Italian Language', p.20)
Bordering countries: Austria, France, Holy See (Vatican City), San Marino, Slovenia and Switzerland
Surrounding seas: Mediterranean, Adriatic, Ionian, Tyrrhenian
Population: 57,715,625
Religion: predominately Roman Catholic with Protestant and Jewish communities and a growing Muslim immigrant community
GDP growth rate: 0.4 per cent
GDP per capita: €18,795
Unemployment: 12 per cent

Further Reading and Major Films

Books

Barzini, Luigi, *The Italians* (Simon & Schuster, 1964)
Clark, Martin, *Modern Italy, 1871–1995* 2nd Edition (ADDIS, 1996)
Dickens, Charles, *Pictures From Italy* (Penguin Classics)
Duggan, Christopher, *A Concise History of Italy* (Cambridge University Press, 1994)

Forster, E.M., *A Room With a View* (Bantam Classics, 1988), *Where Angels Fear to Tread* (Vintage Books, 1992)

Ginsborg, Paul, *A History of Contemporary Italy; Society and Politics 1943–1988* (Penguin, 1990)

Goethe, J.W., *Italian Journey* (Penguin Classics, 1982)

James, Henry, *The Portrait of a Lady* (Penguin Classics), *Italian Hours* (Penguin Classics), *Henry James on Italy* (Grove Press, 1992)

Jones, Tobias, *The Dark Heart of Italy* (Faber and Faber, 2003)

Larner, Monica and Travis Neighbor, *Living, Studying and Working in Italy* (Henry Holt, 1998)

Lawrence, D.H., *Twilight in Italy*, *Sea and Sardinia*, *Etruscan Places* (Penguin Classics)

Linter, Valerio, *A Traveller's History of Italy* (The Windrush Press, 1989)

Martines, Lauro, *April Blood* (Jonathan Cape, 2003)

Parks, Tim, *Italian Neighbors* (Ballantine Books, 1993), *Italian Education* (Grove Press, 1995)

Robb, Peter, *Midnight in Sicily* (Vintage Books, 1999)

Majanlahti, Anthony, *The Families Who Made Rome* (Chatto and Windus, 2004)

Mann, Thomas, *Death in Venice* (Vintage International)

McCarthy, Mary, *The Stones of Florence*, *Venice Observed* (Penguin, 1986)

Morton, H.V., *A Traveller in Rome* and *A Traveller in Southern Italy* (Methuen, 1957, 1969)

Sciascia, Leonardo, *The Moro Affair* (Scholarly Book Services, May 1987)

Mack Smith, Denis, *Modern Italy: A Political History* (University of Michigan Press, 1998)

Stille, Alexander, *Excellent Cadavers: The Mafia and the Death of the First Italian Republic* (Vintage Books, 1996), *Benevolence and Betrayal* (Penguin, 1993)

Stowe, Harriet Elizabeth, *Agnes of Sorrento* (AMS Press, 1971)

Wharton, Edith, *Italian Backgrounds* (Ecco Press, 1989) *Italian Villas and Their Gardens* (De Capo Press, 1977), *Roman Fever* (Virago, 2001)

Yallop, David, *In God's Name* (Poetic Productions, 1984)

Films

Cabiria, considered the first colossal film in the history of cinematography, shot in 1910.

Miseria e Nobiltà is one of the many films by the king of theatrical comedy, Totò. The Neapolitan actor who worked from the late 1930s through the end of 1960 has debatably never been topped.

Roma città aperta (*Rome Open City*) is the 1945 Rossellini's brutal portrayal of Nazis in Italy, shot just one year after the war had ended. The spectacular Anna Magnani is in one of her best roles, along with Aldo Fabrizi.

Ladri di biciclette (*The Bicycle Thief*), 1948, is one of the Neorealist masterpieces.

Riso Amaro (*Bitter Rice*), 1949. Misery and poverty of Italian migrant workers in the northern rice paddies.

La Dolce Vita is one of director Federico Fellini's most renowned films. Marcello Mastroianni plays a young playboy journalist with Anita Eckberg at his side.

I Due Nemici, with Alberto Sordi and David Niven, set in North Africa in 1942, details the personal struggle between an English officer and his Italian counterpart.

Il Sorpasso by director Dino Risi, shot in 1963, is a window on frivolous, yet serious, Italy in the 60s, with Gassman and Trintignant.

Una Giornata Particolare is an Ettore Scola masterpiece with Marcello Mastroianni and Sophia Loren at their most poetic.

Novecento by Bernardo Bertolucci, a wealthy, northern Italian family's view of fascist infection pre-Second World War, with Donald Sutherland, Robert de Niro, Burt Lancaster, Gerard Depardieu and Stefania Sandrelli, filmed in 1976.

Profondo Rosso is the cultish, 1975 Dario Argento thriller that any weak of heart should not see.

Blow up, an Italian mystery about swinging London, sex, work, relationships, drugs and photography with David Hemmings and Vanessa Redgrave directed by Michelangelo Antonioni in 1966.

Il Nuovo Cinema Paradiso, 1988, portrays a young boy's dreams and friendship in Sicily, and the inevitable changes that come with time.

Il Postino, with the exquisite Neapolitan actor Massimo Troisi as a humble postman in a small but beautiful Italian village, was an Italian success beyond the country's borders in 1995.

Mediterraneo, by the new-guard director Gabrielle Salvatores revolves around forgotten soldiers of the Second World War on a Greek island.

La Vita è Bella was the first film Tuscan comedian Roberto Benigni directed, and it earned him Oscars for Best Foreign Language Film and Best Actor. Also see *Pinocchio*, also by Benigni.

Pane e Tulipani (*Bread and Tulips*), Giovanni Soldini, 1999. A housewife gets left behind at a rest stop while on the way home from a bus tour, and hitchhikes past home and on to Venice when nobody comes to pick her up.

L'Imbalsamatore (*The Taxidermist*), went to Cannes in 2002 with a dark tale about warped love and taxidermy on the impoverished periphery of Naples.

Dictionary of Useful and Technical Terms

A

abitabile	habitable
abitazione	housing
abusivo	house or part of a building that is illegally built, or without the proper permit
ACI (Automobile Club d'Italia)	Italy's driving association
acqua	water
acquedotto	aqueduct, or state-supplied water
acquistare su carte	purchase of a property before it has been built, based on blueprints ('off plan')
affittacamere	rooms to let
affittasi	to rent; to let
affresco	frescoes
agente immobiliare	estate agent
agenzia immobiliare	estate agency

agriturismo	farm with rooms to rent
albo degli artigiani	professional order of artisans
albergo	hotel
alimentari	food shop selling cheese, cold meats and canned goods
aliscafo	high-speed boat or hydrofoil
alloggio	lodging
amministratore del condominio	paid official representing an apartment building, condominium administrator
ammobiliato	furnished
ammortizzare	reducing debts, like a mortgage, in smaller payments
ampia metratura	large, in size or metres
anagrafe	bureau of vital statistics or census office
anagrafe canina	registration office for dogs
angolo cottura	small construction in kitchen, or kitchen corner
annessi	attachments or building extensions
ANSA	Italy's news or information agency
anticamera	entranceway
antico	old or antique
anticipo di pagamento	deposit
appartamento	flat or apartment
appartamento ammobiliato	furnished apartment
appartamento in affitto	flat for rent
appartamento di lusso	exclusive apartment
appartamento su due paini	duplex
appartamento vacanze	holiday apartment
arcate	covered walkway, or arcade
archivio	archive
architetto	architect
arco	archway
aria condizionamento	air-conditioning
arredamento	interior furnishings
arredato	furnished
artigiano	artisan, craftsman
ascensore	elevator
assicurazione	insurance
assicurazione contro i terzi	third-party insurance
attaccato	joined, as in two properties, or next door
attico	top-floor apartment with terrace; penthouse
atto di compravendita	conveyance document
attrezzata	equipped
autobus	public bus
autonoleggio	car rental
autorimessa	car park

autostrada	motorway, highway
avvocato	lawyer or solicitor
azienda agricola	working farm

B

bagno	bathroom or toilet
balcone	balcony
banca	bank
bancomat	bank card or automatic cash machine (ATM)
bar	where you get breakfast and (if its is a *bar-tabacchi*) phone cards, cigarettes and stamps
bella figura/bella presenza	something that makes a good impression
belli arti	governed by the Ministry of Culture to preserve Italy's cultural heritage. The *belli arti* can block your plans to restore or build a house
ben conservata	well-preserved
ben tenuto	benefits from good upkeep
benzinaio	petrol station
biblioteca	library
bifamiliare	semi-detached building
biglietti	tickets
biglietti timbrati	validated tickets, like on a bus
bilocale	two-room apartment. Usually a studio apartment with a main room and kitchen
bolletta	bill or invoice
bollo	tax stamp
bombola	gas storage tank; compressed gas
bombolone	storage tank for compressed or liquid gas
bonifico	wire transfer used for paying bills from a bank account
borgo	a hamlet or small town. Can also mean 'neighbourhood.'
borsa	stock exchange
Borsa di Milano	main stock exchange; *see also nuovo mercato*
bosco	forest
box	parking for a single car
breve periodo	short term
buon entrata/buon uscita	'key money' or illegal payment made to buy off previous tenants' rent
buona posizione	good location
buono stato	good condition
BUSARL	official registry of companies

C

cabina	cabin
calce	limescale
caldaia	water heater, boiler
camera	room
camera di commercio	chamber of commerce
camera doppia	double room (twin beds)
camera matrimoniale	room with queen-size bed
camera singola	single room
cameretta	small room
camino	fireplace
cantina	storage cellar or wine cellar
capannone	outdoor barn
caparra	deposit
carabinieri	police force governed by the Defence Ministry
caratteristico	picturesque, quaint, charming
carta bollata	document with tax stamp included
carta d'identità	identification documents
carta da parati	wallpaper
Carta Verde	proof of insurance for cars
cartoleria	stationery supplier
casa	house, home
casa d'epoca	old house, period home
casa padronale	landowner's house in the country; main house
casa popolare	low-income housing
casa di ringhiera	apartments in Milan that look on to a interior courtyard
casa rurale	rural house
casa signorile	exclusive house or property
casa urbana	urban property
casale	farmhouse
cascina	another word for farmhouse
casetta	small house
cassa	cash register, till
cassone	water storage tank
castello	castle
catasto	land registry
catasti	zoning maps
centro	centre of a city
centro storico	historic centre, most expensive area
ceramica	ceramics
certificato di matrimonio	marriage certificate
certificato di morte	death certificate
certificato di nascita	birth certificate
certificato di residenza	residence permit

chiave	key
circoscrizione	a subdivision of the *comune* or municipality
cittadinanza	citizenship
clausola condizionale	conditional clause
codice fiscale	personal taxpayer number
colonna	column
colonnato	row of columns
coltivatore diretto	farmer
commercialista	accountant, also prepares tax returns
complesso residenziale	residential or housing complex
compromesso di vendita	preliminary sales agreement in buying property
comune	municipality or town hall
concessione edilizia	planning permission
condizione	condition
condominio	condominium
condono	a government 'pardon' for illegal building, usually issued when the state is short of funds
contatti	contacts
convivere	living together, sharing an apartment
conguaglio	adjustment. The electricity company uses this term when they bill based on estimated consumption
contatore	meter for utilities
contenuto dell'abitazione	inventory of furnishings
conto	bill
conto corrente	bank account
conto estero	a bank account in foreign currency
contraente	contracting party
contratto	contract
contratto di affitto	lease agreement
contratto preliminaria di vendita	preliminary sales contract
corridoio	corridor or hallway
corso	main street
cortile	courtyard
costruttore	builder
costruzione	building
cotto	terracotta
cucina	kitchen
cucina abitabile	kitchen-diner
cucina a gas	gas cooker
cupola	dome

D

dammusi	cube houses found only on the island of Pantelleria

decoratore	interior decorator
denuncia	police report
deposito	deposit
diritto del coltivatore	farmers' rights. If a neighbour earns 70 per cent or more of his or her income through agriculture, they have first refusal on adjoining property for sale
disdire/disdetta	to cancel
disponibile	available
Ditta Individuale	sole proprietorship business
DOC	wine region that is controlled by geographic origin
DOCG	wine region that is not only controlled but also guarantees geographic origin
doccia	shower
Dogana	Customs
domicilio	address
doppi servizi	two bathrooms
doppi vetri	double-glazing for windows
doppio garage	car parking for two vehicles
due piani	two floors

E

edicola	newspaper kiosk
edificio	building
edilizia	construction yard
elettricista	electrician
elettrodomestici	appliances
ENEL (Ente Nazionale per l'Energia Electtrica)	national electricity company
ENIT (Ente Nazionale Italiano del Turismo)	state tourism office
enoteca	wine merchant
entroterra	hinterland
equo canone	rent control
Escursionisti Esteri (EE)	car licence plates for foreigners who did not pay IVA tax when they bought their car
ettaro	hectare
EUR	modern neighbourhood south of Rome, built by Mussolini, that exemplifies Fascist architecture
euro	as of 1 January 2002, Italy's currency. €1 = 1,936 lire

F

fabbro	metalsmith; locksmith
facciata	façade

fai da te	do-it-yourself
falegname	carpenter
farmacia	pharmacy
fascia blu	ordinance banning traffic from the centre of a city
fattoria	farm
fattura	invoice, bill
Ferragosto	15 August holiday (the Assumption)
ferramenta	hardware store
Ferrovia dello Stato (FS)	railway system
finestra	window
fienile	storage area for hay
fisco	tax authorities
fiume	river
fontana	fountain
fornaio	bakery
fornello	cooker
forno	oven
forno a legna	wood-burning oven
fossa settica	septic tank
francobollo	stamp
frigorifero	refrigerator
fronte mare	facing the sea
fruttivendolo	greengrocer

G

gabinetto	toilet
Gazzetta Ufficiale	published document with all new legislation
geometra	combination of architect and surveyor. Very important figure, exists only in Italy
giardiniere	gardener
giardino	garden
giorno	day
giorno di riposo	rest day; day off
granaio	barn; hay storage
grande	large
grattacielo	skyscraper
Guardia di Finanza	tax police (also perform coastguard duties)

I

ICI (Imposta Comunale sugli Immobili)	property tax
idraulico	plumber
imbianchino	painter
immatricolare	to register a car with the Italian state
impianto	fixtures
imposta	tax
imposta di registro	stamp duty

indipendente	detached
indirizzo	address
ingegnere	engineer
ingresso	entrance
inquilino	tenant
interrato	basement; underground
intonaco	plaster
ipoteca	mortgage
IRAP (Imposta Regionale sulle Attività Produttive)	regional tax
IRPEF (Imposta sul Reddito delle Persone Fisiche)	personal income tax
IRPEG (Imposta sul Reddito delle Persone Guiridiche)	corporation tax
ISCOM (Imposta Servizio Comunale)	tax on communal services
ISD (Imposta sulle Successioni e Donazioni)	gift and inheritance tax
ISTAT	the national statistics institute
IVA (Imposta sul Valore Aggiunto)	Value Added Tax (20 per cent)

K

Kasher	Kosher food, also spelled *cosher* and *casher*

L

La Repubblica	Italy's second-largest circulation daily newspaper
lago	lake
lampadina	light bulb
largo	square
latteria	dairy shop
laurea	university degree
lavabo	washbasin
lavanderia	launderette; dry cleaners
lavastoviglie	dishwasher
lavatrice	washing machine
lavoro	work
lavoro al nero	illegal (black market) work
legname	timber
legno	wood
libretto di circolazione	car registration papers
libero	unoccupied
libreria	bookshop
lira	Italy's old currency, phased out after the euro's introduction on 1 January 2002. €1 = 1,936 lire according to the fixed exchange rate
locanda	inn
loggia	covered space on building

luce	light
lungomare	boardwalk, road near beach
lusso	luxury
M	
macchina	car
macelleria	butcher's shop
mammismo	the tendency of adult 'children' to live at home with their parents
mansarda	top-floor apartment under eaves, with sloping ceilings
manutenzione	maintenance
marca da bollo	tax stamp
mare	sea
marmo	marble
marmo di Carrara	white marble from Carrara
mas	from old Celtic word for 'house', a type of home found in the Alpine north
maso	same as a *mas*
masseria	from old Celtic word for 'house', a type of palace found in the south
mattone	bricks
mediatore	another word for an estate agent
medico	doctor
medico mutualistico	doctor under health insurance plan
mensile	monthly
mercato	market
metrature	size as measured in square metres
metri quadri	square metres
metro	ruler (measure)
Metropolitane	Metro or underground service
mezza pensione	half board, just room and breakfast
Mezzogiorno	the name for the collective south of Italy
misura	size, measure
modernizzare	refurbish, restore
monolocale	one-room apartment, studio apartment
motorino	moped or scooter
moquette	carpet
municipio	town hall
multe	traffic violations or parking tickets
muratore	carpenter, bricklayer, handyman or mason
mura	walls of a city
muro	walls of a house
mutuo	mortgage or medical coverage
mutuo compreso	mortgage included
mutuo per ristrutturazione	loan for reconstruction

N

non-residente	non-resident of Italy (better as a tenant for your property)
notaio	notary. Very important when buying property because he or she conducts basic investigations
nulla osta	'no obstacle' permit
numero di polizza	insurance policy number
numero di telaio	serial number, as on a moped
nuova	new
Nuovo Mercato	Milan's index for high-growth companies

O

occasione	bargain
officina	workshop
oliveto	olive grove
orario	business hours, schedule
orario non-stop/continuato	non-stop business hours, no lunch break
originale	original
ospedale	hospital
ottima posizione	prime location
ottima condizione	prime condition

P

padrone/a	landlord/landlady
paese	town
pagamento	payment
palazzo	building or palace
panetteria	bread shop
parco	park
Partita IVA	VAT registration number for businesses and freelancers
parzialmente arredato	partially furnished
passaggio di proprietà	ownership change, such as when you sell a car
pasticceria	pastry shop
patente	driver's permit, licence
pavimento in cotto	terracotta floor
pavimento	floor
pensione	small hotel
periferie	suburbs
perito agronomo	land surveyor
permessi comunali	planning permits from the town hall
permesso di lavoro	work permit
permesso di soggiorno	permit to stay in Italy for tourism, work, study or living
piano	floor

piano nobile	considered the best floor of a building, the first floor up with the highest ceilings
piano regolatore	zoning plan
piano terra	ground floor ('first' floor in the USA)
piastrelle	tiles
piazza	town square
piazzale	larger square
piccolo	small
pietra	stone
pineto	pine forest
piscina	swimming pool
pitture	painting
più spese	expenses, such as utilities, not included
polizia	police regulated by the Interior Ministry
ponte	bridge
portico	covered walkway
portiere	porter, doorman or woman
portinaio/portineria	the porter's quarters at the entrance of a building
porta	door
porta blindata	armoured door with steel beams that extend on to the wall
Porta Portese	Rome's biggest Sunday flea market
porto	sea port
portone	the main door of a building
posto macchina	car park
pozzo	well
pratica	bureaucratic file
prato	lawn
prefettura	courthouse
premio	insurance premium
prenotazione	reservation, such as for a train or in a restaurant
prestito	loan
preventivo	estimate of work costs, quotation
prezzo	price
prima casa	first house or primary residence
primo piano	first floor
procura	tribunal; power of attorney
progetto	project
pronta consegna	ready to be lived in, or moved into
proposta d'acquisto	initial offer made on a property
proprietà	property

Q

quadro	painting
questura	police station where you apply for a permit to stay

quotazione	quotation (*preventivo* is better)

R

radiatori	radiators
ragioniere	accountant
rate	instalments, as when paying bills
referenziati	references required
regolamento di condominio	condominium conditions or rules
rendita catastale	value of a property
residence	a room or flat for rent on a weekly or monthly basis
residente	resident of Italy
residenza	official residency as registered at the *anagrafe*
restaurare	to restore
restaurato	restored
ricostruire	to be reconstructed, re-built
rilevamento	land survey
rinnovamento	modernization, renovation
riparazione	repair
ripostiglio	storage room, or broom cupboard
riscaldamento	heating
riscaldamento autonomo	means a house has its own boiler and the owner can turn the heat off or on as desired. Owner pays for his/her individual use
riscaldamento centrale	one main boiler heats a building and the apartment owner does not decide when it is turned on or off. Cost is divided equally between all inhabitants
ristrutturare	to restore, refurbish
ritenuta d'acconto	when the 20 per cent IVA tax is withheld from a pay cheque
rocca	fortress
rogito	act or final deed signed in front of a *notaio*
rovina	ruins
rudere	ruins, or pile of rocks of historic significance
rustico	rustic

S

sala	room
sala da pranzo	dining room
saldo	sale
salone	sitting room
salotto	hallway or sitting room
scala	stairs
scalinata	stairway

scaldabagno	same as *caldaio* or boiler, water heater
scatti	phone units or segments of time used to calculate phone bills
scatti di anzianità	wage increase based on length of employment
sconto	discount
scontrino	receipt
semi arredato	partially furnished
semicentro	the area of a city just outside the centre
seminterrato	apartment at basement level
serrande	shutters or metal curtains
servizi	kitchen and bathroom, excluded from the number of rooms listed for a home
sfratto	eviction
sindaco	mayor
sistemare	to fix
società	company
società di capitali	corporation
società di persone	partnership
Società in accomandita semplice (S.a.s)	limited partnership in which liability is determined by the original investment
Società in nome collettivo (S.n.c)	general business partnership. All partners are liable without limit of debts
Società per Azioni (S.p.A)	joint stock corporation, usually to trade on the stock exchange
Società a responsabilità limitata (S.r.l)	limited liability company
soffitta	attic
soffitti a volta	vaulted ceilings
soffitto	ceiling
soggiorno	room, sitting room
soggiorno pranzo	dining room
sorgente	spring source of water
sottodichiarazione	common (illegal) practice of under-declaring a property's value for tax reasons
spese	expenses
spese agenzia	agent's fee
spese del condominio	building, maintenance or condo fees
spese condominiali comprese	maintenance fee included
spiaggia	beach
spiaggia libera	public beach
spiaggia privata	private beach
stanza	room
stanza da letto	bedroom
stato	condition, state
stato di famiglia	family status document (single, married with children, etc.)
stazione	train station

stima	estimate
strada	street
stuttura	structure
strutturalmente	structurally
stucco	plaster or stucco
studio	office or laboratory, den
suolo	ground
supermercato	supermarket
supplemento	surplus to pay, extra charge
supplemento rapido	extra fee to pay on fast trains

T

tabacchi	state-licensed tobacco store where you buy cigarettes, bus tickets, phone cards, postage stamps and tax stamps (*marca da bollo*)
tabelle professionali	salary classifications regulated by the state
Tangenziale	the ring roads around major cities like Milan. In Rome it is called the Grand Raccordo Anulare
tappeto	carpet
targhe	licence plates for a car
targhe alterne	used at time of high smog levels. On alternate days, city authorities allow into the centre cars with an odd number at the end of their licence plate or those with an even number
tassa comunale dei rifiuti	refuse (rubbish) tax
Telecom Italia	once had monopoly on phone service. Now faces competition from other companies
telefono	land-line phone
telefonino	'little phone', meaning mobile phone
terra	ground floor
terrazza	terrace
terreno	land
terreno alberato	land with trees
terreno coltivato	cultivated land
tessera	a subscription, such as for a month's worth of bus tickets
testamento	will, or last testament
tetto	roof
tintoria	dry cleaners
titolo di proprietà	deed of property
toiletta	toilet
torre	tower
torrente	stream
traghetto	ferry boat

trattabile	negotiable
trattazione riservata	closed session negotiation, reserved
travertino	porous marble from Lazio
travi di legno	wooden ceiling-beam
trulli	cone-shaped stone houses found only in Puglia
Tutto Città	the road atlas published for every town and city

U

Ufficio delle Imposte Dirette	tax office where you get your codice fiscale
Ufficio di Stato Civile	same as anagrafe, or census office
ufficio postale	post office
ultimo piano	top floor
umidità	humidity – a common problem in old homes

V

valore	value
valore catastale	value of property for tax purposes
vano	room
vaporetto	water transport in Venice; a boat
vasca	bath
vecchio	old
vendesi	for sale
veranda	porch
vetro	glass
via	street
viale	wider street
vicolo	little street
vicoletto	even smaller street
vigili urbani	traffic police, street police
vigneto	vineyard
villa	house
villetta (villino)	a smaller house, often modern
villagggio	village
vista	view
visto	visa for travel to Italy, or for studying, working or living in Italy
vista sul mare	sea views
vista sul monte	mountain views

Z

zona	zone
zona censuaria	parts into which a town is divided for tax purposes
zona tranquilla	quiet area

Internet Vocabulary

database	*banche dati*
delete	*cancellare*
@	*chiocciolina*
decode	*decifrare*
//	*doppia barra; doppia slash*
colon :	*due punti*
online	*in rete*
email address	*indirizzo elettronico*
underline	*linetta in basso; sottolinea*
dot .	*punto*
network	*rete*
re-start	*riavviare*
to select	*selezionare*
to browse	*sfogliare*
forward slash /	*slash; barra che parte da destra*
shut down	*smetti*
hyphen	*trattino*
user	*utente*
www	*vu vu vu*

Italian Holidays and Celebrations

National Holidays

On national holidays you may find information offices closed, museums open for shorter hours and public transport running a limited service. Be forewarned by checking the dates of your vacation against the list below. (Note that Easter Monday is a mobile feast-day, and changes every year, while all the other holidays keep to the same date.)

Days that are celebrated nationwide are:

> 1 January
> 6 January
> Easter Monday
> 25 April
> 1 May
> 2 June
> 15 August
> 1 November
> 2 November
> 8 December
> 25 December
> 26 December

Major celebrations include:

1 January	*Capodanno* or *San Silvestro*. New Year's Day is celebrated with fireworks and champagne. Some people still throw their old furniture out of their windows to celebrate a new beginning.
6 January	*Befana* or *Epifania*. On the day of the Epiphany a good witch flies into children's rooms and gives them gifts if they've been good or coal (usually in the form of candy) if they've been bad.
January–March	*Carnevale*. Carnival celebrations are taken very seriously in Venice (with a masquerade parade), in Ivrea (where townsfolk pummel each other with oranges) and in Viareggio (where floats resembling popular and unpopular politicians are paraded through town).
February	*Festival della Canzona Italiana*. The seaside town of San Remo is transformed by Italy's biggest music festival.
8 March	*Festa delle Donne*. On Women's Day yellow mimosa flowers are given to favourite females and the women head out to dinner together.
March or April	*Pasqua*. On Easter Sunday, Italians eat lamb and a dove-shaped cake. It's a day that the extended family spends together.
	Pasquetta. Easter Monday is a national holiday and time for more eating picnic style.
25 April	*Anniversario della Liberazione*. On Liberation Day, parades and parties to celebrate Italy's freedom from Germany in 1945.
1 May	*Primo Maggio*. Labour Day is celebrated with parades and a massive outdoor concert in Rome.
June–September	*Biennale di Venezia*. In even-numbered years, this international art event is held through the summer.
2 June	*Festa della Repubblica*. The Celebration of the Italian Republic is honoured with military parades.
July and August	*Palio di Siena*. This Tuscan town holds it famous horse race once in July and then again the following month.
July or August	*La Festa di Noantri*. Rome's Trastevere celebrates with food, games and music.
July or August	*Festival dei Due Mondi*. In Spoleto, Umbria, the 'Festival of Two Worlds' has music and performing arts.
15 August	*Ferragosto*. The Festival of the Assumption is one day when you can count on every Italian being on holiday.
September	*Regatta Storica*. A boat race in Venice on the Grand Canal.
September	*Mostra Internazionale d'Arte Cinematografica*. During the first two weeks of the month, Venice puts on Italy's most important film festival.
1 November	*Ognissanti*. All Saints' Day.
2 November	*Tutti i Morti*. All Soul's Day is when people bring flowers to the tombs of their relatives.

8 December	*L'Immacolata Concezione*. Immaculate Conception.
25 December	*Natale*. Christmas is celebrated with gifts and, more recently, a tree, but tradition calls for a *percepio*, a Nativity scene with handmade figurines.
26 December	*Santo Stefano*. The day after Christmas, or Saint Steven's Day, is the time for a big family lunch.

In addition to public holidays, each town has its Saint's Day off as a public holiday. These are celebrated with fervour and match an individual's *onomastico*, or name day Here are some examples for the major towns and cities of Italy.

Date	Saint	Place Celebrated
25 April	San Marco	Venice
1 May	Sant'Elisio	Cagliari
13 June	Sant'Antonio	Padua
24 June	San Giovanni	Turin, Genova, Florence
29 June	San Pietro	Rome
10–15 July	Santa Rosalia	Palermo
26 July	Santa Anna	Ischia
19 September	San Gennaro	Naples
4 October	San Petronio	Bologna
4 October	San Francesco	Assisi
7 December	Sant'Ambrogio	Milan

Regional Calling Codes

The international country code for calling Italy from outside is 39.

Bari	080
Bologna	051
Brindisi	831
Cagliari	070
Capri	081
Catania	095
Como	031
Florence	055
Genoa	010
Milan	02
Modena	059
Naples	081
Padova	049
Palermo	091
Pantelleria	0923
Perugia	075
Pescara	085
Pisa	050

Pompei	081
Portofino	0185
Reggio Clabria	096
Rome	06
Sondrio	0342
Sorrento	081
Taranto	099
Torino	11
Trieste	040
Turin	011
Vatican City	06
Venice	041
Verona	045
Vicenza	0444

Regional Climate Charts

Average Seasonal Temperatures °Fahrenheit

	Jan	Feb	Mar	Apr	May	June	July	Aug	Sept	Oct	Nov	Dec
Amalfi	55	52	53	57	64	78	78	77	73	70	55	56
Bologna	35	40	48	55	63	74	77	75	68	61	46	36
Florence	42	45	50	55	63	74	78	75	68	60	50	43
Genoa	46	48	52	57	63	69	75	74	69	63	54	48
Milan	34	37	44	50	59	70	78	75	64	54	42	35
Naples	46	47	51	55	63	70	79	77	69	61	54	49
Palermo	54	55	56	60	65	67	78	79	75	69	62	56
Rome	46	48	51	55	62	69	77	75	69	62	55	49
Venice	36	40	46	54	62	68	75	73	66	56	45	38

Average Precipitation in Inches

	Jan	Feb	Mar	Apr	May	June	July	Aug	Sept	Oct	Nov	Dec
Bologna	1.7	1.8	2.4	2.6	2.6	2.1	1.7	2.3	2.4	2.8	3.2	2.4
Como	2.4	2.2	3.2	5.0	6.9	6.4	4.7	6.3	5.6	5.6	3.7	2.1
Florence	2.9	2.7	3.2	3.1	2.9	2.2	1.6	3.0	3.1	3.5	4.4	3.6
Genoa	4.2	3.7	4.2	3.4	3.0	2.1	1.1	3.2	3.9	6.0	4.4	3.2
Milan	2.7	3.0	3.9	4.2	5.2	3.7	2.6	3.8	2.9	4.2	4.2	2.2
Naples	4.1	3.9	3.4	3.0	2.0	1.3	1.0	1.6	3.2	5.1	6.4	4.8
Palermo	2.8	2.6	2.3	1.7	1.0	0.5	0.2	0.5	1.6	3.9	3.7	3.2
Rome	3.2	3.0	2.6	2.2	1.3	0.6	0.6	·1.3	2.7	3.7	4.4	3.5
Venice	2.3	2.1	2.3	2.5	2.7	3.0	2.5	3.3	2.6	2.7	3.4	2.1

Index